The Complete Book of Bible Lists

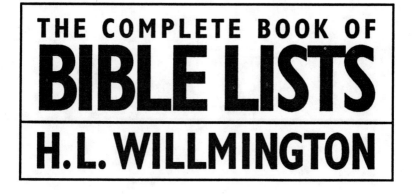

THE COMPLETE BOOK OF
BIBLE LISTS
H. L. WILLMINGTON

Tyndale House Publishers, Inc.
Wheaton, Illinois

Copyright 1987 by H. L. Willmington
All rights reserved
Previously published under the title *Willmington's Book of Bible Lists*

Library of Congress Catalog Card Number 87-50938
ISBN 0-8423-0290-5

Printed in the United States of America

00 99 98 97
6   5   4   3

Dedicated to my peers

THE LIBERTY UNIVERSITY FACULTY

mature champions of God

faithfully training young champions for God

CONTENTS

INTRODUCTION 13

ABOMINATIONS TO GOD ... 15

ALLEGORIES
(Extended Metaphors) 15

ALTARS 16

ANGELS 17
  27 Facts about Angels
  8 Names for the Angels
  7 Heavenly Activities of the Angels
  47 Earthly Activities of the Angels
  10 Old Testament Appearances of the
    Angel of the Lord
  17 Activities of the Archangel
    Gabriel
  4 Activities of the Archangel Michael

ANIMALS 23

ANOINTINGS 27

THE ANTICHRIST 28
  21 Facts about the Coming Antichrist
  6 Names for the Coming Antichrist

APOSTLES 29

AUTHORS OF THE
BOOKS OF THE BIBLE 30

BANQUETS, SUPPERS,
AND FEASTS 31

BAPTISMS 33

BIBLE STATISTICS 34
  Old Testament Statistics
  New Testament Statistics
  10 Longest Books in the Bible
  10 Shortest Books in the Bible
  10 Old Testament Books Most
    Referred to in the New Testament
  10 New Testament Books Containing
    Material from the Greatest Number
    of Old Testament Books
  10 Old Testament Verses Most
    Frequently Cited in the New
    Testament

Scripture's Record List of Individuals
Most Mentioned Men in the Bible
30 Great Topical Chapters

BOATS AND SHIPS 41

BOOKS MENTIONED
IN THE BIBLE 42

BRIDES 43

BROOKS 43

BURIALS AND FUNERALS . 44

CALLED BY GOD TO
SPECIAL SERVICE 46

CAVES 48

CHILDREN 49
  Infants
  Small Children
  Young Boys
  Young Girls

THE CHRISTIAN LIFE 50
  7 Divine Calls to the Christian from
    God
  9 Reasons for Studying Biblical
    Doctrine
  12 Areas to Be Tested at the
    Judgment Seat of Christ
  10 Challenges of the Christian in
    Light of the Rapture
  5 Reasons for Giving Our Money

CHURCHES 53

THE CHURCH'S TASKS 61

CITIES 62

CITY BUILDERS 76

COMMANDS TO BELIEVERS 76

COMMANDS TO
INDIVIDUALS 81

COMMANDS TO ISRAEL ... 84

CONFESSIONS OF SIN 85

CONVERSIONS 87

COUNTERFEITS 88
COUPLES 89
  Couples with Both Husband and
    Wife Named
  Couples with Only the
    Husband Named

COVENANTS 92
CROWNS 94
CURSES 94
DAYS 95
DEACONS 96
DEMON POSSESSIONS 97
DISEASES AND
INFIRMITIES 98
DISPENSATIONS 99
DREAMS AND VISIONS
FROM GOD 100
  Dreams
  Visions

EARTHQUAKES 101
ESCAPES 102
EXCUSES 103
EXECUTED BY GOD 104
  Individuals
  Universal
  Israelites
  Various Nations

FABLES 106
FAMINES 107
FASTS 108
FIRES 109
FOODS 110
FOOLS 113
GARDENS 114
GARMENTS 114
GATES 116
GENEALOGIES 118
GIANTS 119
GIFTS 119
GOD 121
  23 Facts about God
  16 Old Testament Names for God
  15 Things God Sees and Knows
  50 Facts about the Father
  The Trinity and Scriptural
    Evidences for It

GODLESS SONS OF
GODLY FATHERS 127

GODLY SONS OF
GODLESS FATHERS 128
HANDICAPPED
AND DISABLED 128
  Paralysis and Lameness
  Withered Hand
  Blindness
  Deafness

HEAVEN 130
  53 Facts about Heaven
  7 Facts about Our Resurrected Bodies
    in Heaven
  3 Activities in Heaven

HELL 133
HISTORY IN THE BIBLE ..134
  99 Important B.C. Biblical Dates
  60 Important A.D. Biblical Dates
  12 Stages in Bible History
  85 Biblical Phenomena Supported by
    Archaeological Findings
  70 Most Important Events in the
    Bible

THE HOLY SPIRIT 147
  15 Facts about the Holy Spirit
  13 Names for the Holy Spirit
  18 Gifts of the Holy Spirit
  57 Ministries of the Holy Spirit

HYMNS AND SONGS 152
IDOLS AND FALSE GODS .153
JERUSALEM 155
  14 Names for Jerusalem
  History and Significance

JESUS CHRIST 160
  117 Scriptural Names for Christ
  8 Divine Announcements Concerning
    Christ's Birth
  14 Reasons for the Virgin Birth
  25 Proofs of the Humanity of Christ
  37 Proofs of the Deity of Christ
  10 Witnesses for the Sinlessness
    of Christ
  9 Examples of Christ's Humility
  17 Post-Resurrection Appearances
    of Christ
  14 Results of Christ's Resurrection
  16 Signs Suggesting the Return
    of Christ
  6 Reasons for Christ's Second
    Coming
  39 Descriptions of Christ in the 39
    Old Testament Books

27 Descriptions of Christ in the 27
New Testament Books

JOURNEYS 174

JUDGES 176

JUDGMENTS FROM GOD .. 177
Past Judgments
Present-day Judgments
Future Judgments

KINGS AND RULERS 179
Amalekite
Ammonite
Assyrian
Babylonian
Canaanite
Edomite
Egyptian
Herodian
Moabite
Persian and Mede
Philistine
Roman
Syrian
Tyrian
The United Kingdom of Israel
Israel (The Northern Kingdom)
Judah (The Southern Kingdom)
Queens

KISSES 187

LAMPS, LIGHTS, AND
TORCHES 188

LAST WORDS 189

LEPERS 190

LETTERS 190

LIES 192

LOTS 192

MARRIAGES 193

MARTYRS 194

MEASUREMENTS,
WEIGHTS, MONEY 195

MEMORIALS 197

MILITARY MEN 198
General Commanders
Regular Soldiers
Centurions

MIRACLES 199
Performed by the Full Godhead
Performed by Christ
Performed by Angels
Performed by Joseph
Performed by Moses and Aaron
Performed by Joshua
Performed by Gideon
Performed by Samson
Performed by David
Performed by Elijah
Performed by Elisha
Performed by Daniel
Performed by Peter
Performed by Paul

MISSIONARIES AND
EVANGELISTS 208

MOUNTAINS 209

MURDERERS 211

MUSICAL INSTRUMENTS . 213

MUSICIANS 215

NATIONS AND PEOPLES .. 215

NUMBERS 217

OCCUPATIONS 222

OFFERINGS 223

ORDAINED BEFORE BIRTH
FOR SPECIAL SERVICE ... 224

PALACES 224

PARABLES 225
Old Testament Parables
Jesus' Parables
Other New Testament Parables

PARADOXES 229
General
Concerning Christ

PASTORAL DUTIES 230

PASTORS 231

PHARISEES 232

PLAGUES 232
Upon Nations
Upon Individuals

PLANTS 235

PLOTS 238

POLITICAL AND
RELIGIOUS GROUPS 242

POLYGAMISTS 243

PRAYERS 244
Petition
Praise and Thanksgiving
Complaint
10 Elements in the Lord's Prayer

PRAYING 251
17 Reasons for Prayer
8 Qualifications for Prayer

11 Hindrances to Prayer
8 Things to Pray For

PRECIOUS METALS 253
PRIESTS 254
Old Testament
New Testament

PRISONERS 256
PROMISES
TO THE BELIEVER 258
PROPHECIES 259
General Prophecies
Prophecies Fulfilled by Jesus
Prophecies Made by Jesus
Prophecies Concerning Births
Prophecies Concerning Cities
Prophecies Concerning Individuals
Prophecies Concerning Israel
Prophecies Concerning Nations
End-Time Prophecies (A Basic
   Overview)
Prophecies Concerning the Last Days
Prophecies Concerning the Nature of
   the Tribulation
Prophecies Concerning the Events
   Occurring with the Tribulation
Millennial Prophecies

PROPHETS AND
PROPHETESSES 285
Old Testament
New Testament
Prophetesses
False Prophets

THE PSALMS IN SUBJECT
CATEGORIES 289
PUNISHMENTS 290
RAISED FROM THE DEAD   291
REVIVALS AND REFORMS   292
RIVERS 294
ROADS AND HIGHWAYS ... 296
ROCKS AND STONES 297
SALVATION 298
4 Facts about God's Salvation
6 Reasons Why People Are Lost and
   in Need of Salvation
17 Key Words in the Vocabulary of
   Salvation

SATAN AND FALLEN
ANGELS 300
16 Facts about Satan
22 Names for Satan
27 Activities of Satan

20 Facts about Fallen Angels
14 Activities of Fallen Angels
5 Examples of How God Uses Fallen
   Angels for His Glory

SCIENTIFIC ACCURACIES
IN THE BIBLE 306
SEAS 306
SERMONS 307
SEXUALLY IMPURE 308
THE SHEKINAH GLORY
CLOUD OF GOD 310
SHEPHERDS 311
SIGNS 312
SIN 313
Various Sins
7 Consequences of Sin
7 Losses When a Christian Sins

SORCERERS 315
SPEARS AND SWORDS 316
STAFFS, STICKS, AND RODS
.... 317
SUFFERING 318
25 Reasons Why Christians Suffer
13 Proper Reactions to Suffering
5 Sources of Suffering

SUICIDES 321
SUPERNATURAL
CONCEPTIONS 321
SYMBOLS AND EMBLEMS   322
Symbols of Christ
Symbols of the Church and Believers
Symbols of Israel
Symbols of Satan
Symbols of Apostates
Symbols of the Bible
Symbols of the Holy Spirit
Symbols of the Kingdom of Heaven
Symbols of Coming Judgment
Symbols of Wickedness and
   Uncleanness
Symbols of the Antichrist
Symbols of Sorrow
Symbols of the Death and
   Resurrection of Christ
Symbols of Rewards

TEACHERS 328
TEAMS 329
TEMPLES 329
TRAITORS 330
TREES 331

THE TRIBULATION 332
    12 Names for the Coming World
        Calamity
    7 Reasons for the Great Tribulation
    25 Individuals and Groups Appearing
        in the Great Tribulation

TROUBLEMAKERS 334
TRUMPETS 335
TYPES, FORESHADOWS ... 336
    Types of Christ
    Types of the Antichrist
    Types of the Church
    Types of Israel
    Types of the Father
    Types of False Religion
    Types of the Rapture
    Types of the Tribulation
    Types of the Millennium
    Old Testament Individuals Who
        Foreshadow New Testament
        Individuals

VESSELS, PITCHERS,
AND WATER POTS 342
VINEYARDS 344
VOWS 344
WALLS 345
WARS AND BATTLES 346
WEAPONS 350
WEEPING AND MOURNING 350
WELLS 354
WICKED MEN
IN THE OLD TESTAMENT . 355
WICKED MEN
IN THE NEW TESTAMENT . 357
WICKED WOMEN IN THE OLD
AND NEW TESTAMENTS ... 358
WIDOWS 359
WINDOWS 360
WINDSTORMS 361
WORSHIPING GOD 362

INTRODUCTION

This is, literally, a fact-filled volume, featuring over 350 lists of scriptural facts. It differs from other books of Bible lists in that the topics are arranged alphabetically and are carefully cross-referenced so that each list refers the reader to related lists. The list of "Burials and Funerals," for example, refers the reader to the list "Weeping and Mourning."

Each list is arranged in a two-column format, with the items—persons, places, facts, whatever—in the first column and the related Scripture reference in the second column.

How can this storehouse of information be used? It lends itself to use in preparing Sunday school lessons and sermons, in group and individual Bible study, and in personal devotions. Let us suppose that a Sunday school teacher is preparing a lesson on the raising of Lazarus. This was, of course, one of the best-known of Jesus' miracles. If the teacher desires more background material on the number and nature of biblical miracles, along with the persons performing them and the related Scripture references, he or she can turn to the lists of "Miracles." Here are all the miracles of the Bible, arranged according to who performed them. The person will find all the miracles of Jesus in one list and, in the same section, lists of the miracles of Elijah, Elisha, Moses, Peter, and Paul. If the person glanced through the lists of Elijah's miracles, he would find that Elijah also raised a person from the dead. The person would thus learn more about Jesus' different miracles and also more about other raisings from the dead.

If a person was interested in aspects of the Christian life, he or she could turn to the section on "The Christian Life," which not only contains several lists in itself but which also refers the reader to related lists—"The Church's Tasks," "Commands to Believers," "Praying," and "Salvation."

The examples could be easily multiplied. The alphabetical arrangement and the cross-referencing system make it the most usable of any book of Bible lists. Suffice it to say that this comprehensive reference tool is made for anyone who is interested in studying and understanding Scripture in all its richness.

ABOMINATIONS TO GOD

1. The evil-minded person	Prov. 3:22; 11:20
2. A false balance	Prov. 11:1
3. The sacrifices of the wicked	Prov. 15:8; 21:27
4. The thoughts of the wicked	Prov. 15:26
5. The justification of the wicked and the condemnation of the just	Prov. 17:15
6. A proud look	Prov. 6:17
7. A lying tongue	Prov. 6:17; 12:22
8. Hands that shed innocent blood	Prov. 6:17
9. A heart that devises wicked imaginations	Prov. 6:18
10. Feet that are swift in running to mischief	Prov. 6:18
11. A false witness	Prov. 6:19
12. One who sows discord among brethren	Prov. 6:19

ALLEGORIES (EXTENDED METAPHORS)
See also Fables, Parables

1. The Shepherd Psalm	Ps. 23
2. The grape vine	Ps. 80:8-14
3. God's vineyard	Isa. 5:1-7
4. The great eagle	Ezek. 17:1-10

5. The lioness   Ezek. 19:1-9
6. The bread of life   John 6:26-51
7. The sheepfold and shepherd   John 10
8. The vine   John 15:1-7
9. The Christian foundation   1 Cor. 3:10-15
10. The whole armor of God   Eph. 6:10-17
11. Hagar and Sarah   Gal. 4:21-31

ALTARS
See also Offerings

1. Built by Noah   Gen. 8:20
2. Built by Abraham in Shechem, in   Gen. 12:7-8;
   Hebron, and in Moriah   13:18; 22:2, 9
3. Built by Isaac   Gen. 26:25
4. Built by Jacob at Shechem and at   Gen. 33:20; 35:1-7
   Bethel
5. Built by Moses   Exod. 17:15
6. Built by Balak   Num. 23:1, 4, 14
7. Built by Joshua   Josh. 8:30
8. Built by the tribes living east of Josh. 22:10
   Jordan
9. Built by Gideon   Judg. 6:24
10. Built by Manoah   Judg. 13:20
11. Built by Israel   Judg. 21:4
12. Built by Samuel   1 Sam. 7:15, 17
13. Built by Saul   1 Sam. 14:35
14. Built by David   2 Sam. 24:25
15. Built by Jeroboam   1 Kings 12:32-33
16. Built by Ahab   1 Kings 16:32
17. Built by Elijah   1 Kings 18:31-32

18. Built by Uriah	2 Kings 16:11
19. Built by Manasseh	2 Kings 21:3
20. Built by Zerubbabel	Ezra 3:2

Note: There were four basic kinds of altars: (1) earthen, (2) stone, (3) wood covered with brass, and (4) wood covered with gold.

ANGELS
See also Satan and Fallen Angels

27 Facts about Angels

1. They are mentioned 273 times in 34 biblical books.	
2. They were all created by God.	Gen. 2:1; Neh. 9:6; Eph. 3:9; Col. 1:16
3. They report directly to God.	Job 1:6; 2:1
4. They were present at the Creation of the world.	Job 38:1, 4, 7
5. They announced Jesus' birth to the shepherds.	Luke 2:10-14
6. They do not marry.	Matt. 22:30
7. They were created to live forever.	Rev. 4:8
8. Their purpose is to glorify God.	Rev. 4:8
9. Some angels help human beings.	Heb. 1:14
10. Some angels harm human beings.	Mark 5:1-5
11. They are spirit beings.	Ps. 104:4; Heb. 1:7, 14
12. They are invisible beings.	Rom. 1:18-32; Col. 2:18; Rev. 19:10; 22:9

13. They are innumerable.

Deut. 33:2; Ps 68:17; Dan. 7:9-10; Matt. 26:53; Heb. 12:22; Rev. 5:11

14. They possess intelligence.

Dan. 9:21-22; 10:14; Rev. 19:10; 22:8-9

15. They possess will.

Isa. 14:12-15; Jude 6

16. They display joy.

Job 38:7; Luke 2:13

17. They display desire.

1 Pet. 1:12

18. They are stronger than men.

Ps. 103:20; 2 Thess. 1:7; 2 Pet. 2:11

19. They are more intelligent than men.

Dan. 9:21-22; 10:14

20. They are swifter than men.

Dan. 9:21; Rev. 14:6

21. They are not omnipresent.

Dan. 10:12

22. They are not omnipotent.

Dan. 10:13; Jude 9

23. They are not omniscient.

Matt. 24:36

24. Some are cherubim.

Ezek. 1:1-28; 10:20

25. Some are seraphim.

Isa. 6:1-8

26. The majority remained true to God.

Rev. 5:11-12

27. They will join all believers in the heavenly Jerusalem.

Heb. 12:22-23

8 Names for the Angels

1. Ministers, signifying their religious virtues and spiritual service

Ps. 103:20-21; 104:4

2. Host, speaking of their military service

Gen. 32:1-2; Josh. 5:14; 1 Sam. 17:45; Ps. 89:8

3. Chariots, which may refer to their swiftness

2 Kings 6:16-17; Ps. 68:17; Zech. 6:5

4. Watchers, speaking of their duties as supervisors and agents

Dan. 4:13, 17

5. Sons of the mighty, which may refer to their awesome strength and power

Ps. 29:1; 89:6

6. Sons of God

Gen. 6:2, 4; Job 1:6, 2:1; 38:7

7. Holy Ones, saints, referring to their total separation to the will of God

Ps. 89:7; Dan. 8:13

8. Stars, which may indicate both their number and their brightness

Job 38:7; Ps. 148:2-3; Rev. 12:3-4

7 Heavenly Activities of the Angels

1. They worship God.

1 Kings. 22:19; Ps. 29:1-2; Isa. 6:3; Rev. 4:8; 19:4

2. They observe the people of God.

Luke 12:8-9; 15:10; 1 Cor. 4:9; 11:10; Eph. 3:10; 1 Tim. 5:21; 1 Pet. 1:12

3. They inquire into the prophetical plan of God.

Dan. 12:5-6

4. They perform the will of God.

Ps. 104:4; Dan. 7:10

5. They witness the wrath of God.

Rev. 14:10

6. They rejoice in God's work of creation.

Job 38:7; Rev. 4:11

7. They rejoice in God's work of redemption.

1 Tim. 3:16; Rev. 5:11-12

47 Earthly Activities of the Angels

1. They ministered to Daniel.

Dan 7:16; 10:5, 11

2. They ministered to Zechariah.

Zech. 1:9; 13-14, 19; 2:3; 5:5-10; 6:4-5

3. They ministered to Zacharias.

Luke 1:11-20

4. They ministered to Mary.

Luke 1:26-33

5. They ministered to Joseph.

Matt. 1:20; 2:13, 19

6. They ministered to the shepherds.

Luke 2:9-12

7. They ministered to the women at the tomb.

Luke 24:4-7

8. They ministered to the apostles.

Acts 1:10-11

9. They ministered to Philip.

Acts 8:26

10. They ministered to Cornelius.

Acts 10:3-6

11. They ministered to John.

Rev. 17:1; 21:9

12. They protected Lot from the Sodomites.

Gen. 19:10-11

13. They protected Elisha from the Syrians.

2 Kings 6:15-17

14. They comfort.

1 Kings 19:5; Acts 27:23-24

15. They deliver.

Acts 5:19; 12:7

16. They minister to the believer at the moment of death.

Luke 16:22

17. They judged the Egyptians.

Exod. 12:13; 23

18. They judged the Sodomites.

Gen. 19:13

19. They judged the Assyrians.

2 Kings 19:35

20. They judged Herod.

Acts 12:23

21. They will judge the earth during the Tribulation.

Rev. 8–10

22. They hold back the four winds of heaven.

Rev. 7:1

23. They pronounce the seven trumpet judgments.

Rev. 8:2

24. They cast Satan and his angels out of heaven.

Rev. 12:7-8

25. They announce the eternal hell awaiting all unbelievers.

Rev. 14:10

26. They predict the fall of Babylon.

Rev. 14:8

27. They announce the fall of Babylon.

Rev. 18:1-2

28. They pour out the seven vial judgments.

Rev. 15:1

29. They announce Armageddon. — Rev. 19:17

30. They accompany Christ at his second coming. — 2 Thess. 1:7-8

31. They gather the unsaved for eternal hell. — Matt. 13:39-43

32. They bind Satan in the bottomless pit. — Rev. 20:1-2

33. They fought for Israel. — Judg. 5:20

34. They gave the law to Israel. — Deut. 33:2; Acts 7:53; Gal. 3:19; Heb. 2:2

35. They seal the 144,000 Israelites. — Rev. 7:1-4

36. They will regather faithful Israel. — Matt. 24:31

37. They worship Christ. — Heb. 1:6

38. They were made by him and for him. — Col. 1:17

39. They predicted his birth. — Matt. 1:20-21; Luke 1:31

40. They announced his birth. — Luke 2:9-14

41. They helped protect him. — Ps. 91:11; Matt. 2:13

42. They ministered to him in the wilderness. — Matt. 4:11

43. They ministered to him in the garden. — Luke 22:43

44. They rolled away the tombstone. — Matt. 28:2

45. They announced his resurrection. — Matt. 28:5-6

46. They predicted his second coming. — Acts 1:10-11

47. They are in total subjection to him. — 1 Pet. 3:22

10 Old Testament Appearances of the Angel of the Lord

1. He wrestled with Jacob. — Gen. 32:24-30

2. He redeemed Jacob from all evil. — Gen. 48:16

3. He spoke to Moses from the burning bush. — Exod. 3:2

4. He protected Israel at the Red Sea. — Exod. 14:19

5. He prepared Israel for the Promised Land. — Exod. 23:20-23; Isa. 63:9; 1 Cor. 10:1-4

6. He commissioned Gideon.   Judg. 6:11-12

7. He ministered to Elijah.   1 Kings 19:7

8. He reassured Joshua.   Josh. 5:13-15

9. He saved Jerusalem.   Isa. 37:36

10. He preserved three godly Hebrew   Dan. 3:25
    men.

17 Activities of the Archangel Gabriel

1. He explained the vision of the ram   Dan. 8:16
   and goat battle to Daniel.

2. He explained the 70 weeks to Daniel.   Dan. 9:21-27

3. He predicted the birth of John the   Luke 1:13
   Baptist to Zacharias.

4. He predicted the birth of Jesus to   Luke 1:26
   Mary.

5. He assured Joseph of Mary's purity.   Matt. 1:20

6. He warned Joseph about the plot of   Matt. 2:13
   Herod.

7. He told Joseph about the death of   Matt. 2:19-20
   Herod.

8. He announced the birth of Christ to   Luke 2:9-14
   the shepherds.

9. He strengthened Christ in the Garden   Luke 22:43
   of Gethsemane.

10. He rolled the stone back at the   Matt. 28:2
    Resurrection.

11. He freed the apostles from prison.   Acts 5:19

12. He sent Philip to the desert of Gaza to   Acts 8:26
    meet the eunuch.

13. He instructed Cornelius to send for   Acts 10:3
    Peter.

14. He freed Peter from prison.   Acts 12:7

15. He executed wicked Herod for   Acts 12:23
    blasphemy.

16. He reassured Paul on the deck of a   Acts 27:23
    sinking ship.

17. He will sound the trumpet at the Rapture. — 1 Thess. 4:16

4 Activities of the Archangel Michael

1. He helped a lesser-ranked angel get through to answer Daniel's prayer. — Dan. 10:13, 21

2. He will stand up for Israel during the Tribulation. — Dan. 12:1

3. He disputed with Satan concerning the dead body of Moses. — Jude 9

4. He fights against Satan in the heavenlies. — Rev. 12:7

ANIMALS

1. Adder (a type of snake) — Prov. 23:32
2. Ant — Prov. 6:6; 30:25
3. Antelope ("wild bull" in some translations) — Isa. 51:20
4. Ape — 1 Kings 10:22
5. Asp (a type of cobra) — Isa. 11:8
6. Ass — John 12:14
7. Badger (also translated "coney") — Exod. 25:5; Lev. 11:5
8. Bat — Isa. 2:20
9. Bear — 1 Sam. 17:34-37; 2 Kings 2:24; Isa. 11:7; Dan. 7:5; Rev. 13:2
10. Bees — Judg. 14:8
11. Behemoth — Job 40:15
12. Camel — Gen. 24:10; Matt. 3:4; 19:24; 23:24
13. Chameleon — Lev. 11:30

14. Chamois (mountain sheep) Deut. 14:5

15. Cock Matt. 26:34

16. Cockatrice Isa. 11:8

17. Cormorant (a large black water bird) Lev. 11:17

18. Crane Isa. 38:14

19. Cricket (sometimes translated "beetle") Lev. 11:22

20. Crocodile (translated in various ways) Ps. 74:14; Ezek. 29:3; 32:2

21. Cuckow (seagull) Lev. 11:16

22. Dog Judg. 7:5; 1 Kings 21:23-24; Eccles. 9:4; Matt. 15:26-27; 7:6; Luke 16:21; 2 Pet. 2:22; Rev. 22:15

23. Dove Gen. 8:8; 2 Kings 6:25; Matt. 3:16; 10:16; John 2:16

24. Eagle Exod. 19:4; Isa. 40:31; Ezek. 1:10; Dan. 7:4; Rev. 4:7; 12:14

25. Elephant 1 Kings 10:22

26. Falcon (kite) Lev. 11:14

27. Fish Exod. 7:18; Jon. 1:17; Matt. 14:17; 17:27; Luke 24:42; John 21:9

28. Flea 1 Sam. 24:14; 26:20

29. Fly Eccles. 10:1; see also Exod. 8:16-19

30. Fox Judg. 15:4; Neh. 4:3; Matt. 8:20; Luke 13:32

31. Frog Exod. 8:2; Rev. 16:13

32. Gazelle (often translated "roe" and "roebuck") Deut. 12:15

33. Gecko (lizard)	Lev. 11:30
34. Gnat	Matt. 23:24
35. Goat	Gen. 15:9; 37:31; Dan. 8:5; Lev. 16; Matt. 25:33
36. Hare (a rodent)	Lev. 11:6
37. Hart	Deut. 14:5
38. Hawk	Job 39:26
39. Heron (stork)	Deut. 14:18
40. Hoopoe (lapwing)	Lev. 11:19
41. Hornet	Exod. 23:28; Deut. 7:20; Josh. 24:12
42. Horse	1 Kings 4:26; 2 Kings 2:11; Rev. 6:2-8; 19:14
43. Horseleech	Prov. 30:15
44. Hyena (sometimes translated "beast")	Eccles. 3:18-19
45. Kite (a bird of prey)	Lev. 11:14
46. Leopard	Isa. 11:6; Jer. 13:23; Dan. 7:6; Rev. 13:2
47. Leviathan	Job 41:1
48. Lice	Exod. 8:16
49. Lion	Judg. 14:8; 1 Kings 13:24; Isa. 65:25; Dan. 6:7; 1 Pet. 5:8; Rev. 4:7; 13:2
50. Lizard	Lev. 11:30
51. Locust	Exod. 10:4; Joel 1:4; Matt. 3:4; Rev. 9:3
52. Mole (a burrowing rat)	Isa. 2:20
53. Moth	Matt. 6:19; Isa. 50:9; 51:8
54. Mule	2 Sam. 18:9; 1 Kings 1:38
55. Osprey (a fish hawk)	Lev. 11:13

56. Ossifrage (largest of the vultures)	Lev. 11:13
57. Ostrich	Lam. 4:3
58. Owl (sometimes translated "swan")	Isa. 34:14
59. Ox (bullock)	1 Sam. 11:7; 15:14; 2 Sam. 6:6; 1 Kings 19:20-21; Isa. 1:3; Dan. 4:25, 32; Luke 14:5, 19
60. Partridge	1 Sam. 26:20
61. Peacock	1 Kings 10:22
62. Pelican	Ps. 102:6
63. Pygarg (a desert animal)	Deut. 14:5
64. Quail	Exod. 16:13; Num. 11:31
65. Raven	Gen. 8:7; 1 Kings 17:4
66. Scorpion	1 Kings 12:11, 14; Luke 10:19; Rev. 9:3, 5, 10
67. Serpent	Gen. 3:1; Exod. 4:3; Num. 21:9; Rev. 12:9
68. Sheep	Exod. 12:5; Gen. 4:2; Luke 15:4; John 10:7
69. Snail	Ps. 58:8
70. Sparrow	Matt. 10:31
71. Spider	Isa. 59:5
72. Swallow	Isa. 38:14
73. Swine	Matt. 7:6; 8:32; Luke 15:15-16
74. Tortoise	Lev. 11:29
75. Turtledove	Gen. 15:9; Luke 2:24
76. Unicorn (wild ox)	Num. 23:22
77. Viper	Isa. 30:6
78. Weasel	Lev. 11:29

79. Whale	Gen. 1:21
80. Wolf	Isa. 11:6; Matt. 7:15
81. Worm	Job 7:5; 17:14; 21:26; Isa. 14:11; 66:24; Jon. 4:7; Mark 9:43-48

Note: Biblical animals are not always easy to identify, and the names may vary from one translation to another.

ANOINTINGS

1. Of a stone by Jacob	Gen. 28:18; 31:13
2. Of the high priest by Moses	Exod. 28:41; 29:7
3. Of the tabernacle by Moses	Exod. 40:9
4. Of Saul by Samuel	1 Sam. 9:16; 10:1
5. Of David by Samuel, by the men of Judah, and by all of Israel	1 Sam. 16:12; Ps. 89:20; 2 Sam. 2:4, 7; 5:3
6. Of Solomon by Zadok	1 Kings 1:39
7. Of Christ	
a. by the Father	Ps. 2:2; 45:7; Luke 4:18; Acts 4:27; 10:38; Heb. 1:9
b. by the Holy Spirit	Matt. 3:16
c. by an immoral woman	Luke 7:38
d. by Mary of Bethany	John 11:2
8. Of all believers by the Holy Spirit	2 Cor. 1:21
9. Of Lucifer by God (prior to his fall)	Ezek. 28:14
10. Of sick believers by church elders	James 5:14

Note: There are four basic kinds of anointings: (1) oil—Exod. 40:9, (2) blood—Lev. 8:23-24; 9:9, (3) water—Lev. 8:6, and (4) spiritual—2 Cor. 1:21.

THE ANTICHRIST
See also Prophecies, The Tribulation

21 Facts about the Coming Antichrist

1. He will be an intellectual genius. — Dan. 8:23
2. He will be an oratorical genius. — Dan. 11:36
3. He will be a political genius. — Rev. 17:11-12
4. He will be a commercial genius. — Dan. 11:43; Rev. 13:16-17
5. He will be a military genius. — Rev. 6:2; 13:2
6. He will be a religious genius. — 2 Thess. 2:4; Rev. 13:8
7. He will begin by controlling the Western power block. — Rev. 17:12
8. He will make a seven-year covenant with Israel but will break it after three and a half years. — Dan. 9:27
9. He will attempt to destroy all of Israel. — Rev. 12
10. He will destroy the false religious system so that he may rule unhindered. — Rev. 17:16-17
11. He will set himself up as God. — Dan. 11:36-37; 2 Thess. 2:4, 11; Rev. 13:5
12. He will briefly rule over all nations. — Ps. 2; Dan. 11:36; Rev. 13:16
13. He will be utterly crushed by the Lord Jesus Christ at the Battle of Armageddon. — Rev. 19
14. He will be the first creature thrown into the lake of fire. — Rev. 19:20
15. He will be a master of deceit. — 2 Thess. 2:10
16. He will profane the temple. — Matt. 24:15
17. He will be energized by Satan himself. — Rev. 13:2

18. He will do everything according to his own selfish will. Dan. 11:36

19. He will not regard the God of his fathers. Dan. 11:37

20. He will not have the desire of women. Dan. 11:37

21. His god will be the god of power. Dan. 11:38

6 Names for the Coming Antichrist

1. The little horn Dan. 7:8
2. The willful king Dan. 11:36
3. The man of sin 2 Thess. 2:3
4. The son of perdition 2 Thess. 2:3
5. The wicked one 2 Thess. 2:8
6. The beast Rev. 11:7

APOSTLES

1. Simon Peter, fisherman, the brother of Andrew John 1:40

2. Andrew, fisherman, the brother of Simon Peter John 1:40

3. John, fisherman, the brother of James Matt. 4:21

4. James, fisherman, the brother of John Matt. 4:21

5. Philip, who introduced his friend Nathanael to Jesus John 1:43

6. Nathanael, also called Bartholomew John 1:45

7. Matthew, tax collector, also called Levi Luke 5:27

8. Thaddaeus, also called Judas or Jude Matt. 10:3

9. James the Less, son of Alphaeus, possibly the brother of Matthew Matt. 10:3

10. Simon the Zealot, member of a radical Jewish party Matt. 10:4

11. Thomas, a twin   John 11:16
12. Judas Iscariot, the traitor   John 6:70
13. Matthias, elected to take Judas   Acts 1:26
    Iscariot's place
14. Paul, apostle to the Gentiles   Rom. 11:13
15. Barnabas, Paul's first missionary   Acts 13:2
    companion
16. Silas, Paul's second missionary   1 Thess. 2:7
    companion
17. James, half brother of Christ and head   Gal. 1:19
    of the Jerusalem church

AUTHORS OF THE BOOKS OF THE BIBLE

1. Moses wrote Genesis, Exodus, Leviticus, Numbers, Deuteronomy.
2. Joshua wrote the book named after him.
3. Job may have written his own story.
4. Samuel may have written Judges, Ruth, and 1 Samuel.
5. David wrote most of the Psalms.   2 Sam. 23:2
6. Sons of Korah wrote Psalms 42, 44–49, 84–85, 87.
7. Asaph wrote Psalms 50, 73–83.
8. Heman wrote Psalm 88.
9. Ethan wrote Psalm 89.
10. Hezekiah wrote Psalms 120–123, 128–130, 132, 134–136.   Isa. 38:20
11. Solomon wrote Psalms 72, 127, Proverbs 1–29, Ecclesiastes, Song of Songs.
12. Agur wrote Proverbs 30.

13. Lemuel wrote Proverbs 31.

14. Jeremiah wrote Jeremiah, probably Lamentations, and possibly 1 and 2 Kings.

15. Ezra wrote Ezra and possibly 1 and 2 Chronicles and 2 Samuel.

16. Mordecai may have written Esther.

17. Luke wrote Acts as well as the Gospel of Luke.

18. John wrote the Gospel of John, 1 John, 2 John, 3 John, and Revelation.

19. Paul wrote Romans, 1 Corinthians, 2 Corinthians, Galatians, Ephesians, Philippians, Colossians, 1 Thessalonians, 2 Thessalonians, 1 Timothy, 2 Timothy, Titus, and Philemon.

20. Apollos may have written Hebrews.

21. The books of Old Testament prophecy were written by the prophets whose names they bear. The New Testament Epistles and Gospels, with the exceptions noted above, were also named after their authors.

BANQUETS, SUPPERS, AND FEASTS

1. Abraham's feast for some angels		Gen. 18:1-8
2. Lot's feast for some angels		Gen. 19:3
3. Abraham's feast for Isaac		Gen. 21:8
4. Laban's feast for Jacob		Gen. 29:22

5. Joseph's feast for his brethren	Gen. 43:16-34
6. Samson's wedding feast	Judg. 14:10-18
7. David's feast for Abner	2 Sam. 3:20
8. Israel's feast for David	1 Chron. 12:39
9. Solomon's thanksgiving feast	1 Kings 3:15
10. Solomon's dedication feast	1 Kings 8:65
11. Elisha's ordination feast	1 Kings 19:21
12. Ahasuerus's feast for his nobles	Esther 1:3-12
13. Ahasuerus's feast for Esther	Esther 2:17-18
14. Esther's feast for Haman	Esther 7:1-10
15. Job's feast for his children	Job 1:13
16. Belshazzar's feast for his nobles	Dan. 5
17. Herod's feast for his nobles	Mark 6:21
18. Jesus' feast for 5,000 men	Matt. 14:15-21
19. Jesus' feast for 4,000 men	Matt. 15:32-39
20. A certain king's feast for his son	Matt. 22:1-14; Luke 14:16-24
21. Simon's feast for Jesus	Mark 14:3; John 12:1-2
22. The wedding feast in Cana	John 2:1-12
23. A Pharisee's feast for Jesus	Luke 7:36-50
24. Matthew's feast for Jesus	Luke 5:29
25. A father's feast for his repentant son	Luke 15:23
26. The upper room Passover feast	John 13
27. The Emmaus feast	Luke 24:30
28. The Upper Room post-Calvary feast	Luke 24:42-43
29. Jesus' feast for seven of his disciples	John 21:12-13
30. The feast at Armageddon	Rev. 19:17-18
31. The marriage feast of the Lamb	Rev. 19:9
32. The Levitical Old Testament feasts	
a. The weekly Sabbath feast	Exod. 20:8-11; Lev. 23:1-3
b. The seventh-year Sabbath feast	Exod. 23:10-11; Lev. 25:2-7

c. The fiftieth-year (Jubilee) Sabbath feast — Lev. 25:8-16

Note: These three speak of God's creation, as they come in cycles of seven, just as God rested on the seventh day from his creative acts. The next six feasts continue to explain and unfold God's perfect work among mankind.

d. Passover, which points to Calvary — Lev. 23:4-8; 1 Cor. 5:7

e. The Feast of the First Fruits, which points to the Resurrection — Lev. 23:9-14; 1 Cor. 15:23

f. Pentecost, which points to the coming of the Holy Spirit at Pentecost — Lev. 23:15-22; Acts 2

g. The Feast of Trumpets, which points to Jesus' Second Coming — Lev. 23:23-25; 1 Thess. 4:13-18

h. The Day of Atonement feast, which points to the Tribulation — Lev. 23:26-32; Rev. 6–19

i. The Feast of Tabernacles, which points to the Millennium — Lev. 23:33-44; Rev. 20:1-6

33. The post-Levitical feasts

a. Purim, a yearly feast to celebrate the deliverance of the Jews in Persia from Haman — Esther 9

b. The Feast of Dedication to celebrate the restoration of the temple from Antiochus Epiphanes — John 10:22

BAPTISMS

1. The baptism of sin upon Christ at Calvary — Luke 12:50; Matt. 20:20-23

2. The baptism of the Holy Spirit upon believers at Pentecost — Acts 1:5; 2:1-4; Matt. 3:11

3. The baptism of God's wrath upon this world during the Tribulation — Matt. 3:12; 13:30; Rev. 6:16-17

4. The baptism of all Christians by the Holy Spirit into the body of Christ — 1 Cor. 12:13

5. The baptism of Israel unto Moses — 1 Cor. 10:2

6. The baptism of John the Baptist for repentance — Mark 1:4; Acts 13:24

7. The baptism of Jesus by John and by the Father with the Holy Spirit — Matt. 3:15-16

8. The water baptism of new converts in the Book of Acts

   a. At Pentecost, when 3,000 were baptized by Peter and the apostles — Acts 2:41

   b. At Samaria, where many were baptized by Philip the evangelist — Acts 8:12

   c. At Gaza, where the Ethiopian eunuch was baptized by Philip — Acts 8:38

   d. At Damascus, where Paul was baptized by Ananias — Acts 9:18

   e. At Caesarea, where Peter baptized Cornelius and his friends — Acts 11:48

   f. At Philippi, where Paul baptized Lydia and the Philippian jailor — Acts 16:15, 33

   g. At Corinth, where Paul baptized Crispus, Gaius, Stephanas, and others — Acts 18:8; 1 Cor. 1:14, 16

   h. At Ephesus, where Paul baptized some followers of John the Baptist — Acts 19:3-5

BIBLE STATISTICS

Old Testament Statistics

1. 39 books
2. 929 chapters
3. 23,214 verses

4. 593,493 words
5. Longest book—Psalms
6. Shortest book—Obadiah
7. 17 historical books
8. 5 poetical books
9. 17 prophetical books

New Testament Statistics
1. 27 books
2. 260 chapters

Note: It was not until A.D. 1250 that the Bible was divided into chapters. At that time Cardinal Hugo incorporated chapter divisions into the Latin Bible. His divisions, although for convenience, were not always accurate; however, essentially those same chapter divisions have persisted to this day. In 1551 Robert Estienne introduced a Greek New Testament with the inclusion of verse divisions. He did not fix verses for the Old Testament. The first entire English Bible to have verse divisions was the Geneva Bible in 1560.

3. 7959 verses
4. 181,253 words
5. Longest book—Acts
6. Shortest book—3 John
7. 4 Gospels
8. 1 historical book
9. 22 epistles

10 Longest Books in the Bible
1. Psalms—150 chapters, 2461 verses, 43,743 words
2. Jeremiah—52 chapters, 1364 verses, 42,659 words
3. Ezekiel—48 chapters, 1273 verses, 39,407 words
4. Genesis—50 chapters, 1533 verses, 38,267 words
5. Isaiah—66 chapters, 1292 verses, 37,044 words
6. Numbers—36 chapters, 1288 verses, 32,902 words
7. Exodus—40 chapters, 1213 verses, 32,602 words
8. Deuteronomy—34 chapters, 959 verses, 28,461 words
9. 2 Chronicles—36 chapters, 822 verses, 26,074 words
10. Luke—24 chapters, 1151 verses, 25,944 words

10 Shortest Books in the Bible

1. 3 John—1 chapter, 14 verses, 299 words
2. 2 John—1 chapter, 13 verses, 303 words
3. Philemon—1 chapter, 25 verses, 445 words
4. Jude—1 chapter, 25 verses, 613 words
5. Obadiah—1 chapter, 21 verses, 670 words
6. Titus—3 chapters, 46 verses, 921 words
7. 2 Thessalonians—3 chapters, 47 verses, 1042 words
8. Haggai—2 chapters, 38 verses, 1131 words
9. Nahum—3 chapters, 47 verses, 1285 words
10. Jonah—4 chapters, 48 verses, 1321 words

10 Old Testament Books Most Referred to in the New Testament

1. Isaiah, referred to 419 times in 23 New Testament books
2. Psalms, 414 times in 23 books
3. Genesis, 260 times in 21 books
4. Exodus, 250 times in 19 books
5. Deuteronomy, 208 times in 21 books
6. Ezekiel, 141 times in 15 books
7. Daniel, 133 times in 17 books
8. Jeremiah, 125 times in 17 books
9. Leviticus, 107 times in 15 books
10. Numbers, 73 times in 4 books

10 New Testament Books Containing Material from the Greatest Number of Old Testament Books

1. Revelation, material from 32 Old Testament books
2. Luke, 31
3. John, 26
4. Acts, 25
5. Mark, 24
6. Romans, 23
7. Hebrews, 21

8. 1 Corinthians, 18
9. James, 17
10. 1 Peter, 15

10 Old Testament Verses
Most Frequently Cited in the New Testament

1. Psalm 110:1, quoted 18 times

Matt. 22:44; 26:64; Mark 12:36; 14:62; 16:19; Luke 20:42-43; 22:69: Acts 2:34-35; Rom. 8:34; 1 Cor. 15:25; Eph. 1:20; Col. 3:1; Heb. 1:3, 13; 8:1; 10:12-13; 12:2

2. Ezekiel 1:26-28, quoted 12 times

Rev. 4:2-3, 9-10; 5:1, 7, 13; 6:16; 7:10, 15; 19:14; 21:5

3. Daniel 12:1, quoted 11 times

Matt. 24:21; Mark 13:19; Phil. 4:3; Jude 9; Rev. 3:5; 7:14; 12:7; 13:8; 16:18; 17:8; 20:12

4. Isaiah 6:1, quoted 11 times

Rev. 4:2, 9-10; 5:1, 7, 13; 6:16; 7:10, 15; 19:4; 21:5

5. 2 Chronicles 18:18, Psalm 47:8, and 1 Kings 22:19, each quoted 11 times

Rev. 4:2, 9-10; 5:1, 7, 13; 6:16; 7:10, 15; 19:4; 21:5

6. Psalm 2:7, quoted 10 times

Matt. 3:17; 17:5; Mark 1:11; 9:7; Luke 3:22; 9:35; John 1:49; Acts 13:33; Heb. 1:5; 5:5

7. Isaiah 53:7, quoted 10 times

Matt. 26:63; 27:12, 14; Mark 14:60-61; 15:4-5; 1 Cor. 5:7; 1 Pet. 2:23; Rev. 5:6, 12; 13:8

8. Amos 3:13, quoted 10 times	Rev. 1:8; 4:8, 13; 11:17; 15:3; 16:7, 14; 19:6, 15; 21:22
9. Amos 4:13, quoted 10 times	2 Cor. 6:18; Rev. 1:8; 4:8; 11:17; 15:3; 16:7, 14; 19:6, 15; 21:22
10. Leviticus 19:18, quoted 10 times	Matt. 5:43; 19:19; 22:39; Mark 12:31, 33; Luke 10:27; Rom. 12:19; 13:9; Gal. 5:14; James 2:8

Scripture's Record List of Individuals

1. Earliest: Adam, world's first human being	Gen. 2:7
2. Oldest: Methuselah, son of Enoch, who lived to be 969	Gen. 5:27
3. Strongest: Samson, carnal Nazarite whom God used to deliver Israel from the Philistines	Judg. 14:6; 15:5
4. Wisest: Solomon, king of Israel and son of David	1 Kings 3:12
5. Richest: Solomon	1 Kings 10:23
6. Tallest: Goliath, over nine feet tall, killed in battle by David	1 Sam. 17:4
7. Shortest: Zacchaeus, who climbed a sycamore tree to see Jesus	Luke 19:3-4
8. Fattest: Eglon, Moabite king killed by the judge Ehud	Judg. 3:17
9. Meekest: Moses, Israel's great lawgiver and author of Scripture's first five books	Num. 12:3
10. Cruelest: Manasseh, who shed blood from one end of Judah to the other but later repented	2 Chron. 33:1-13
11. Fastest: Asahel, described in Scripture as "light of foot as a wild roe"	2 Sam. 2:18

12. Greatest of the prophets: John the Baptist, forerunner of Christ — Matt. 11:11

13. Guiltiest: Judas, who betrayed the Savior for 30 pieces of silver — Matt. 27:3-5

14. Proudest: Nebuchadnezzar, Babylonian king who destroyed Jerusalem and was later humbled by God himself — Dan. 4

15. Most beautiful: Esther, Jewish queen who saved her people from the first holocaust attempt in history — Esther 2:7

16. Most traveled: Paul, the great theologian and missionary — Acts 13:4; 15:36; 18:23

17. Most sorrowful: Jeremiah, persecuted by his own countrymen for preaching on sin and who saw his beloved Jerusalem destroyed — Jer. 9:1; Lam. 1:12

18. Most persecuted: Job, attacked by Satan, totally misunderstood by his wife, and criticized by his friends — Job 1–2

19. Most lovestruck: Jacob, who agreed to work seven years for the hand of Rachel — Gen. 29:18-20

20. Most frightened: Belshazzar, whose knees knocked as the handwriting on the wall appeared — Dan. 5:6

21. Most rash: Jephthah, who vowed to offer a special sacrifice if God would allow him to win a battle; the sacrifice turned out to be his daughter — Judg. 11:30

22. Most doubtful: Thomas, who said he could not believe in Christ's resurrection until he saw and touched the Savior — John 11:16; 20:24-29

Most Mentioned Men in the Bible

1. David, mentioned 1118 times
2. Moses, 740

3. Aaron, 339
4. Saul, 338
5. Abraham, 306
6. Solomon, 295
7. Jacob, 270
8. Joseph, 208
9. Joshua, 197
10. Paul, 185
11. Peter, 166
12. Joab, 137
13. Jeremiah, 136
14. Samuel, 135
15. Isaac, 127

Jesus, of course, is mentioned more than anyone else in the Scriptures.

30 Great Topical Chapters

1. The Ten Commandments chapter	Exod. 20
2. The reassurance chapter	Josh. 1
3. The faithfulness of God chapter	Josh. 14
4. The shepherd chapter	Ps. 23
5. The confession of sin chapter	Ps. 51
6. The praise of God chapter	Ps. 103
7. The Word of God chapter	Ps. 119
8. The wisdom chapter	Prov. 8
9. The virtuous woman chapter	Prov. 31
10. The majesty of God chapter	Isa. 40
11. The great invitation chapter	Isa. 55
12. The Beatitudes chapter	Matt. 5
13. The Lord's Prayer chapter	Matt. 6
14. The sower and seed chapter	Matt. 13
15. The protection of the sheep chapter	John 10
16. The comfort chapter	John 14

17. The abiding chapter	John 15
18. The justification chapter	Rom. 5
19. The sanctification chapter	Rom. 6
20. The glorification chapter	Rom. 8
21. The marriage chapter	1 Cor. 7
22. The gifts chapter	1 Cor. 12
23. The love chapter	1 Cor. 13
24. The Resurrection chapter	1 Cor. 15
25. The fruit of the Spirit chapter	Gal. 5
26. The faith chapter	Heb. 11
27. The chastisement chapter	Heb. 12
28. The tongue chapter	James 3
29. The reason for suffering chapter	1 Pet. 4
30. The fellowship chapter	1 John 1

BOATS AND SHIPS

1. Noah's ark, used to save humanity during the Flood	Gen. 7:1
2. Moses' ark, the tiny boat in which Moses, aged three months, was placed to escape death	Exod. 2:3
3. The ship Jonah boarded to go to Tarshish	Jon. 1:3
4. The boat James and John were in when Christ called them to follow him	Matt. 4:21-22
5. Peter's boat, which Jesus used to preach from	Luke 5:3
6. The boat Jesus used to tell his parable on the sower and the seed	Matt. 13:2

7. The boat in which Jesus rebuked the angry sea Matt. 8:24

8. The boat Jesus entered after walking on the sea John 6:21

9. The boat in which Paul was shipwrecked en route to Rome Acts 27:41

BOOKS MENTIONED IN THE BIBLE

The Bible is itself a collection of 66 inspired books. But in the Bible several other books are mentioned:

1. The Book of Wars Num. 21:14

2. The Book of Jasher Josh. 10:13

3. The Chronicles of David 1 Chron. 27:24

4. The Book of Gad 1 Chron. 29:29

5. The Book of the Prophet Iddo 2 Chron. 13:22

6. The Book of Nathan 1 Chron. 29:29

7. The Book of Jehu 2 Chron. 20:34

8. The record book of Ahasuerus, which indirectly helped save the Jews in Persia Esther 2:23; 6:1

9. The Book of Remembrance Mal. 3:16

10. The Book of Life Dan. 12:1; Phil. 4:3; Rev. 20:12; 22:19

11. The Book of Judgment Dan. 7:10; Rev. 20:12

12. The seven-sealed book Rev. 5:1

13. An angel's book Rev. 10:2

BRIDES
See also Couples, Marriages

1. Eve, bride of Adam, married in Eden	Gen. 3:20
2. Rebekah, bride of Isaac, married in Beersheba	Gen. 24:67
3. Rachel, bride of Jacob, married in Haran	Gen. 29:18
4. Zipporah, bride of Moses, married in Midian	Exod. 2:21
5. Ruth, bride of Boaz, married in Bethlehem	Ruth 4:13
6. Esther, bride of Ahasuerus, married in Persia	Esther 2:16
7. Mary, bride of Joseph, married in Nazareth	Matt. 1:24
8. Bride at Cana	John 2:1
9. The Church, bride of Christ, to be married in heaven	Rev. 19:7

BROOKS
See also Rivers

1. Jabbok, where Jacob wrestled with God	Gen. 32:22
2. Eshcol, where the 12 spies of Israel cut down a sample of the marvelous fruit of the Promised Land	Num. 13:23
3. Sinai, the stream at the base of the mountain where Moses disposed of the golden calf Israel had made	Deut. 9:21
4. Besor, where David and his mighty men camped briefly en route to do battle with the Amalekites	1 Sam. 30:9

5. Cherith, where Elijah was fed by ravens · 1 Kings 17:3-4

6. Kishon, where Deborah and Barak defeated Sisera · Judg. 4:13

7. Kidron, which the Savior crossed en route to Gethsemane · John 18:1

BURIALS AND FUNERALS
See also Weeping and Mourning

1. Sarah: Abraham bought a cave from a pagan, and wept over the body of his beloved wife, who died at the age of 127. · Gen. 23:1-20

2. Abraham: Isaac and Ishmael attended and buried him alongside Sarah in the cave of Machpelah. He died at age 175. · Gen. 25:7-11

3. Deborah: Jacob buried his mother's old nurse under an oak tree in Bethel. · Gen. 35:8-9

4. Rachel: Jacob buried her just outside the city of Bethlehem, and set a pillar upon her grave. · Gen. 35:16-20

5. Isaac: Esau and Jacob met and buried their father next to Abraham in Hebron. · Gen. 35:27-29

6. Jacob: Joseph and his brothers carried their father out of Egypt back into Canaan and buried him at Hebron. · Gen. 50:1-13

7. Joseph: At his command, Joseph was buried by his sons in Egypt, but predicted that his bones would someday be carried back to Palestine. · Gen. 50:22-26

8. Miriam: Moses and Aaron buried their sister at Kadesh. — Num. 20:1

9. Aaron: Moses and Aaron's son, Eleazar, buried the first high priest of Israel on Mount Hor. Israel then mourned him for 30 days. — Num. 20:23-29

10. Moses: God himself attended Moses' funeral and buried him on Mount Pisgah. Apparently Michael the archangel and Satan were at this funeral. — Deut. 34; Jude 9

11. Joshua: Israel's great warrior was buried on a hill belonging to the tribe of Ephraim. — Josh. 24:29-30

12. Samuel: All Israel gathered at Ramah to bury their beloved prophet. Both Saul and David may have attended, but not at the same time. — 1 Sam. 25:1

13. David: Solomon buried his great father in the city of David after hearing his dying words of admonition. — 1 Kings 2:1-11

14. The widow of Zarephath's son: This marked the first biblical resurrection from the dead. Elijah performed it. — 1 Kings 17:17-24

15. The Shunammite's son: This marked the second biblical resurrection. — 2 Kings 4:18-37

16. A nameless man: This burial proved to be premature, for after the body came into contact with the buried bones of Elisha, the man was revived. — 2 Kings 13:20-21

17. The daughter of Jairus: She was never buried, for Jesus raised her. — Mark 5:35-43; Luke 8:41-42, 49-56; Matt. 9:18-26

18. The widow of Nain's son: Another dead person raised by Jesus. — Luke 7:11-18

19. Lazarus: He had already been buried for four days, and was raised, still wearing his graveclothes, by Jesus. — John 11:1-46

20. Dorcas: This good woman, whose   Acts 9:36-42
body had been lying in an upper
chamber, was raised by Peter.

CALLED BY GOD TO SPECIAL SERVICE
See also Ordained before Birth for Special Service

1. Noah, called to build a ship   Gen. 6:14

2. Abraham, called to leave his home for   Gen. 12:1-2
a strange land

3. Isaac, called to stay in Palestine and   Gen. 26:1-5
carry on his father's faith

4. Jacob, called to be true to his   Gen. 28:12-15
grandfather's faith

5. Joseph, called to exercise spiritual   Gen. 37:5-9
authority over his brothers

6. Moses, called to free Israel from   Exod. 3:1-12
Egyptian bondage

7. Aaron, called to become Israel's first   Lev. 8:2
high priest

8. Eleazar, called to assume   Num. 3:32; 20:28;
responsibility over the tabernacle and   34:17
to become Israel's high priest

9. Phinehas, called to receive God's   Num. 25:10-13
covenant of peace for his family

10. Joshua, called to lead Israel into   Josh. 1:1-9
Canaan

11. Othniel, called to defeat the   Judg. 3:9-10
Mesopotamians

12. Ehud, called to defeat the Moabites   Judg. 3:15

13. Deborah and Barak, called to defeat   Judg. 4:4-9
the Canaanites

14. Gideon, called to defeat the   Judg. 6:11-16
Midianites

15. Jephthah, called to defeat the   Judg. 11:29
    Ammonites
16. Samson, called to defeat the   Judg. 13:24-25
    Philistines
17. Samuel, called to replace Eli   1 Sam. 3:1-14
18. Saul, called to be Israel's first king   1 Sam. 9
19. David, called to be Israel's finest king   1 Sam. 16
20. Solomon, called to serve God as did   1 Kings 3:1-14
    his father
21. Jeroboam, called to be king over the   1 Kings 11:26-40
    ten tribes of Israel
22. Elijah, called to preach judgment   1 Kings 17:1-4
    against sin
23. Elisha, called to be the successor to   2 Kings 2:1-13
    Elijah
24. Jehu, called to rule over the ten tribes   2 Kings 9:1-6
    of Israel
25. Ezra, called to teach the Word of God   Ezra 7:6-10
    to the returning Jews
26. Nehemiah, called to build the wall   Neh. 2:18
    around Jerusalem
27. Esther, called to save her people from   Esther 4:13-16
    extermination by the Persians
28. Isaiah, called to become God's   Isa. 6:1-13
    greatest prophet
29. Jeremiah, called to be a prophet to the   Jer. 1:4-10
    nations
30. Ezekiel, called to be Israel's   Ezek. 3:10-27
    watchman on the wall
31. Daniel, called to interpret dreams   Dan. 2:19-23
32. Hosea, called to marry a harlot   Hosea 1:1-2
33. Amos, called to preach against the   Amos 1:1
    sins of the ten tribes
34. Jonah, called to warn Nineveh about   Jon. 1:1-2
    coming judgment unless it repented
35. John the Baptist, called to prepare the   Luke 1:76-80
    way for Christ

36. Peter and Andrew, called to follow Christ — Matt. 4:18-20

37. James and John, called to follow Christ — Matt. 4:21-22

38. Philip, called to follow Christ — John 1:43

39. Nathanael, called to follow Christ — John 1:44-51

40. Matthew, called to follow Christ — Matt. 9:9

41. The rich young ruler, called to sell his goods and follow Christ — Matt. 19:16-21

42. Matthias, called to take the place of Judas Iscariot — Acts 1:23-26

43. Stephen, called to function as a deacon and evangelist — Acts 6:5, 8-15

44. Philip, called to function as a deacon and evangelist — Acts 6:5; 8:5-8

45. Saul, called to become the church's first missionary-evangelist-pastor — Acts 9:15-16; 13:1-2

46. Barnabas, called to help Paul — Acts 11:22-30

47. John Mark, called to help Paul — Acts 13:5; 15:39

48. Silas, called to help Paul — Acts 15:40

49. Timothy, called to help Paul and later pastor a church — Acts 16:1-3

50. Apollos, called to be an evangelist and pastor — Acts 18:24-26

51. Jude, called to write the Book of Jude — Jude 3

CAVES

1. The cave Lot fled to after Sodom's destruction — Gen. 19:30

2. Machpelah, where Sarah, Abraham, Isaac, Rebekah, Leah, and Jacob were buried — Gen. 23:19; 25:9; 35:29; 49:30-31

3. Makkedah, where five wicked kings hid	Josh. 10:16-17
4. Adullam, where David escaped from Saul	1 Sam. 22:1
5. Engedi, where David spared Saul	1 Sam. 24:1-8
6. The cave where Obadiah hid 150 prophets of God	1 Kings 18:4
7. The cave where God spoke to Elijah	1 Kings 19:9-18
8. The cave where God spoke to Moses	Exod. 33:21-23
9. The cave where Lazarus was buried	John 11:38
10. The cave where Jesus was entombed	Matt. 27:59-60

CHILDREN

Infants

1. David and Bathsheba's son, who died in infancy	2 Sam. 12:15-18
2. Harlot's baby, a case that proved Solomon's wisdom	1 Kings 3:16-27
3. Ichabod, Phinehas's son and Eli's grandson, whose name means, "the glory of the Lord has departed"	1 Sam. 4:19-21

Small Children

1. Jeroboam's son, taken by God to punish Jeroboam	1 Kings 14:12-13
2. Isaiah's first son, who was with his father when the virgin birth prophecy was given	Isa. 7:3, 14
3. Isaiah's second son, whose name, Maher-shalal-hash-baz, is the longest in the Bible	Isa. 8:1-4

4. Nobleman's son, whom Jesus healed without being present — John 4:46-53

5. Child used by Jesus as illustration of the kingdom of God — Matt. 18:1-6; Mark 9:36-37; Luke 9:46-48

Young Boys

1. Boy raised by Elijah in what was history's first resurrection — 1 Kings 17:17-24

2. Boy raised by Elisha in what was history's second resurrection — 2 Kings 4:17-37

3. Boy who betrayed David by helping Absalom — 2 Sam. 17:18

4. Micha, son of Mephibosheth and grandson of Jonathan — 2 Sam. 9:12

5. Boy with fishes and loaves used by Christ to feed the 5000 — John 6:9

6. Demonic lad whose heartbroken father asked Jesus to heal him after the disciples proved unable to heal him — Matt. 17:14-18; Mark 9:24

Young Girls

1. Jairus's daughter, raised from the dead by Jesus — Mark 5:35-42

2. Rhoda, the first person to hear from Peter after he was released from prison — Acts 12:13

THE CHRISTIAN LIFE
See also The Church's Tasks, Commands to Believers, Praying, Salvation, Worshiping God

7 Divine Calls to the Christian from God

1. The call to salvation — Rom. 8:28-30

2. The call to sanctification — 1 Thess. 4:3; 5:23-24

3.	The call to service	John 15:16; 1 Cor. 1:26; Eph. 2:10
4.	The call to separation	2 Cor. 6:14-18
5.	The call to sonship	1 John 3:1
6.	The call to subjection	Rom. 13:4-5
7.	The call to suffering	John 16:33; Acts 14:22; Phil. 1:29; 3:10; 1 Thess. 3:3; 1 Pet. 2:21

9 Reasons for Studying Biblical Doctrine

1.	It will help settle us.	Eph. 4:14
2.	It will help save us from theological food poisoning.	1 Tim. 4:13-16
3.	It will help us reflect God.	2 Tim. 2:15
4.	It will help us equip ourselves.	2 Tim. 3:13-17; Eph. 6:10-17
5.	We will understand the history of Israel.	1 Cor. 10:1-5
6.	We will understand the restoration of Israel.	Rom. 11:25
7.	We will understand spiritual gifts.	1 Cor. 12:1
8.	We will understand the return of Christ.	1 Thess. 4:13-17
9.	We will understand the destruction of this earth.	2 Pet. 3:8, 10

12 Areas to Be Tested at the Judgment Seat of Christ

1.	How we treat other believers	Heb. 6:10; Matt. 10:41-42
2.	How we exercise our authority over others	Heb. 13:17; James 3:1
3.	How we employ our God-given abilities	1 Cor. 12:4, 11; 2 Tim. 1:6; 1 Pet. 4:10
4.	How we use our money	1 Cor. 16:2; 2 Cor. 9:6-7; 1 Tim. 6:17-19

5. How we spend our time — Ps. 90:12; Eph. 5:16; Col. 4:5; 1 Pet. 1:17

6. How much we suffer for Jesus — Matt. 5:11-12; Mark 10:29-30; Rom. 8:18; 2 Cor. 4:17; 1 Pet. 4:12-13

7. How we run that particular race which God has chosen for us — 1 Cor. 9:24; Phil. 2:16; 3:13-14; Heb. 12:1

8. How effectively we control the old nature — 1 Cor. 9:25-27

9. How many souls we witness to and win to Christ — Prov. 11:30; Dan. 12:3; 1 Thess. 2:19-20

10. How we react to temptation — James 1:2-3; Rev. 2:10

11. How much the doctrine of the Rapture means to us — 2 Tim. 4:8-9

12. How faithful we are to the Word of God and the flock of God — Acts 20:26-28; 2 Tim. 4:1-2; 1 Pet. 5:2-4

10 Challenges of the Christian in Light of the Rapture

1. To attend the services of the Lord regularly — Heb. 10:25

2. To observe the Lord's Supper with the Rapture in mind — 1 Cor. 11:26

3. To love believers and all men — 1 Thess. 3:12-13

4. To be patient — James 5:8

5. To live a separated life — 1 John 3:2-3

6. To refrain from judging others — 1 Cor. 4:5

7. To preach the Word — 2 Tim. 4:1, 2

8. To comfort the bereaved — 1 Thess. 4:16, 18

9. To win souls — Jude 21-23

10. To be concerned with heaven — Col. 3:1-4

5 Reasons for Giving Our Money

1. That God's work might be supported — 1 Tim. 5:17-18
2. That our lives might be blessed — Prov. 3:9-10; 28:20; Mal. 3:10; Luke 6:38; 2 Cor. 9:6
3. That other Christians might be challenged — 2 Cor. 9:2
4. That the Father might be glorified — 2 Cor. 9:12
5. That needy saints may be provided for — Acts 11:29; 1 John 3:17

CHURCHES
See also Pastors

1. The church in Jerusalem
   a. Began at Pentecost with at least 3120 members and was pastored by James, half brother of Christ — Acts 2:47, 41; 15:13
   b. Performed many wonders and signs — Acts 2:43; 5:12-16
   c. Had believers who had all things in common — Acts 2:44-45; 4:32-35
   d. Had believers who were in one accord — Acts 2:46
   e. Spent a good deal of time in prayer — Acts 2:42; 3:1; 4:24; 12:5-17
   f. Witnessed at every opportunity — Acts 3:12; 5:42; 4:33
   g. Radiated Jesus — Acts 4:13; 6:15
   h. Was kept pure by God — Acts 5:1-11; 8:18-24
   i. Grew constantly — Acts 2:47; 5:14; 4:4; 12:24

j. Endured persecution — Acts 4:1-3; 4:14-21; 5:17-41; 7:54-60; 8:1-3; 12:1-4

k. Appointed deacons — Acts 6:1-7

l. Practiced baptism and the Lord's Supper — Acts 2:41, 46

m. Sent forth missionaries — Acts 8:5, 14; 11:22; 13:1-3; 15:22, 27

n. Was the site of the important meeting on circumcision — Acts 15

o. Had Spirit-led believers — Acts 2:1-18; 4:31; 13:2-4; 15:28

p. Preached the word — Acts 2:16-36; 3:13-26; 7:1-53; 6:4; 5:42

q. Contended for the faith — Acts 15:1-21

r. Apparently later compromised with the Judaizers — Acts 21:18-25

2. The church in Antioch of Syria

a. Founded during the persecution which followed the martyrdom of Stephen — Acts 11:19

b. Experienced a great ingathering of souls — Acts 11:21

c. Received Barnabas, sent by the Jerusalem church to check it out — Acts 11:22

d. First pastored by Barnabas — Acts 11:23

e. Had many new members added at this time — Acts 11:24

f. Had Paul as associate pastor — Acts 11:25

g. Where Paul and Barnabas worked for a year — Acts 11:26

h. Where believers were first called Christians — Acts 11:26

i. Took up a large love offering for the needy believers in Jerusalem — Acts 11:30

    j. The home church of the first two   Acts 13:1-3; 14:26
        Christian missionaries, Paul and
        Barnabas

    k. Later became their headquarters,   Acts 14:26; 15:35
        both after their first missionary trip
        and following the Jerusalem
        Council

    l. Home church of Silas   Acts 15:34

    m. Where Paul set Peter straight on   Gal. 2:11
        matters of legalism

3. The church in Antioch of Pisidia

    a. Begun by Paul during his first   Acts 13:14
        missionary journey

    b. Where Paul preached his first   Acts 13:16
        recorded sermon

    c. Formed from the converts coming   Acts 13:43
        out of this meeting

    d. Where Paul turned from the Jews   Acts 13:46

    e. Where Paul related his heavenly   Acts 13:47
        calling as a light to the Gentiles

4. The church in Lystra

    a. Organized during Paul's first   Acts 14:6
        missionary journey

    b. The scene of Paul's healing of the   Acts 14:10-11
        impotent man, which led to Paul's
        almost being worshiped

    c. The scene of Paul's stoning   Acts 14:19;
                                                 2 Tim. 3:11

    d. Where Paul picked up Timothy   Acts 16:1-3
        during his second missionary
        journey

5. The church in Derbe   Acts 14:20-22

6. The church in Iconium

    a. Where Paul led many to Christ   Acts 14:2
        during his first journey

    b. Where he also worked great signs   Acts 14:3
        and wonders

    c. Where Paul was driven from by the unbelieving Jews   Acts 14:5

7. The church in Philippi

    a. Organized by Paul in the home of a woman convert named Lydia   Acts 16:15, 40

    b. The scene of Paul's healing of a demon-possessed girl   Acts 16:18

    c. Where the jailor became a convert   Acts 16:33

    d. Paul wrote a letter to this church.   Phil. 1:1

    e. Timothy ministered to this church.   Phil. 2:19

    f. Sent Epaphroditus to minister to Paul while the apostle was in prison   Phil. 2:25

    g. Was in danger of legalism   Phil. 3:1-3

    h. Paul wrote and asked the "true yokefellow" to help two quarreling church women named Euodias and Syntyche.   Phil. 4:1-3

    i. Helped to supply the material needs of Paul   Phil. 4:15, 18

8. The church in Thessalonica

    a. Founded during Paul's second missionary journey   Acts 17:1

    b. Witnessed a great harvest of souls   Acts 17:4

    c. Paul was accused here of turning the world upside down.   Acts 17:6

    d. In spite of their zeal, the believers were not good Bible students.   Acts 17:11

    e. Paul wrote two letters to this church.   1 Thess. 1:1; 2 Thess. 1:1

    f. The believers there had a reputation for witnessing.   1 Thess. 1:8

    g. They were persecuted by the unbelieving Jews for their faith.   1 Thess. 2:14

    h. Timothy ministered to this church.   1 Thess. 3:1-2

    i. There were some lazy members in this church.   2 Thess. 3:10

    j. There were some busybodies.   2 Thess. 3:11

    k. There were some disobedient   2 Thess. 3:14-15
       members.

9. The church in Berea, commended for   Acts 17:11
   its knowledge of and love for the
   Word of God

10. The church in Athens. It is not certain   Acts 17:34
    whether a local assembly came into
    being after Paul's sermon on Mars
    Hill, but if so, a convert named
    Dionysius probably led it.

11. The church in Corinth

    a. Founded during Paul's second   Acts 18:1
      journey

    b. Paul was aided by Aquila and   Acts 18:2
      Priscilla.

    c. Crispus, the chief ruler of the   Acts 18:8
      Jewish synagogue, was one of the
      first converts.

    d. His successor, Sosthenes, later was   Acts 18:17;
      also evidently saved.   see 1 Cor. 1:1

    e. Paul stayed here 18 months.   Acts 18:11

    f. To this church Paul wrote several   1 Cor. 5:9; 2 Cor.
      letters, two of which are included   10:9-10
      in the New Testament.

    g. This church experienced almost
      total confusion in regard to:

        (1) baptism   1 Cor. 1:12

        (2) earthly wisdom   1 Cor. 1:26

        (3) carnality and strife   1 Cor. 3:1-3

        (4) judging others unfairly   1 Cor. 4:7

        (5) immorality   1 Cor. 5:1

        (6) taking other believers to court   1 Cor. 6:1-4

        (7) marriage   1 Cor. 7:1

        (8) Christian liberty   1 Cor. 8–9

        (9) the Lord's Supper   1 Cor. 11:17-34

(10) spiritual gifts   1 Cor. 12–14

(11) the doctrine of the   1 Cor. 15
      resurrection

(12) tithing   1 Cor. 16

h. Later pastored by Apollos   1 Cor. 3:6

12. The church in Ephesus

a. Founded during Paul's second   Acts 18:19
   journey

b. May have been pastored by
   Apollos, Timothy, and the apostle
   John

c. Where Paul wrought many miracles   Acts 19:11-41
   and saw much fruit

d. Where Paul went soul-winning   Acts 20:17-21
   door-to-door

e. The only Christian church ever to
   receive letters from two New
   Testament writers: Paul wrote a
   letter to them (Eph. 1:1), and John
   the apostle would later direct a
   portion of his book Revelation to
   them (Rev. 2:1-7). According to
   John's letter, this church:

   (1) worked hard and possessed
        patience

   (2) had high church standards

   (3) suffered for Christ

   (4) hated the deeds of the
        licentious Nicolaitans

   (5) had left their first love

   (6) needed to remember, repent,
        and return to Christ

13. The church in Troas. Here Paul raised   Acts 20:7-12
    up Eutychus, a believer who had gone
    asleep during Paul's sermon and had
    fallen down from the third loft of the
    building.

14. The church in Rome

    a. Origin and founder of this church unknown

    b. Where Priscilla and Aquila labored, the church meeting in their home — Rom. 16:3-5

    c. Had a ringing testimony throughout all the land — Rom. 1:8

    d. Paul mentions having many personal friends in this church. The names of 26 individuals may be counted in Romans 16.

15. The churches in Galatia

    a. Organized by Paul during his first journey

    b. Had all fallen victim to the legalistic Judaizers, who would continually plague Paul's gospel of grace — Gal. 1:6-9

    c. The Letter to the Galatians was written to these churches. — Gal. 3:1

16. The church in Colosse

    a. Founded during Paul's stay in Ephesus, probably by Epaphras — Col. 2:1; 1:7, 12-13

    b. Philemon and Onesimus were members. — Col. 4:9; Philem. 1-2

    c. Paul commanded the Colossian epistle to be read to the Laodicean church, and ordered the one he wrote them to be read to the Colossian church. — Col. 4:16

17. The church in Babylon — 1 Pet. 5:13

    a. Wherever this church was located, it was filled with suffering believers. — 1 Pet. 1:6

    b. Some of this suffering was due to sin. — 1 Pet. 4:15-17

18. The church in Smyrna   Rev. 2:8-11

    a. The believers had suffered much for Christ.

    b. They had been slandered by those from the synagogue of Satan.

    c. Satan had imprisoned some of them.

19. The church in Pergamos   Rev. 2:12-17

    a. The believers were located in the very center of satanic worship.

    b. They had remained loyal to Christ in spite of martyrdom.

    c. They were, however, tolerating some in the church who were guilty of sexual sins.

    d. They were also tolerating those who held the doctrine of the Nicolaitans.

20. The church in Thyatira   Rev. 2:18-29

    a. The believers had performed many good deeds.

    b. But they permitted a false prophetess named Jezebel to teach that sexual sin was not a serious matter.

21. The church in Sardis   Rev. 3:1-6

    a. This church had a reputation, but was dead.

    b. They were to strengthen what little good remained.

22. The church in Philadelphia   Rev. 3:7-13

    a. Even though this church was not strong, its members had obeyed God's Word.

    b. This they had done during persecution.

23. The church in Laodicea   Rev. 3:14-22
    a. This was the least faithful church mentioned in the New Testament.
    b. The people were neither hot nor cold.
    c. They bragged about their wealth, claiming they had need of nothing, but in reality they were wretched, miserable, poor, blind, and naked.
    d. God admonished them to totally repent and allow him to re-enter fellowship with them.

THE CHURCH'S TASKS
See also The Christian Life, Worshiping God

---

1. To love God	Rev. 2:4
2. To glorify God	Eph. 1:5-6, 11-12, 14; 3:21; 2 Thess. 1:12
3. To display God's grace	Eph. 2:7; 3:6, 10; 1 Pet. 2:9
4. To evangelize the world	Matt. 28:19-20; Mark 16:15; Luke 24:47; John 20:21; Acts 1:8
5. To baptize believers	Matt. 28:19
6. To instruct believers	Matt. 28:19; Phil. 4:8-9; 1 Tim. 4:6; 5:17; 2 Tim. 2:2, 24-25
7. To edify believers	1 Cor. 14:16; Eph. 4:11-12, 16; 1 Thess. 5:11; 2 Pet. 3:18; Jude 20

8. To discipline believers

9. To provide fellowship for believers — Acts 2:42; 1 Cor. 1:9; 2 Cor. 8:4; 13:14; Gal. 2:9; Phil. 1:5; 2:12; 1 John 1:3, 6-7

10. To care for its own in time of need — 2 Cor. 8–9; 1 Tim. 5:1-16; James 1:27

11. To provoke Israel to jealousy — Rom. 11:11-14

12. To prepare rulers for the millennial kingdom — Rom. 8:17; 2 Tim. 2:12

13. To act as a restraining and enlightening force in this present world — Matt. 5:13-16; 2 Thess. 2:6-7

14. To promote all that is good — Gal. 6:10

CITIES

1. Acre (Ptolemais)
   a. Paul stopped here on his final trip to Jerusalem. — Acts 21:7
   b. Important because of its excellent harbor and ease of access to the plain of Esdraelon

2. Alexandria, the home of Apollos — Acts 18:24-26

3. Anathoth, the home of Jeremiah — Jer. 1:1

4. Antioch of Pisidia, where Paul preached his first recorded sermon during the first missionary journey — Acts 13:14-52

5. Antioch of Syria
   a. Where the disciples were first called Christians — Acts 11:19-26
   b. Where the first missionaries were sent forth — Acts 13:1-3

6. Antipatris, where the soldiers who took Paul captive from Jerusalem to Caesarea stopped for the night
Acts 23:31

7. Arad, where men took some of the children of Israel prisoners; Israel vowed to destroy them for this.
Compare Num. 21:1-2 with 33:40; Josh. 12:14; Judg. 1:16

8. Arimathea, home of Joseph, who, along with Nicodemus, claimed the body of our Lord
Matt. 27:57-60

9. Ashdod, one of the five main Philistine cities, where the Ark of the Covenant caused the destruction of the pagan god Dagon
1 Sam. 5:1-8

10. Ashkelon, another key Philistine city
1 Sam. 6:17
    a. Birthplace of Herod the Great
    b. Where Samson slew 30 men
Judg. 14:19

11. Ashtaroth, home of a number of giants
Deut. 1:4; Josh. 9:10

12. Athens, capital city of Greece, where Paul preached his Mars Hill sermon
Acts 17:15-34

13. Babylon
    a. Capital city of the Babylonian Empire
    b. Home of the Tower of Babel and original headquarters of all false religions
Rev. 17
    c. Where Daniel and Ezekiel lived and wrote their Old Testament books

14. Beer-sheba, the southern limit of Israel (Judg. 20:1), actually a cluster of wells in the open desert; place where Abraham made a covenant with Abimelech and to which Hagar fled
Gen. 21:14, 31

15. Berea, a place of Scripture-loving believers, visited by Paul during his first missionary journey
Acts 17:10-12

16. Bethany
   a. Where Lazarus was raised from the dead — John 11
   b. Where Mary anointed the feet of Jesus — John 12:1-11
   c. Where the Lord blessed his disciples just prior to his ascension — Luke 24:50

17. Bethel
   a. Where Abraham worshiped God when he came to Palestine — Gen. 12:8; 13:3-4
   b. Where Jacob dreamed his "ladder dream" — Gen. 28:11-19
   c. Where Jacob was commanded to return — Gen. 35:1, 8, 15
   d. Where Jeroboam set up golden calf images — 1 Kings 12:26-29
   e. Where Elisha was mocked by some children — 2 Kings 2:1-3, 23-24

18. Bethlehem
   a. Burial place of Rachel — Gen. 35:15-18
   b. Home of Boaz and Ruth — Book of Ruth
   c. Birthplace of David and the site of his anointing — 1 Sam. 16:4-13
   d. Birthplace of Jesus — Micah 5:2; John 7:42; Luke 2
   e. Birthplace of Mary and Joseph — Luke 2:1-4

19. Beth-peor, site of the last sermon and burial place of Moses — Deut. 4:44-46; 34:1-6

20. Bethphage, where Jesus mounted the donkey he rode into Jerusalem — Matt. 21:1

21. Bethsaida
   a. Home of Philip, Andrew, and Peter — John 1:44
   b. One of the cities upbraided by Jesus — Luke 10:11-14
   c. Where Jesus healed a blind man — Mark 8:22-26

22. Beth-shan, where the bodies of Saul   1 Sam. 31:8-13
    and Jonathan were nailed to the wall

23. Beth-shemesh
    a. Birthplace of Samson   Judg. 13:2-25
    b. Where a number of men were slain   1 Sam. 6:19-21
       for looking into the Ark of God

24. Caesarea
    a. Home of Cornelius   Acts 10:1-18
    b. Where God struck down Herod   Acts 12:19-23
       Agrippa I
    c. Home of Philip the evangelist and   Acts 21:10-13
       his daughters
    d. Where Paul witnessed to Felix   Acts 24:25
    e. Where Paul witnessed to Agrippa   Acts 26:28

25. Caesarea Philippi, where Jesus heard   Matt. 16:33
    Peter's great confession

26. Cana
    a. Home of Nathanael   John 21:2
    b. Where Jesus performed his first   John 2:1-11
       miracle, that of turning water into
       wine
    c. Where Jesus performed his second   John 4:46-54
       miracle, that of healing the
       nobleman's son

27. Capernaum
    a. Main headquarters of Jesus' earthly   Matt. 4:13; 9:1
       ministry
    b. Where Jesus chose Matthew   Matt. 9:9
    c. Where Jesus delivered his great   John 6:24-71
       Bread of Life sermon
    d. Where Jesus performed at least
       nine of his 36 recorded miracles:
       (1) Healing of the centurion's   Matt. 8:5-13
           servant
       (2) Healing of Peter's mother-in-   Matt. 8:14-15
           law

      (3)   Healing of a demoniac   Mark 1:21-27

      (4)   Healing of a palsied man who   Mark 2:1-5
            was lowered from the roof

      (5)   Healing of the woman with   Matt. 9:22
            internal bleeding

      (6)   Healing of Jairus's daughter   Matt. 9:25

      (7)   Healing of two blind men   Matt. 9:29

      (8)   Healing of a dumb demoniac   Matt. 9:33

      (9)   The miracle of the tribute   Matt. 17:24-27
            money

28. Colosse

   a. The church in this city received a
      letter from Paul.

   b. Home of Philemon and Onesimus   Col. 4:9

29. Corinth

   a. Home of Aquila and Priscilla   Acts 18:1-2

   b. Where God appeared to Paul in a   Acts 18:9-10
      vision

   c. Where Paul visited on his second Acts 18:11
      journey and spent 18 months

   d. The church in this city received two
      of Paul's epistles.

30. Cyrene, home of Simon, who carried   Matt. 27:32
    Jesus' cross

31. Damascus

   a. Home of Abraham's faithful   Gen. 15:2
      servant

   b. Where Elisha visited a sick king   2 Kings 8:7

   c. Israel's King Ahaz built a pagan   2 Kings 16:10
      altar in Jerusalem after seeing a
      similar one in Damascus.

   d. City connected with Paul's   Acts 9:1-18
      conversion

32. Dan

   a. City marking the northern limit of 1 Sam. 3:20
      Israel

b. One of two cities where Jeroboam set up his golden calves — 1 Kings 12:29

33. Derbe, a stopping point during Paul's first missionary journey — Acts 16:1

34. Dothan
   a. Where Joseph was sold into slavery — Gen. 37:17
   b. Where the Lord struck the Syrian army with blindness at the request of Elisha — 2 Kings 6:18

35. Ekron, one of the five main Philistine cities whose leaders hurriedly rid themselves of the troublesome Ark of God — 1 Sam. 10–12

36. Emmaus, where Jesus appeared to two disciples after his resurrection — Luke 24:13-31

37. Endor, where Saul visited the witch — 1 Sam. 28:7-14

38. En-gedi, near where David hid from Saul in a cave — 1 Sam. 24:1-22

39. Ephesus
   a. Visited by Paul during his second missionary journey — Acts 18:19
   b. Where Apollos was instructed by Aquila and Priscilla — Acts 18:24-26
   c. Where Paul met some of John the Baptist's disciples — Acts 19:1-7
   d. Where the gospel led to a book-burning ceremony and a confrontation with the worshipers of the pagan goddess Diana — Acts 19:18-41

40. Ezion-geber, home of Solomon's navy — 1 Kings 9:26; 22:48

41. Gath, Philistine city, hometown of Goliath — 1 Sam. 17:4

42. Gaza
   a. Philistine city which had its main gates along with the gateposts pulled up and carried away by Samson — Judg. 16:1-3

    b. Where Samson was imprisoned   Judg. 16:21
       after his betrayal by Delilah

    c. Area where Philip met the   Acts 8:26
       Ethiopian eunuch

43. Gerar

    a. Where Abraham lied the second   Gen. 20
       time about Sarah

    b. Where Isaac lied about Rebekah   Gen. 26

44. Gibeah, hometown of Saul   1 Sam. 10:26

45. Gibeon

    a. City that tricked Joshua into sparing   Josh. 9:1-27
       it

    b. Where the sun stood still   Josh. 10:12-13

    c. Where God appeared to Solomon   1 Kings 3:4-15
       and granted him wisdom

46. Gilgal

    a. The first stop of Israel after they   Josh. 4:19
       crossed the River Jordan west

    b. Where Joshua heard Caleb's   Josh. 14:6-15
       testimony

    c. Where Saul was publicly   1 Sam. 11:14-15
       proclaimed king

    d. Where Saul intruded into the office   1 Sam. 13:4-14
       of the priesthood

    e. Where Saul lied to Samuel about   1 Sam. 15:12-23
       killing the enemy

    f. Where Elisha cured a pot of   2 Kings 4:38-41
       poisonous stew

47. Gomorrah, a wicked city near Sodom   Gen. 19:24-25
    which was destroyed along with it

48. Haran

    a. City where Abraham got bogged   Gen. 11:31; 12:4
       down for awhile after his call to
       Canaan

    b. Home of Rebekah, and the home of   Gen. 24:10; 28–29
       Jacob for 20 years. Here all his
       sons except Benjamin were born.

49. Hazor, headquarters of Israel's enemy, Sisera — Judg. 4:1-2

50. Hebron
    a. Where Abraham built an altar to God — Gen. 13:18
    b. Burial place of Sarah, Abraham, Isaac, and Jacob — Gen. 23:2, 19: 25:9; 35:37-29; 50:13
    c. Where David was anointed king over Judah — 2 Sam. 2:1-3
    d. Where David was anointed king over all Israel — 2 Sam. 5:1-5
    e. Where Joab killed Abner — 2 Sam. 3:27
    f. Headquarters of Absalom during his brief rebellion — 2 Sam. 15:7-10
    g. One of the six cities of refuge — Josh. 20:7

51. Iconium, a stop during Paul's first missionary journey — Acts 13:51

52. Jabesh-gilead, a city saved from a cruel fate by King Saul — 1 Sam. 11

53. Jericho
    a. Home of Rahab the harlot — Josh. 2
    b. City shouted down by Israel — Josh. 6
    c. Location of a school of the prophets — 2 Kings 2:5, 15
    d. City from which Elijah departed into heaven — 2 Kings 2:1-5
    e. Where Jesus healed a blind man named Bartimaeus — Luke 18:35
    f. Where Jesus met Zacchaeus — Luke 19:1-10
    g. City Jesus used to illustrate his Good Samaritan parable — Luke 10:30-37

54. Jerusalem — see separate entry

55. Jezreel
    a. Home of Naboth — 1 Kings 21:1-29
    b. Place of Jezebel's death — 2 Kings 9:10, 30-37

     c. Where Jehu killed two kings,   2 Kings 8:29;
       Joram of the north, and Ahaziah of   9:24, 27
       the south

56. Joppa

     a. Where Jonah attempted to flee from   Jon. 1:3
       God's command

     b. Where Peter raised Dorcas from the   Acts 9:36-41
       dead

     c. Where Peter received his "sheet"   Acts 9:43
       vision concerning the Gentiles

57. Kerioth, birthplace of Judas Iscariot.

58. Kirjath-jearim, where the Ark of the   1 Sam. 6:21; 7:1-2
    Covenant was kept for 20 years

59. Laodicea, home of one of the seven
    churches mentioned in Revelation
    3:14

60. Lydda, where Peter cured Aeneas   Acts 9:32-35

61. Lystra

     a. Home of Timothy   Acts 16:1-4

     b. Where Paul was stoned   Acts 14:19; 2 Tim.
       3:11

62. Magdala, home of Mary Magdalene   Luke 8:2; Mark
      16:9

63. Masada

     a. Where David hid from Saul   1 Sam. 24:22;
      1 Chron. 12:8

     b. King Herod's winter headquarters

     c. Site of the Jews' last stand during
       the A.D. 66–73 revolt against the
       Romans. The 960 besieged Jews
       killed themselves rather than
       surrender.

64. Michmash, site of Israel's great   1 Sam. 14:1-23
    victory over the Philistines

65. Miletus, a seaport town where Paul   Acts 20:15-38
    met with some Ephesian elders

66. Mizpah
    a. Where Jacob and Laban parted   Gen. 31:49
    b. The hometown of Jephthah   Judg. 11:34
    c. Where 11 tribes declared war on Benjamin   Judg. 21:1-8
    d. Where Samuel gathered Israel for prayer and rededication   1 Sam. 7:5-7
    e. Where Saul was introduced to Israel as their first king   1 Sam. 10:17-24

Note: Saul was anointed at Ramah by Samuel, introduced at Mizpah, and publicly crowned at Gilgal. 1 Sam. 9:15-16; 10:1; 11:15

67. Myra, where Paul changed ships as a prisoner en route to Rome   Acts 27:5-6

68. Nain, where Jesus raised a widow's son from the dead   Luke 7:11-18

69. Nazareth
    a. Where the angels announced the birth of Jesus to both Mary and Joseph   Luke 1:26; Matt. 1:19-20
    b. Where Jesus grew into manhood   Luke 2:39-40
    c. Where he preached his Isaiah 61 sermon   Luke 4:16-30
    d. Where he was rejected by the townspeople, because "a prophet is not without honor, save in his own country"   Matt. 13:53-58; Mark 6:1-6

70. Nineveh
    a. Ancient capital of Assyria, where Jonah was sent by God to preach   Jon. 1
    b. Referred to by Jesus as an Old Testament example of repentance   Matt. 12:41

71. Nob
    a. Where David took refuge during his flight from Saul   1 Sam. 21:1
    b. Where Saul murdered 85 priests of the Lord   1 Sam. 22:18

72. Paphos, a city in southwest Cyprus where Paul worked his first recorded miracle — Acts 13:6-12

73. Perga, where John Mark left Paul and Barnabas to return home — Acts 13:13

74. Pergamos, an Asian city with a church that was among the seven churches in Revelation — Rev. 2:12

75. Petra
    a. Home of Esau — Gen. 36:1
    b. Home of some proud and treacherous Edomites — Book of Obadiah
    c. The possible refuge of saved Israel during the Tribulation — Rev. 12:14; Zech. 14:5; Isa. 63:1

76. Philadelphia, an Asian city with a church that was among the seven churches in Revelation — Rev. 3:7-13

77. Philippi
    a. Paul wrote a letter to the church in this city.
    b. Paul led three to Christ here. These conversion stories are well-known:
        (1) A Jewish woman, Lydia — Acts 16:14-15
        (2) A demon-possessed Greek girl — Acts 16:16-19
        (3) The jailor — Acts 16:25-34

78. Rabbah-ammon, where Uriah was murdered — 2 Sam. 11:2-17

79. Ramah
    a. Home of Samuel's parents — 1 Sam. 1:19
    b. Where Israel gathered to demand a king — 1 Sam. 8:4-5
    c. Permanent headquarters of Samuel — 1 Sam. 15:34; 16:13
    d. Where Samuel was buried — 1 Sam. 25:1

80. Rome
    a. The church in this city received the greatest theological epistle ever

written, Paul's Letter to the
Romans.

b. Where Paul was martyred

c. Where Peter was martyred

81. Salamis, a city in southeast Cyprus where Paul preached during his first missionary journey — Acts 13:4-5

82. Samaria

a. Capital city of the northern kingdom, built by King Omri — 1 Kings 16:24; 2 Kings 3:1

b. Where Ahab built his beautiful ivory palace — 1 Kings 16:31-33

c. Where Elijah confronted Ahab about the murder of Naboth — 1 Kings 21:18

d. Where Ahab, mortally wounded, died beside a pool — 1 Kings 22:37-38

e. Where Elisha led some blinded Syrian soldiers — 2 Kings 6:19

f. The city saved by four lepers — 2 Kings 7:1-20

g. Where Naaman was healed of leprosy — 2 Kings 5:3-14

h. Where Jehu killed all the Baal worshipers — 2 Kings 10:17-28

i. Where Philip the evangelist led a great revival — Acts 8:5-25

83. Shechem

a. Where Jacob buried his household's false gods — Gen. 35:4

b. Where Simeon and Levi tricked their enemies — Gen. 34

c. Where Joseph's bones were buried — Josh. 24:32

d. One of the six cities of refuge — Josh. 20:7-8

e. Where Joshua gave his farewell address — Josh. 24:1

f. Headquarters of Abimelech's evil doings — Judg. 9

    g. Where Rehoboam was crowned king   1 Kings 12:1

84. Shiloh

    a. Home of the tabernacle after Israel conquered Palestine   Josh. 18:1

    b. Where Joshua divided up the land among the tribes   Josh. 18:2-10; 19:51; 21:1-3

    c. Where the remaining Benjaminite warriors found wives   Judg. 21:16-23

    d. Where Hannah prayed for a son   1 Sam. 1

    e. Where God called to young Samuel   1 Sam. 3:21

    f. Where Jeroboam's wife attempted to trick Ahijah the prophet   1 Kings 14:1-18

85. Shunem, home of woman whose son Elisha raised   2 Kings 4:8

86. Sidon

    a. Home of Jezebel   1 Kings 16:31-33

    b. Home of the Canaanite woman whose daughter Jesus healed   Matt. 15:21-28

87. Smyrna, a city in Asia that had one of the seven churches mentioned in Revelation   Rev. 2:8-11

88. Sodom

    a. Abraham refused to enter into a pact with the wicked king of this perverted city.   Gen. 14:21-24

    b. Destroyed by God with fire and brimstone   Gen. 19

89. Succoth

    a. Jacob's home for awhile after meeting up with Esau   Gen. 33:17

    b. City punished by Gideon because of its refusal to feed his hungry troops   Judg. 8:5-16

90. Sychar, home of the Samaritan woman who talked with Jesus at the well   John 4:7-26

91. Tarsus, birthplace of Paul — Acts 9:11; 21:39; 22:3

92. Tekoa
   a. Home of a crafty woman who attempted to reconcile David and Absalom — 2 Sam. 14:2-4
   b. Home of Amos the prophet — Amos 1:1

93. Thessalonica
   a. Paul established a church here during his second missionary journey. — Acts 17:1-9
   b. He later wrote two epistles to this church.

94. Thyatira
   a. Home of Lydia — Acts 16:14
   b. Location of one of the seven churches in Revelation — Rev. 2:18-24

95. Tiberias, the town at the mouth of the Jordan River and the Sea of Galilee — John 6:1; 21:1

96. Troas
   a. Where Paul received his Macedonian vision — Acts 16:11
   b. Where Paul revived Eutychus — Acts 20:6-12
   c. Where Paul left his cloak — 2 Tim. 4:13

97. Tyre
   a. Home of Hiram, the supplier for Solomon's temple — 1 Kings 5:1-11; 9:11-14
   b. City of Ezekiel's great prophecy — Ezek. 26
   c. Where God struck down Herod with a plague — Acts 12:20
   d. Where Paul knelt down by the seashore and prayed — Acts 21:2-6

98. Ur, birthplace of Abraham — Gen. 11:27, 28; 15:7; Neh. 9:7

99. Zarephath, home of a widow with whom Elijah stayed — 1 Kings 17:9-24; Luke 4:26

100. Zoar, a city near the cave where Lot
     and his daughters stayed after
     Sodom's destruction

CITY BUILDERS

1. Cain built a city called Enoch east of   Gen. 4:17
   Eden.
2. Nimrod built Babylon.   Gen. 10:8-11; 11:4
3. Enslaved Israelites built treasure cities   Exod. 1:11
   of Pithom and Raamses.
4. Solomon built Gezer and Beth-horon.   1 Kings 9:1-17
5. Jeroboam built Shechem and Penuel.   1 Kings 12:25
6. Rehoboam rebuilt Bethlehem.   2 Chron. 11:6
7. Baasha rebuilt Ramah.   1 Kings 15:17
8. Omri built Samaria.   1 Kings 16:23-24
9. Hiel rebuilt Jericho.   1 Kings 16:34
10. Azariah built Elath.   2 Kings 14:22
11. Nebuchadnezzar rebuilt Babylon.   Dan. 4:30

COMMANDS TO BELIEVERS
See also The Christian Life, Praying, Worshiping God

1. Abstain from all appearances of evil.   1 Thess. 5:22
2. Abstain from all fleshly lusts.   1 Pet. 2:11
3. Avoid troublemakers.   Rom. 16:17
4. Avoid profane and vain babblings.   1 Tim. 6:20
5. Avoid false science.   1 Tim. 6:20

6. Avoid foolish questions.	Titus 3:9
7. Avoid arguments about the law.	Titus 3:9
8. Be reconciled to a brother.	Matt. 5:24
9. Be wise as serpents.	Matt. 10:16
10. Be harmless as doves.	Matt. 10:16
11. Be thankful.	Col. 3:15
12. Be patient toward all men.	1 Thess. 5:14; 2 Tim. 2:24
13. Be ready to give an answer of the hope that is in you.	1 Pet. 3:15
14. Be transformed.	Rom. 12:2
15. Be patient in tribulation.	Rom. 12:12
16. Be children in [avoiding] malice.	1 Cor. 14:20
17. Be men in understanding.	1 Cor. 14:20
18. Be steadfast.	1 Cor. 15:58
19. Be unmovable.	1 Cor. 15:58
20. Be always abounding in God's work.	1 Cor. 15:58
21. Be of one mind.	Rom. 12:16
22. Be separate from the unclean.	2 Cor. 6:17
23. Be angry and sin not.	Eph. 4:26
24. Be filled with the Spirit.	Eph. 5:18
25. Be anxious for nothing.	Phil. 4:6
26. Be an example to other believers.	1 Tim. 4:12
27. Be gentle to all men.	2 Tim. 2:24
28. Be ready to teach.	2 Tim. 2:24
29. Be content with what you have.	Heb. 13:5
30. Be vigilant.	1 Pet. 5:8
31. Do not be like the hypocrites in prayer.	Matt. 6:5
32. Do not be afraid of men.	Luke 12:4
33. Do not be conformed to this world.	Rom. 12:2
34. Do not be children in understanding.	1 Cor. 14:20
35. Do not be deceived by evil companions.	1 Cor. 15:33

36. Do not be unequally yoked with unbelievers. — 2 Cor. 6:14-18

37. Do not be drunk with wine. — Eph. 5:18

38. Do not be weary in well-doing. — 2 Thess. 3:13

39. Do not be slothful. — Heb. 6:12

40. Do not be influenced by strange doctrines. — Heb. 13:9

41. Beware of false prophets. — Matt. 7:15; Phil. 3:2

42. Beware of [evil] men. — Matt. 10:17

43. Beware of covetousness. — Luke 12:15

44. Beware of backsliding. — 2 Pet. 3:17

45. Do not bid false teachers Godspeed. — 2 John 10-11

46. Bring up children in the Lord. — Eph. 6:4

47. Cast your cares upon God. — 1 Pet. 5:7

48. Have confidence in God. — Heb. 10:35

49. Come out from among the world. — 2 Cor. 6:17

50. Count it joy when you are tempted. — James 1:2

51. Treat others as you expect to be treated. — Matt. 7:12

52. Desire the milk of the Word. — 1 Pet. 2:2

53. Do all to God's glory. — 1 Cor. 10:31; Col. 3:17, 23

54. Do all things without murmuring or disputing. — Phil. 2:14

55. Earnestly contend for the faith. — Jude 3

56. Give no place to Satan. — Eph. 4:27

57. Give thanks. — Eph. 5:20; Phil. 4:6

58. Give time to reading. — 1 Tim. 4:13

59. Give no offense. — 1 Cor. 10:32

60. Give freely. — 2 Cor. 9:6-7

61. Give as God has prospered. — 1 Cor. 16:2

62. Give willingly. — 2 Cor. 8:12

63. Give purposely. — 2 Cor. 9:7

64. Do not grieve the Holy Spirit.	Eph. 4:30
65. Grow in grace.	2 Pet. 3:18
66. Have no fellowship with darkness.	Eph. 5:11
67. Have compassion.	Jude 22
68. Have a good conscience.	1 Pet. 3:16
69. Hold forth the Word of life.	Phil. 2:16
70. Hold fast sound words.	2 Tim. 1:13
71. Honor fathers.	Eph. 6:2
72. Honor mothers.	Matt. 19:19
73. Honor widows.	1 Tim. 5:3
74. Honor rulers.	1 Pet. 2:17
75. Lay aside all envy.	1 Pet. 2:1
76. Lay aside all evil speaking.	1 Pet. 2:1
77. Do not lay up treasures on earth.	Matt. 6:19
78. Let your light shine.	Matt. 5:16
79. Let everyone deny himself.	Matt. 16:24
80. Let him share with the needy.	Luke 3:11
81. Let everyone obey civil laws.	Rom. 13:1
82. Let no man deceive himself.	1 Cor. 3:18
83. Let everyone examine himself at communion.	1 Cor. 11:28
84. Let your requests be made known to God.	Phil. 4:6
85. Let your speech be with grace.	Col. 4:6
86. Do all things in decent order.	1 Cor. 14:40
87. Let those who are taught support the teacher.	Gal. 6:6
88. Let wives be subject to their husbands.	Eph. 5:22; Col. 3:18
89. Let husbands love their wives.	Eph. 5:25
90. Let wives reverence their husbands.	Eph. 5:33
91. Let everyone be swift to hear, slow to speak, slow to wrath.	James 1:19
92. Let the afflicted pray.	James 5:13

93.	Let the adorning of women be more inward than outward.	1 Pet. 3:3-4
94.	Don't let the left hand know what the right hand is doing.	Matt. 6:3
95.	Do not let sin reign in the body.	Rom. 6:12
96.	Do not let the sun go down on your wrath.	Eph. 4:26
97.	Follow things that edify.	Rom. 14:19
98.	Walk in the Spirit.	Gal. 5:25
99.	Do not provoke one another.	Gal. 5:26
100.	Do not be weary in well-doing.	Gal. 6:9
101.	Come boldly to the throne of grace.	Heb. 4:16; 10:19-23
102.	Do not forsake assembling together in worship.	Heb. 10:25
103.	Exhort one another.	Heb. 10:25
104.	Lay aside every weight.	Heb. 12:1
105.	Run with patience the race before us.	Heb. 12:1
106.	Look to Jesus.	Heb. 12:2
107.	Offer the sacrifice of praise to God continually.	Heb. 13:15
108.	Do not judge one another in doubtful things.	Rom. 14:1
109.	Do not cause others to stumble.	Rom. 14:13
110.	Mark troublemakers.	Rom. 16:17; Phil. 3:17
111.	Pray for your persecutors.	Matt. 5:44; Luke 6:28
112.	Pray for laborers.	Matt. 9:38; Luke 10:2
113.	Present your body to God.	Rom. 12:1
114.	Put on the new man.	Eph. 4:24; Col. 3:10
115.	Put on the whole armor of God.	Eph. 6:11, 13
116.	Do not quench the Spirit.	1 Thess. 5:19
117.	Consider yourself dead to sin.	Rom. 6:11

118. Redeem the time.   Eph. 5:16
119. Resist the devil.   James 4:7; 1 Pet. 5:9
120. Restore backsliders in meekness.   Gal. 6:1
121. Strengthen feeble knees.   Heb. 12:12
122. Study to show yourself approved to God.   2 Tim. 2:15
123. Take no anxious thought of tomorrow.   Matt. 6:34
124. Take the Lord's Supper.   1 Cor. 11:24-26
125. Be careful not to despise little ones.   Matt. 18:10
126. Be aware of yourself and your doctrine.   1 Tim. 4:16
127. Withdraw from disorderly people.   2 Thess. 3:6, 14

COMMANDS TO INDIVIDUALS

1. To Adam
   a. Be fruitful, and multiply, and replenish the earth, and subdue it.   Gen. 1:28
   b. But of the tree of the knowledge of good and evil, you shall not eat.   Gen. 2:17
2. To Noah
   a. Make an ark of gopher wood.   Gen. 6:14
   b. And of every living thing of all flesh, two of every sort you shall bring into the ark.   Gen. 6:19
   c. Come with all your house into the ark.   Gen. 7:1
   d. Go forth from the ark.   Gen. 8:16
   e. Be fruitful, and multiply, and replenish the earth.   Gen. 9:1

3. To Abraham

    a. Go out from your country unto a land I will show you. — Gen. 12:1

    b. This shall not be your heir. — Gen. 15:4

    c. Take an heifer. — Gen. 15:9

    d. Your name shall be Abraham. — Gen. 17:5

    e. And you shall circumcise the flesh of your foreskin. — Gen. 17:11

    f. You shall not call her name Sarai, but Sarah. — Gen. 17:15

    g. Take your son and offer him for a burnt offering. — Gen. 22:2

4. To Isaac: Do not go down into Egypt. — Gen. 26:2

5. To Jacob

    a. Your name shall no longer be called Jacob, but Israel. — Gen. 32:28

    b. Arise, go up to Bethel, and dwell there. — Gen. 35:1

    c. Fear not to go down into Egypt. — Gen. 46:3

6. To Moses

    a. Take off your shoes. — Exod. 3:5

    b. You shall say to the children of Israel, I AM hath sent me to you. — Exod. 3:14

    c. Cast your rod on the ground. — Exod. 4:3

    d. Put your hand into your bosom. — Exod. 4:6

    e. Go, and I will be with your mouth. — Exod. 4:12

    f. Take your rod, and stretch out your hand upon the waters of Egypt. — Exod. 7:19

    g. Each man take a lamb. — Exod. 12:3

    h. Lift up your rod over the sea and divide it. — Exod. 14:16

    i. Smite the rock. — Exod. 17:6

    j. Write this for a memorial in a book. — Exod. 17:14

    k. Let them make me a sanctuary. — Exod. 25:8

    l. Go, get down; for your people have — Exod. 32:7
       corrupted themselves.

    m. Behold, there is a place by me, and — Exod. 33:21
       you shall stand upon a rock.

    n. Take Aaron and the anointing oil. — Lev. 8:2

    o. Gather seventy men of the elders of — Num. 11:16
       Israel.

    p. Send men, that they may search the — Num. 13:2
       land of Canaan.

    q. Speak unto the rock. — Num. 20:8

    r. Strip Aaron of his garments, and — Num. 20:26
       put them upon Eleazar his son.

    s. Make a fiery serpent and set it upon — Num. 21:8
       a pole.

    t. Take Joshua and lay hands upon — Num. 27:18
       him.

    u. Get up unto Mount Nebo. — Deut. 32:49

7. To Joshua

    a. Moses my servant is dead; now — Josh. 1:2
       arise, go over Jordan.

    b. Have I not commanded you? Be — Josh. 1:9
       strong and courageous; do not be
       afraid, or dismayed.

    c. Circumcise again the children of — Josh. 5:2
       Israel.

    d. Go around the city once. Do this — Josh. 6:3-4
       for six days and the seventh day
       you shall circle the city seven
       times.

    e. Get up; why do you lie upon your — Josh. 7:10
       face?

8. To Gideon

    a. Proclaim in the ears of the people, — Judg. 7:3
       saying, Whoever is fearful and
       afraid, let him return and depart.

b. The people are still too many; bring them down to the water, and I will try them there. — Judg. 7:4

9. To Samuel

a. I will send you a man out of the land of Benjamin, and you shall anoint him to be captain over my people Israel. — 1 Sam. 9:16

b. Look not on his appearance, for the Lord looks on the heart. Arise, anoint him: for this is he. — 1 Sam. 16:7, 12

10. To David

a. And the Lord said, Go up to Hebron. — 2 Sam. 2:1

b. You shall not build me a house to dwell in. — 1 Chron. 17:4

11. To Elijah

a. Go and hide yourself by the brook Cherith. — 1 Kings 17:3

b. Get thee to Zarephath. — 1 Kings 17:9

c. Go, show yourself to Ahab. — 1 Kings 18:1

d. Rise up and eat, because the journey is too great for you. — 1 Kings 19:7

COMMANDS TO ISRAEL

1. You shall have no other gods before me. — Exod. 20:3

2. You shall not make any graven image. — Exod. 20:4

3. You shall not take the name of the Lord your God in vain. — Exod. 20:7

4. Remember the Sabbath day, to keep it holy. — Exod. 20:8

5. Honor your father and mother.	Exod. 20:12
6. You shall not kill.	Exod. 20:13
7. You shall not commit adultery.	Exod. 20:14
8. You shall not steal.	Exod. 20:15
9. You shall not bear false witness.	Exod. 20:16
10. You shall not covet.	Exod. 20:17
11. You shall love the Lord your God with all your heart, and with all your soul, and with all your might.	Deut. 6:5
12. These words which I command you shall be in your heart.	Deut. 6:6
13. You shall teach [God's words] diligently unto your children.	Deut. 6:7
14. You shall fear the Lord your God, and serve him.	Deut. 6:13
15. Circumcise the foreskin of your heart, and be no longer stiffnecked.	Deut. 10:16
16. Whatever I command you, observe and do it. You shall not add to or subtract from it.	Deut. 12:32

CONFESSIONS OF SIN

1. Judah's confession of the sin of immorality	Gen. 38:26
2. Pharaoh's confession of his persecution of Israel	Exod. 10:16

Note: Not all confessions in the Bible were genuine!

3. Moses' confession of Israel's golden calf sin	Exod. 32:30-32
4. Balaam's confession of his disobedience to God	Num. 22:34

5. Achan's confession of his goods stolen from Jericho — Josh. 7:20

6. Saul's confession of his sparing of the spoils of war and of his murderous intents toward David — 1 Sam. 15:24, 30; 26:21

7. David's confession of his sin with Bathsheba and his sin in numbering Israel — 2 Sam. 12:13; Ps. 51:4; 2 Sam. 24:10, 17

8. Shimei's confession of his sin of cursing David — 2 Sam. 19:20

9. Manasseh's confession of his evil reign on Judah's throne — 2 Chron. 33:11-13

10. Isaiah's confession of his personal sins and those of Israel — Isa. 6:5; 59:12

11. Jeremiah's confession of his personal sins and those of Israel — Jer. 3:25

12. Daniel's confession of his personal sins and those of Israel — Dan. 9:20

13. Ezra's confession of his personal sins and those of Judah — Ezra 10:1

14. Nehemiah's confession of his personal sins and those of Judah — Neh. 1:6

15. Job's confession of his self-righteousness — Job 42:6

16. The Prodigal Son's confession of his riotous living — Luke 15:18

17. Peter's confession of his denial of Christ — Matt. 26:75

18. Judas's confession of his remorse in betraying Christ — Matt. 27:4

19. A Corinthian believer's confession of his immorality — 1 Cor. 5:1-13; 2 Cor. 2:1-11; 7:9-10

CONVERSIONS

1. Abraham	Gen. 12:1-3; 15:6
2. Jacob	Gen. 28:19-22
3. Rahab	Josh. 2:9
4. Ruth	Ruth 1:16
5. Samuel	1 Sam. 3:1-10
6. David	1 Sam. 16:13
7. Widow of Zarephath	1 Kings 17:24
8. Shunammite woman	2 Kings 4:30
9. Naaman	2 Kings 5:14-15
10. Manasseh	2 Chron. 33:10-13, 18-19
11. Cyrus	Ezra 1:2-4; Isa. 44:28
12. Nebuchadnezzar	Dan. 3:28-29; 4:1-2, 34-35, 37
13. Darius	Dan. 6:25-27
14. King of Nineveh	Jon. 3:5-9
15. A centurion	Matt. 8:10, 13
16. Matthew	Matt. 9:9
17. A Canaanite woman	Matt. 15:28
18. Another centurion	Matt. 27:54
19. The Gadarene maniac	Mark 5:15
20. A woman with internal bleeding	Mark 5:34
21. The father of a demoniac son	Mark 9:24
22. Bartimaeus	Mark 10:52
23. A scribe	Mark 12:34
24. Mary Magdalene	Mark 16:9
25. A paralytic	Luke 5:20
26. An immoral woman	Luke 7:38
27. A leper	Luke 17:12-19
28. A publican	Luke 18:13-14
29. Zacchaeus	Luke 19:8

30. A woman with an 18-year infirmity	Luke 13:12-13
31. A dying thief	Luke 23:42
32. Peter	John 1:42
33. Andrew	John 1:40
34. Philip	John 1:43
35. Nathanael	John 1:49
36. Nicodemus	John 3
37. The Samaritan woman	John 4:29
38. A nobleman	John 4:53
39. An adulterous woman	John 8:11
40. A blind man	John 9:38
41. Martha	John 11:27
42. A lame man	Acts 3:8
43. The Ethiopian eunuch	Acts 8:37
44. Saul	Acts 9:6
45. Cornelius	Acts 10:44
46. Sergius Paulus	Acts 13:12
47. Lydia	Acts 16:14-15
48. A demoniac girl	Acts 16:18
49. The Philippian jailor	Acts 16:32-34
50. Crispus	Acts 18:8
51. Apollos	Acts 18:24-25

COUNTERFEITS

1. False worship	Matt. 15:8-9
2. False Christs	Matt. 24:4-5, 24
3. False apostles	2 Cor. 11:13
4. False ministers	2 Cor. 11:14-15
5. False gospel	Gal. 1:6-12

6. False Christians	Gal. 2:3-4
7. False miracle workers	2 Thess. 2:7-12
8. False science	1 Tim. 6:20
9. False commandments	Titus 1:13-14
10. False doctrines	Heb. 13:9
11. False religion	James 1:26
12. False prayer	James 4:3
13. False religious teachers	2 Pet. 2:1
14. False prophets	1 John 4:1

COUPLES
See also Brides, Marriages

Couples with Both Husband and Wife Named

1. Adam and Eve, world's first couple	Gen. 3:20
2. Abraham and Sarah, father and mother of Israel	Gen. 11:29
3. Isaac and Rebekah, son and daughter-in-law of Abraham	Gen. 24:67
4. Jacob and Rachel, father of Israel's 12 tribes and his beloved wife	Gen. 29:18
5. Joseph and Asenath, beloved son of Jacob and his Egyptian wife	Gen. 41:45
6. Amram and Jochebed, parents of Moses	Exod. 2:1-2; 6:20
7. Moses and Zipporah, great lawgiver and his Midianite wife	Exod. 2:21
8. Elimelech and Naomi, mother-in-law and father-in-law to Ruth	Ruth 1:2
9. Boaz and Ruth, great-grandparents of King David	Ruth 4:13

10. Elkanah and Hannah, parents of   1 Sam. 1:1-2
    Samuel

11. Saul and Ahinoam, Israel's first king   1 Sam. 14:50
    and his wife

12. Nabal and Abigail, foolish farmer and   1 Sam. 25:3
    his wise wife

13. David and Bathsheba, parents of   2 Sam. 11:27
    Solomon

14. Rehoboam and Maachah, Solomon's   2 Chron. 11:20;
    son who ruled Judah with his idol-   1 Kings 15:13
    worshiping wife

15. Ahab and Jezebel, northern kingdom's   1 Kings 16:30-31
    worst king and queen

16. Joram and Athaliah, son of   2 Kings 8:16-24
    Jehoshaphat married to the godless
    daughter of Jezebel

17. Jehoiada and Jehosheba, godly high   2 Chron. 22:11
    priest and wife who saved Joash

18. Hosea and Gomer, godly prophet and   Hos. 1–3
    his promiscuous wife

19. Ahasuerus and Esther, Persian king   Esther 2:16
    and his Jewish queen

20. Haman and Zeresh, wicked Persian   Esther 5:14; 6:13
    politician and his wife

21. Zacharias and Elisabeth, parents of   Luke 1:5
    John the Baptist

22. Joseph and Mary, legal father and   Luke 1:27
    actual mother of Jesus

23. Zebedee and Salome, parents of James   Matt. 4:21; 27:56
    and John

24. Chuza and Joanna, the steward of   Luke 8:3
    Herod Antipas and his wife, who both
    supported Jesus financially during his
    earthly ministry

25. Herod Antipas and Herodias, ruler of   Matt. 14:3
    Galilee and his wicked wife, who
    brought about the death of John the
    Baptist

26. Ananias and Sapphira, killed for lying   Acts 5:1
    to the apostles

27. Aquila and Priscilla, godly couple   Acts 18:2
    who helped the apostle Paul

28. Felix and Drusilla, the Roman   Acts 24:24
    governor at Caesarea and his Jewish
    wife, whom Paul preached before

29. Agrippa II and Bernice, a king   Acts 25:13
    (Herod's great-grandson) and his
    wife, whom Paul preached to at
    Caesarea

Couples with Only the Husband Named

1. Cain and his wife, the first murderer,   Gen. 4:17
   who married his sister

2. Lot and his wife, nephew of Abraham   Gen. 19:26
   whose wife perished outside Sodom

3. Job and his wife, suffering patriarch   Job 2:9-10
   who had a cynic for a wife

4. Manoah and his wife, parents of   Judg. 13:2
   Samson

5. Samson, strong man who never lived   Judg. 14
   with his Philistine wife

6. Phinehas and his wife, parents of the   1 Sam. 4:4, 19-21
   infant son called Ichabod

7. Solomon and his first wife, an   1 Kings 3:1
   Egyptian

8. Jeroboam and his wife, the northern   1 Kings 14:1
   kingdom's first royal couple

9. Naaman, a leprous Syrian soldier, and   2 Kings 5:1-3
   his faithful wife

10. Isaiah and his wife, a prophetess   Isa. 8:3

11. Amaziah, godless priest of Bethel,   Amos 7:10-17
    and his harlot wife

12. Ezekiel and his wife, who died   Ezek. 24:18
    suddenly

13. Belshazzar, wicked Babylonian king,   Dan. 5:10-12
    whose wife—or mother—advised him
    to seek counsel from Daniel

14. Pilate, Roman governor whose wife   Matt. 27:19
    had a dream of warning

15. Cleopas and his wife, couple to whom   Luke 24:13-35;
    the resurrected Christ appeared   John 19:25

COVENANTS

A covenant *(berith* in Old Testament Hebrew, *diatheke*
in New Testament Greek) is a promise or an agreement
between God and man. A covenant may be conditional or
unconditional. There are eight important covenants in the
Bible:

1. The covenant with all repenting   See Titus 1:1-2;
   sinners to save them through Christ.   Heb. 13:20
   This covenant is unconditional (no
   strings attached).

2. The covenant with Adam   Gen. 1:28; 2:15-
     16; 3:15-19

   a. Before the Fall—that he could
      remain in Eden as long as he
      obeyed. This was conditional.

   b. After the Fall—that God would
      someday send a Savior. This was
      unconditional.

3. The covenant with Noah   Gen. 8:21-22
   a. That the earth would not be
      destroyed by water again.
   b. That the seasons would continue
      until the end. This was
      unconditional.

4. The covenant with Abraham   Gen. 12:2-3, 7;
     13:14-17; 15:5, 18;
     17:8

    a. That God would make Abraham the founder of a great nation.

    b. That God would someday give Palestine forever to Abraham's seed. This was unconditional.

5. The covenant with Moses and Israel — Exod. 19:3-8; Lev. 26; Deut. 28

    a. That Israel could have the land at that time to enjoy if they obeyed.

    b. That Israel would forfeit all God's blessings if they disobeyed. This was conditional.

6. The covenant with David — 2 Chron. 13:5; 2 Sam. 7:12-16; 23:5

    a. That from David would come an everlasting throne.

    b. That from David would come an everlasting kingdom.

    c. That from David would come an everlasting king. This was unconditional.

7. The covenant with the Church — Matt. 16:18; 26:28; Luke 22:20; Heb. 13:20-21

    a. That Christ would build his Church with his own blood.

    b. That all the fury of hell would not destroy it.

    c. That he would perfect all the members of his Church. This was unconditional.

8. The new covenant with Israel — Jer. 31:31-34; Isa. 42:6; 43:1-6; Deut. 1:1-9; Heb. 8:7-12

    a. That God would eventually bring Israel back to himself.

    b. That he would forgive their iniquity and forget their sin.

    c. That he would use them to reach
       and teach Gentiles.

    d. That he would establish them in
       Palestine forever. This was
       unconditional.

CROWNS

1. The crown of the high priest	Exod. 29:6; 39:30
2. The crown of thorns	Matt. 27:29
3. The crown of a soul-winner	Phil. 4:1; 1 Thess. 2:19
4. The crown of righteousness	2 Tim. 4:8
5. The crown of life	James 1:12; Rev. 2:10; 3:11
6. The crown of heaven's King of kings	Rev. 14:14; 19:12
7. The crown of incorruption	1 Cor. 9:25
8. The crown of glory	1 Pet. 5:4
9. The crown of demons	Rev. 9:7
10. The crown of Satan	Rev. 12:3
11. The crown of the Antichrist	Rev. 6:2; 13:1

CURSES

1. Upon the serpent	Gen. 3:14-15
2. Upon the ground	Gen. 3:17-18; 5:29; 8:21
3. Upon nature	Rom. 8:19-22
4. Upon Cain	Gen. 4:11

5. Upon Canaan	Gen. 9:25
6. Upon disobedient Israel	Deut. 28:15
7. Upon the enemies of Israel	Gen. 12:3
8. Upon a fruitless fig tree	Mark 11:21
9. Upon all unbelievers	Matt. 25:41
10. Upon false preachers	Gal. 1:8
11. Upon Jehoiakim	Jer. 22:18-19; 36:30
12. Upon all who attempt to remain under the law	Gal. 3:10
13. Upon Christ, for our sin	Gal. 3:13

DAYS

There are at least ten important "days," all yet in the future, that this world will experience. Some of these days refer to a 24-hour period, while others stand for a much longer period of time.

1. The day of the Rapture, probably a literal 24-hour day	Rom. 13:12; Eph. 4:30; Phil. 1:6, 10; 2:16; 2 Pet. 1:19
2. The judgment seat of Christ day, probably a literal 24-hour day that will include only Christians	1 Cor. 3:13; 5:5; 2 Tim. 1:18; 4:8; 1 John 4:17
3. The day of the Lord, a "day" that covers the entire Tribulation, a period of seven years	Joel 1:15; 2:1-2, 11, 31; Acts 2:20; 2 Thess. 2:3; Rev. 6:17
4. The day of Christ's second coming, which will probably be a literal 24-hour day	Matt. 24:36; 26:29; 1 Thess. 5:2-4; 2 Thess. 1:10
5. The day of Armageddon, probably a literal 24-hour day	Rev. 16:14

6. The resurrection of the just day, probably a literal 24-hour day that will include all Old Testament saints and tribulational believers — John 6:39-40, 44-54; 11:24

7. The fallen angel judgment day, probably a literal 24-hour day — Jude 6

8. The day of Christ, a "day" that covers the entire Millennium, a period of 1000 years — 1 Cor. 1:8; 2 Cor. 1:14; 2 Tim. 1:12

9. The Great White Throne judgment day, probably a literal 24-hour day — Matt. 7:22; 11:22; John 12:48; Acts 17:31; Rom. 2:5, 16: 2 Pet. 2:9

10. The new creation day, probably a literal 24-hour day — 2 Pet. 3:7-12

DEACONS
See Acts 6:5

1. Stephen, who became the first martyr
2. Philip, who became an evangelist and whose four daughters were prophetesses
3. Prochorus
4. Nicanor
5. Timon
6. Parmenas
7. Nicolas

DEMON POSSESSIONS
See also Satan and Fallen Angels

1. Man of Capernaum, healed by Christ in the synagogue on the Sabbath — Mark 1:24; Luke 4:35

2. Maniac of Gadara, possessed by and healed of a legion of demons — Matt. 8:28-32; Mark 5:2-13; Luke 8:33

3. A mute man healed by Christ, causing the multitudes to rejoice — Matt. 9:32-33

4. A girl from Tyre and Sidon, healed at the request of her heartbroken mother — Matt. 15:28; Mark 7:29

5. A boy at the base of Mount Hermon, healed at the request of his heartbroken father — Matt. 17:18; Mark 9:25; Luke 9:42

6. A blind and deaf man whom Christ was accused of healing by the power of Beelzebub — Matt. 12:22; Luke 11:14

7. Woman with an 18-year infirmity, healed by Christ in a synagogue on the Sabbath — Luke 13:10-13

8. Mary Magdalene, healed by Christ of seven demons — Mark 16:9; Luke 8:2

9. Judas Iscariot, possessed by Satan himself — Luke 22:3; John 6:70; 13:27

10. A slave girl with powers of divination, healed by Paul at Philippi — Acts 16:16-18

11. Sceva's sons, renegade Jews at Ephesus — Acts 19:15

12. The Antichrist, world dictator during the Great Tribulation — Rev. 16:13

13. False prophet, evil helper of the Antichrist — Rev. 16:13

DISEASES AND INFIRMITIES
See also Handicapped and Disabled, Lepers

1. Barrenness, as suffered by Sarah, Hannah, and Elisabeth — Gen. 16:1; 1 Sam. 1:6; Luke 1:7

2. Blains and boils, as suffered by the Egyptians during the sixth plague, by King Hezekiah, and by Job — Exod. 9:9-10; 2 Kings 20:7; Job 2:7

3. Botch (may have been syphilis), as suffered by the Egyptians — Deut. 28:27; 28:35

4. Canker (cancer) — 2 Tim. 2:17

5. Dropsy — Luke 14:2

6. Dwarfism — Lev. 21:20

7. Dysentery, as suffered by the father of Publius — Acts 28:8

8. Emerods (tumors), as suffered by the Philistines who captured the Ark of the Covenant — 1 Sam. 5:6

9. Fever, as suffered by:
   a. Peter's mother-in-law — Matt. 8:14-15
   b. A little boy — John 4:52

10. Internal bleeding, as suffered by a Capernaum woman for 12 years — Matt. 9:20

11. Itch (eczema) — Deut. 28:27

12. Sores (ulcerated openings) as suffered by:
    a. Old Testament Israel — Isa. 1:6
    b. Lazarus the beggar — Luke 16:20
    c. The ungodly in the Tribulation — Rev. 16:2

13. Sunstroke, as perhaps suffered by the Shunammite woman's son — 2 Kings 4:19

14. Worms (a possible reference to intestinal roundworm infection), as suffered by Herod — Acts 12:21-23

DISPENSATIONS

1. The dispensation of innocence (from the creation of man to the Fall of man)   Gen. 1:28–3:6

2. The dispensation of conscience (from the Fall to the Flood)   Gen. 4:1–8:14

3. The dispensation of civil government (from the Flood to the dispersion at Babel)   Gen. 8:15–11:9

4. The dispensation of promise or patriarchal rule (from Babel to Mount Sinai)   Gen. 11:10; Exod. 18:27

5. The dispensation of the Mosaic Law (from Mount Sinai to the Upper Room)   Exod. 19; Acts 1:26

6. The dispensation of the bride of the Lamb, the Church (from the Upper Room to the Rapture)   Acts 2:1; Rev. 3:22

7. The dispensation of the wrath of the Lamb—the Tribulation (from the Rapture to the Second Coming)   Rev. 6:1–20:3

8. The dispensation of the rule of the Lamb—the Millennium (from the Second Coming through the Great White Throne judgment)   Rev. 20:4-15

9. The dispensation of the new creation of the Lamb—the world without end (from the Great White Throne judgment throughout all eternity)   Rev. 21–22

DREAMS AND VISIONS FROM GOD

Dreams

1. Jacob received the confirmation of the Abrahamic covenant in a dream. — Gen. 28:12

2. Solomon received both wisdom and a warning in a dream. — 1 Kings 3:5; 9:2

3. Joseph in the New Testament received three messages in three dreams:

   a. Assuring him of Mary's purity — Matt. 1:20

   b. Commanding him to flee to Egypt — Matt. 2:13

   c. Ordering him to go back to Palestine — Matt. 2:19-22

4. The wise men were warned of Herod's evil intentions in a dream. — Matt. 2:12

Visions

1. Jacob was instructed to go to Egypt in a vision. — Gen. 46:2-3

2. David was warned of judgment in a vision. — 1 Chron. 21:16

3. Isaiah saw God's holiness in a vision. — Isa. 6:1-8

4. Daniel saw the great Gentile powers in a vision. — Dan. 7–8

5. Daniel saw the glories of Christ in a vision. — Dan. 10:5-9

6. Daniel saw the rise and fall of Alexander the Great in a vision. — Dan. 8

7. Ezekiel saw the regathering of Israel in a vision. — Ezek. 37

8. Ananias was ordered to minister to Saul in a vision. — Acts 9:10

9. Cornelius was instructed to send for Peter in a vision. — Acts 10:3-6

10. Peter was ordered to minister to Cornelius in a vision. — Acts 10:10-16

11. Paul was requested to go to Macedonia in a vision.   Acts 16:9

12. Paul was comforted at Corinth in a vision.   Acts 18:9

13. Paul was comforted at Jerusalem in a vision.   Acts 23:11

14. Paul viewed the glories of the third heaven in a vision.   2 Cor. 12:1-4

15. John the apostle received the Book of Revelation in a vision.   Rev. 1:10

EARTHQUAKES

1. As experienced by Israel at the giving of the Law from Mount Sinai   Exod. 19:18

2. As experienced by Elijah in a cave   1 Kings 19:11

3. As experienced in the days of Uzziah   Zech. 14:5; Amos 1:1

4. As experienced by a centurion at the crucifixion   Matt. 27:54

5. As experienced by the Roman tomb guard at the Resurrection   Matt. 28:2-4

6. As experienced by the Philippian jailor at midnight   Acts 16:26

7. As will be experienced by this world during the Tribulation:

    a. At the opening of the sixth seal   Rev. 6:12

    b. At the opening of the seventh seal   Rev. 8:5

    c. At the raising of the two witnesses   Rev. 11:13

    d. At the pouring out of the seventh vial at Armageddon   Zech. 14:4-5; Rev. 16:16-21

ESCAPES

1. A captive of Chedorlaomer escaped and told Abraham about the imprisonment of Lot. Gen. 14:12-13

2. Lot escaped the judgment upon Sodom. Gen. 19:17-20

3. Ehud escaped after killing Eglon. Judg. 3:26

4. Sisera escaped from Barak and Deborah, only to be killed by a woman named Jael. Judg. 4:17

5. A servant of Job escaped and told his master some terrible news. Job 1:15-19

6. David escaped on many occasions:
   a. From Saul in the palace room 1 Sam. 19:10
   b. From Saul by being let down from a bedroom window 1 Sam. 19:12
   c. From the king of Gath 1 Sam. 22:1
   d. From the city of Keilah, whose citizens would have handed him over to Saul 1 Sam. 23:13

7. A young man claimed to have escaped from a Philistine victory over Israel with news of how Saul met his death 2 Sam. 1:3

8. Jesus escaped the murderous intent of the wicked Pharisees:
   a. After preaching in Nazareth Luke 4:28-30
   b. After preaching in Jerusalem John 10:39

9. Peter escaped from a Roman prison. Acts 12:7

10. Paul escaped the waiting Jews by being lowered from the Damascus city wall in a basket. Acts 9:25; 2 Cor. 11:33

11. All believers can escape present-day temptation. 1 Cor. 10:13

12. All believers will escape a future wrath. 1 Thess. 5:9

EXCUSES

1. As offered by Adam for disobeying God — Gen. 3:12
2. As offered by Eve for disobeying God — Gen. 3:13
3. As offered by Lot for wanting to stay in doomed Sodom — Gen. 19:19
4. As offered by Moses for not wanting to go into Egypt — Exod. 3:11; 4:1, 10
5. As offered by Aaron for constructing the golden calf — Exod. 32:22-24
6. As offered by ten spies for not entering the Promised Land — Num. 13:31-33
7. As offered by Israel for wanting a king — 1 Sam. 8:5
8. As offered by Saul for assuming priestly duties — 1 Sam. 13:11-12
9. As offered by Saul for sparing an enemy God told him to destroy — 1 Sam. 15:21
10. As offered by Elijah for hiding in a cave — 1 Kings 19:10
11. As offered by three invited guests for not attending a wedding — Luke 14:18-20
12. As offered by an unfaithful servant for fruitless labor — Matt. 25:24-25
13. As offered by Felix for not accepting Christ — Acts 24:25

EXECUTED BY GOD
See also Judgments from God

Individuals

1. Er, killed for being so wicked — Gen. 38:7

2. Onan, killed for not obeying the command to produce children by his brother's widow — Gen. 38:8-9

3. Lot's wife, turned to a pillar of salt because she looked back at Sodom — Gen. 19:26

4. Nadab and Abihu, killed for offering strange fire on the altar — Lev. 10:2

5. Ten spies, killed for their unbelief and rebellion — Num. 14:37

6. A Sabbath-breaker, killed for gathering wood on the Sabbath — Num. 15:32-36

7. Korah, swallowed up by the earth for attempting an insurrection against Moses — Num. 16:30-32

8. Nabal, killed for his arrogance and stupidity — 1 Sam. 25:38

9. Saul, killed for his total disobedience, including murder and consulting a medium — 1 Chron. 10:13-14

10. Uzzah, killed because of his carelessness concerning the Ark of the Covenant — 2 Sam. 6:7

11. Jeroboam's son, killed because of the wickedness of his father — 1 Kings 14:12

12. Jeroboam, killed because of his apostate leadership — 2 Chron. 13:20

13. Jehoram, stricken with a fatal disease because of his apostate leadership — 2 Chron. 21:18-19

14. Hananiah, killed for betraying his office of a prophet — Jer. 28:15-17

15. Herod Agrippa I, killed for elevating himself above mortal man   Acts 12:23

16. Ananias and Sapphira, struck down for lying to the Holy Spirit   Acts 5:1-10

Universal

1. Flood in Noah's day, sent because of universal corruption and violence   Gen. 6–9

2. Tribulational judgment, will occur because of universal corruption and violence   Rev. 6–19

Israelites

1. Death due to worshiping the golden calf   Exod. 32:27

2. Death due to complaining, punished by a judgment of fire from God   Num. 11:1

3. Death due to lust, punished by a great plague   Num. 11:31-35

4. Death due to unbelief of the ten unfaithful spies   Num. 14:37

5. Death of Korah and his followers, who were swallowed up by the ground because of their rebellion   Num. 16:32

6. Death due to rebellion, punished by a plague of poisonous serpents   Num. 21:6

7. Death of 24,000 Israelites due to immorality   Num. 25:9

8. Death of over 50,000 Israelites due to looking into the Ark   1 Sam. 6:19

9. Death of 70,000 Israelite men due to David's census   2 Sam. 24:15

10. Death by fire of 100 Israelite soldiers due to Ahaziah's order   2 Kings 1

Various Nations

1. Sodomites, destroyed by fire for their gross immorality   Gen. 19:24

2. The Egyptians' firstborn, destroyed because the door frames of the Egyptians' homes were not covered with the blood of the lamb — Exod. 12:29

3. The Egyptians army, drowned in the Red Sea for attempting to destroy Israel — Exod. 14:27-28

4. Philistines, who experienced plagues because of their possession of the Ark of the Covenant — 1 Sam. 5:8-9

5. Philistine soldiers, who died for attempting to destroy Israel — 1 Sam. 7:10

6. Ethiopian troops, destroyed by God as a result of the prayer of Judean king Asa — 2 Chron. 14:12

7. Moabites and Ammonites, destroyed as a result of the prayer of Jehoshaphat — 2 Chron. 20:1-22

8. Assyrian troops, destroyed by an angel of the Lord as a result of the prayer of Hezekiah — 2 Kings 19:35

9. Gog and Magog, to be destroyed as they attempt to invade Israel — Ezek. 38–39

FABLES
See also Allegories, Parables

1. The fable of the bramble tree, related by Jotham to ridicule the mad dog ruler Abimelech — Judg. 9:7-15

2. The fable of the thistle bush, related by Jehoash, king of Israel, to Amaziah, king of Judah to ridicule him — 2 Kings 14:8-9

FAMINES

1. The famine in Palestine that caused Abraham to go into Egypt — Gen. 12:10

2. The famine in Palestine that caused Isaac to go into Philistia — Gen. 26:1

3. The famine in Palestine that caused Jacob's eleven sons to go into Egypt — Gen. 41:54-57

4. The famine in Palestine that caused Naomi to go into Moab — Ruth 1:1

5. The famine in David's day, caused by Saul's bloodstained house — 2 Sam. 21:1

6. The famine in Elijah's day, caused by the sins of Ahab and Israel — 1 Kings 17:1

7. The famines in Elisha's day

   a. First famine, resulting in Elisha working a miracle of purifying some poisonous stew — 2 Kings 4:38

   b. Second famine, resulting in the salvation of a city through four lepers — 2 Kings 6:25

   c. Third famine, resulting in a woman, a servant, and a king knowing that there was still a prophet of God in Israel — 2 Kings 8:1-6

8. The famine in Jerusalem, caused by Nebuchadnezzar's siege — 2 Kings 25:2; Jer. 14

9. The famine in Nehemiah's day, resulting in a sermon by Nehemiah and an ensuing revival of the people — Neh. 5:3-13

10. The famine in Paul's day, resulting in help being sent by outside Christians to the believers in Judea — Acts 11:28

11. The famine in the Tribulation, which will contribute to the death of millions — Rev. 6:5-8

FASTS

1. Moses' 40-day fast as he prayed concerning Israel's sin — Deut. 9:9, 18, 25-29; 10:10

2. David's fast as he lamented over Saul's death — 2 Sam. 1:12

3. David's fast as he lamented over Abner's death — 2 Sam. 3:35

4. David's fast as he lamented over his child's sickness — 2 Sam. 12:16

5. Elijah's 40-day fast after he fled from Jezebel — 1 Kings 19:7-18

6. Ahab's fast as he humbled himself before God — 1 Kings 21:27-29

7. Darius's fast as he worried over Daniel's fate — Dan. 6:18-24

8. Daniel's fast as he read Jeremiah's prophecy and prayed for Judah's sins — Dan. 9:1-19

9. Daniel's fast as he prayed over a mysterious vision God had given him — Dan. 10:3-13

10. Esther's fast as she sorrowed over Haman's wicked plot to destroy her people — Esther 4:13-16

11. Ezra's fast as he wept over the sins of the returning remnant — Ezra 10:6-17

12. Nehemiah's fast as he wept over the broken-down walls of Jerusalem — Neh. 1:4–2:10

13. The Ninevites' fast after they heard the preaching of Jonah — Jon. 3

14. Anna's fast as she awaited the Messiah — Luke 2:37

15. Jesus' 40-day fast before the temptation — Matt. 4:1-11

16. John's disciples' fast — Matt. 9:14-15

17. The elders' fast in Antioch, prior to the sending out of Paul and Barnabas — Acts 13:1-5

18. Cornelius's fast as he sought out God's plan of salvation — Acts 10:30

19. Paul's three-day fast after his experience on the Damascus Road — Acts 9:9

20. Paul's 14-day fast while on a sinking ship — Acts 27:33-34

FIRES

1. The fire from heaven that destroyed Sodom and Gomorrah — Gen. 19:24

2. The fire Abraham built to sacrifice Isaac — Gen. 22:7

3. The burning bush fire from which Moses received his call — Exod. 3:2

4. The fire of the seventh Egyptian plague — Exod. 9:24

5. The guiding pillar fire that led Israel by night — Exod. 13:21

6. The fire that appeared at the giving of the Law — Exod. 19:8

7. The fire ordered by Moses to destroy the golden calf — Exod. 39:20

8. The fire God sent to consume Aaron's offerings — Lev. 9:24

9. The strange fire of Nadab and Abihu — Lev. 10:1

10. The judgment fire of God at Taberah to punish Israel — Num. 11:1

11. The judgment fire that consumed Korah and 250 of his followers — Num. 16:35

12. The fire ordered by Joshua to destroy Jericho — Josh. 6:24

13. The fire ordered by Joshua to consume Achan — Josh. 7:15, 25

14. The fire made by Samson to burn the grain fields of the Philistines — Judg. 15:5

15. The Mount Carmel fire that consumed Elijah's offering — 1 Kings 18:38

16. The fire that God was not in, as witnessed by Elijah in a cave — 1 Kings 19:12

17. The fire that destroyed a hundred soldiers and protected Elijah — 2 Kings 1:7-11

18. The fire used to transport Elijah home to glory — 2 Kings 2:11

19. The fire and chariots that surrounded and protected Elisha — 2 Kings 6:17

20. The fire of Manasseh in Hinnom, used to burn up his own children — 2 Kings 21:6

21. The fire of Nebuchadnezzar that would not burn three Hebrew believers — Dan. 3:25

22. The fire Simon Peter warmed his hands over when he denied the Savior — John 18:18

23. The fire where Paul shook off a venomous snake — Acts 28:5

24. The fire at the judgment seat of Christ — 1 Cor. 3:13

25. The all-consuming judgment fire of God, to be used in destroying his enemies — 2 Thess. 1:8; Heb. 12:29; Rev. 20:15

26. The fire God will use in purifying this earth — 2 Pet. 3:7

FOODS

1. Spices, herbs, and seasonings
   a. anise — Matt. 23:23
   b. coriander — Exod. 16:31; Num. 11:7

    c. cumin   Isa. 28:25; Matt. 23:23

    d. mint   Matt. 23:23

    e. mustard   Matt. 13:31; 17:20

    f. rue   Luke 11:42

    g. salt   Job 6:6

2. Vegetables

    a. beans   2 Sam. 17:28; Ezek. 4:9

    b. cucumbers   Num. 11:5; Isa. 1:8

    c. garlic   Num. 11:5

    d. gourds   2 Kings 4:39

    e. leeks   Num. 11:5

    f. lentils   Gen. 25:34

    g. melons   Num. 11:5

    h. millet   Ezek. 4:9

    i. onions   Num. 11:5

3. Fruits

    a. almonds   Gen. 43:11

    b. figs   Jer. 24:1-3

    c. grapes   Deut. 23:24

    d. nuts   Gen. 43:11

    e. olives   Deut. 8:8

    f. pomegranates   Num. 13:23

    g. sycamore fruit   Amos 7:14

4. Grains

    a. barley   Ruth 3:17

    b. corn   Gen. 41:35

    c. wheat   Rev. 6:6; 1 Sam. 6:13

5. Fish   John 6, 21

6. Fowl

    a. partridge   1 Sam. 26:20; Jer. 17:11

      b. pigeon   Gen. 15:9; Lev. 1:14

      c. turtledove   Lev. 12:8

      d. quail   Exod. 16:13; Num. 11:31-32; Ps. 105:40

      e. sparrow   Luke 12:6

7. Locusts   Lev. 11:22; Matt. 3:4

8. Meat animals
      a. calf   Luke 15:23
      b. goat   Gen. 27:9
      c. lamb   2 Sam. 12:4
      d. oxen   1 Kings 19:21
      e. sheep   2 Sam. 17:29
      f. venison   Gen. 27:7

9. Various foods and drinks
      a. butter   Judg. 5:25; Isa. 7:15

      b. cheese   1 Sam. 17:18

      c. eggs   Luke 11:12

      d. honey   1 Sam. 14:25; 1 Kings 14:3; Matt. 3:4

      e. milk   Gen. 18:8; Isa. 55:1

      f. wine   John 2

FOOLS

1. Nabal, surly husband of Abigail who later married David   1 Sam. 25:2-3

2. Saul, Israel's first king, who attempted to kill David   1 Sam. 26:21

3. Disbelieving fool who denies God's existence   Ps. 14:1

4. Slandering fool who badmouths believers   Prov. 10:18

5. Disobedient fool who despises his father's instruction   Prov. 15:5

6. Self-centered fool, blinded to his own faults   Prov. 12:15

7. Sexually impure fool who allows a harlot to destroy his soul   Prov. 7:7-27

8. Mocking fool who laughs at the seriousness of sin   Prov. 14:9

9. Short-tempered fool who cannot control his temper   Prov. 14:17

10. Meddling fool who deliberately stirs up strife   Prov. 20:3

11. Thoughtless fool who attempts to build his life upon foundations other than God's Word   Matt. 7:26

12. Unprepared fool who makes no spiritual plans for the future   Matt. 25:3

13. Rich fool who assumes his life will continue indefinitely   Luke 12:20

14. Philosophical fool who substitutes worship of things for worship of God   Rom. 1:22

15. Ignorant fool who does not know of God's power to raise dead bodies   1 Cor. 15:36

16. Legalistic fool who returns to the bondage of the law after enjoying the blessings of grace   Gal. 3:1

GARDENS

1. The garden of God, the home of Lucifer before he became Satan, and the headquarters for God's holy mountain — Ezek. 28:11-17

2. The Garden of Eden, home of the first human couple, planted by God, located in Mesopotamia, and including within it the tree of life and the tree of knowledge of good and evil — Gen. 2:8–3:24

3. The Garden of Gethsemane, where Jesus prayed before his arrest and where Judas kissed him — Matt. 26:36; John 18:1

4. The garden of the Resurrection, where Jesus was laid in a cave tomb and where he later appeared to Mary Magdalene — John 19:41–20:18; Matt. 28:2-4; Mark 16:9-11; Luke 24:12

GARMENTS

1. The leafy garments with which Adam and Eve attempted to clothe themselves — Gen. 3:7

2. The animal garments with which God later clothed them — Gen. 3:21

3. The many-colored coat of Joseph — Gen. 37:3, 31-32

4. The coat Joseph was wearing when it was torn by Potiphar's wife — Gen. 39:12

5. The garments of the high priest of Israel — Exod. 28:4-43; 39:1-31; Lev. 8:7-9; 16:4

6. The garments taken from Aaron and put upon Eleazar — Num. 20:28

7. The "goodly Babylonish garment"   Josh. 7:21
   stolen by Achan

8. The garment with which Boaz covered   Ruth 3:9
   Ruth

9. The coat that Hannah brought for   1 Sam. 2:19
   Samuel each year to the sanctuary at
   Shiloh

10. The robe given to David by Jonathan   1 Sam. 18:4
    to seal their friendship covenant

11. The beautiful linen robe David wore   1 Chron. 15:27
    when he carried the Ark of God to
    Jerusalem

12. Tamar's many-colored garment which   2 Sam. 13:18-19
    she tore after being attacked by
    Ammon

13. Saul's robe which David cut during   1 Sam. 24:11
    the wicked king's sleep

14. Jeroboam's torn garment, ripped into   1 Kings 11:29-31
    12 pieces by the prophet Ahijah to
    symbolize the coming fragmentation
    of the kingdom of Israel

15. The robe of Ahab's which   2 Chron. 18:29
    Jehoshaphat foolishly wore into battle

16. The "filthy garments" of Joshua the   Zech. 3:3
    high priest as he stood before God

17. The rustic garments of John the   Matt. 3:4
    Baptist

18. The robe given to the returning   Luke 15:22
    Prodigal Son by his father

19. The unused wedding garment in the   Matt. 22:11
    parable of the wedding feast

20. The linen cloth discarded by a young   Mark 14:51
    man who ran away naked at
    Gethsemane

21. The fisherman's coat of Simon Peter   John 21:7

22. The scarlet robe Jesus wore as the   Matt. 27:28;
    Roman soldiers mocked him   John 19:2, 5

23. A gorgeous robe placed on Jesus by Herod in mockery — Luke 23:11

24. The seamless garment for which the soldiers at the foot of the cross gambled — Matt. 27:35

25. The cloak of Paul that he requested while in a Roman prison — 2 Tim. 4:13

26. The white robes of those martyred during the Tribulation — Rev. 6:11; 7:9

GATES

1. The gate at Sodom where Lot met the two angels — Gen. 19:1

2. The gate at Bethlehem where Boaz arranged to marry Ruth — Ruth 4:1

3. The gate at Shalem where Shechem agreed to be circumcised, as requested by Jacob's two sons — Gen. 34:20

4. The gate of Jericho, sealed to keep all Israelite soldiers out — Josh. 2:5, 7

5. The gate at Gaza, which Samson ripped from its foundations and carried away — Judg. 16:2-3

6. The gate at Shiloh, where the aged Eli fell and died upon hearing the news concerning Israel's defeat and the capture of the Ark of the Covenant by the Philistines — 1 Sam. 4:18

7. The gate of Gath, where David pretended to be insane — 1 Sam. 21:13

8. The gate of Samaria, where four lepers made a decision that would later save the starving city   2 Kings 7:3

9. The palace gate in Persia, where Mordecai overheard a plot against the king's life which later would be used by God in saving all the Jews in Persia   Esther 2:21-23

10. The gate of the rich man's home, where Lazarus begged for bread   Luke 16:20

11. The temple's Beautiful Gate, where Peter healed a cripple   Acts 3:2

12. Jerusalem's Sheep Gate   Neh. 3:1

13. Jerusalem's Fish Gate   Neh. 3:3

14. Jerusalem's Valley Gate   Neh. 3:13

15. Jerusalem's Dung Gate   Neh. 3:14

16. Jerusalem's Fountain Gate   Neh. 3:15

17. Jerusalem's Water Gate   Neh. 3:26

18. Jerusalem's Horse Gate   Neh. 3:28

19. Jerusalem's East Gate   Neh. 3:29

20. Jerusalem's Miphkad Gate   Neh. 3:31

21. 12 gates in the New Jerusalem, each guarded by an angel and inscribed with the name of one of the tribes of Israel   Rev. 21:12-13

22. Symbolic gates in the Bible

     a. The gate of salvation   Matt. 7:13

     b. The gate of damnation   Matt. 7:13

     c. The gate of death   Job 38:17; Isa. 38:10; Ps. 9:13; 107:18

     d. The gate of heaven   Ps. 24:7, 9; Gen. 28:17

     e. The gate of hell   Matt. 16:18

GENEALOGIES

1. Cain's	Gen. 4:16-24
2. Adam's	Gen. 5:1-32
3. Japheth's	Gen. 10:1-5; 1 Chron. 1:5-7
4. Ham's	Gen. 10:6-20; 1 Chron. 1:8-16
5. Shem's	Gen. 10:22-31; 11:10-30; 1 Chron. 1:17-27
6. Abraham's	Gen. 25:1-4, 12-18; 1 Chron. 1:28-34
7. Isaac's	Gen. 25:19-23
8. Jacob's	Gen. 49:1-27; 1 Chron. 2:1-2
9. Esau's	Gen. 36:1-43; 1 Chron. 1:35-42
10. Judah's	1 Chron. 2:3-12; 4:1-4
11. Simeon's	1 Chron. 4:24-38
12. Reuben's	1 Chron. 5:1-8
13. Levi's	1 Chron. 6:1-53
14. Issachar's	1 Chron. 7:1-5
15. Benjamin's	1 Chron. 7:6-12
16. Naphtali's	1 Chron. 7:13
17. Asher's	1 Chron. 7:30-40
18. Jesse's	1 Chron. 2:13-17
19. Caleb's	1 Chron. 2:18-20, 42-55
20. David's	1 Chron. 3:1-24
21. Ephraim's	1 Chron. 7:20-27
22. Pharez's	Ruth 4:18-22
23. Jesus'	
a. The genealogy of Mary	Luke 3:23-38
b. The genealogy of Joseph	Matt. 1:1-17

GIANTS

1. Anak, founder of a race of giants that inhabited the Holy Land — Deut. 9:2

2. Sheshai, Ahiman, and Talmai, Anak's three sons, defeated by Caleb — Josh. 15:14

3. Sippai, a Philistine giant warrior, slain by the Israelite soldiers — 1 Chron. 20:4

4. Goliath, a Philistine giant, over 9 feet tall, killed by David in battle — 1 Sam. 17

5. Lahmi, brother of Goliath, killed by an Israelite in battle — 1 Chron. 20:5

6. Og, king of Bashan who slept in an iron bed, 14 feet long and 6 feet wide — Deut. 3:11

7. Ishbi-benob, a giant, killed by Abishai, with a spear tip weighing more than 12 pounds — 2 Sam. 21:16

8. A Philistine giant with 12 toes and 12 fingers, killed by David's nephew — 1 Chron. 20:6

GIFTS

1. Abraham's tithes to Melchizedek, given to show honor to the first ruler of Jerusalem — Gen. 14:20

2. Jacob's gift of livestock to Esau, given to make up for cheating Esau out of his blessing — Gen. 32:13-15

3. The gifts of Israel's 12 tribal leaders—silver and gold items and livestock—to the tabernacle, given to please God — Num. 7:12-89

4. The spices, jewels, and gold given by the queen of Sheba to Solomon to assure good relations between Israel and Sheba — 1 Kings 10:1-2, 10

5. The office of third ruler in the kingdom, offered by Belshazzar to Daniel, though Daniel refused — Dan. 5:16-17

6. The gifts of silver, gold, and clothing, given by the Syrian king to an Israelite king to secure the healing of the leper Naaman — 2 Kings 5:4-6

7. The gold, frankincense, and myrrh offered by the wise men to the infant Jesus because of their worship — Matt. 2:11

8. The jar of costly perfume with which Mary of Bethany anointed Jesus because of her devotion — John 12:2-8; Matt. 26:7-13

9. The flask of expensive perfume offered by an immoral woman to Jesus because of her devotion — Luke 7:37-38

10. The gifts of wicked unbelievers to each other during the Tribulation, given to celebrate the death of God's two witnesses — Rev. 11:10

11. The body, given as a living gift to the Lord by believers — Rom. 12:1-3

12. Christ, the Father's gift to the world — John 3:16; 2 Cor. 9:15

13. The gifts of the Holy Spirit to the believer, given to glorify the Father and to edify the believer and the church: — Rom. 12:6-8; 1 Cor. 12:4-31; Eph. 4:7-16

   a. apostleship

   b. prophecy

   c. miracles

   d. healing

   e. tongues

   f. interpretation of tongues

g. knowledge
h. wisdom
i. discerning of spirits
j. giving
k. exhortation
l. ministering
m. showing of mercy
n. ruling
o. faith
p. teaching
q. evangelism
r. pastor-teacher

GOD

23 Facts about God

1. God is self-existent.	Exod. 3:13-14
2. God is self-sufficient.	Ps. 50:10-12
3. God is eternal.	Deut. 33:27; Ps. 90:2
4. God is infinite.	1 Kings 8:22-27; Jer. 23:24
5. God is omnipresent.	Ps. 139:7-12
6. God is omnipotent.	Gen. 18:14; Rev. 19:6
7. God is omniscient.	Ps. 139:2-6; Isa. 40:13-14
8. God is wise.	Prov. 3:19; 1 Tim. 1:17
9. God is immutable.	Heb. 1:10-12; 13:8
10. God is sovereign.	Isa. 46:9-11

11. God is incomprehensible.	Job 11:7-19; Rom. 11:33
12. God is holy.	Lev. 19:2; 1 Pet. 1:15
13. God is righteous and just.	Ps. 119:137
14. God is true.	John 17:3; Titus 1:1-2
15. God is faithful.	Deut. 7:9; Ps. 89:1-2
16. God is light.	James 1:17; 1 John 1:5
17. God is good.	Ps. 107:8
18. God is merciful.	Ps. 103:8-17
19. God is gracious.	Ps. 111:4; 1 Pet. 5:10
20. God is love.	John 3:16; Rom. 5:8
21. God is spirit.	John 4:24
22. God is one.	Deut. 6:4-5; Isa. 44:6-8
23. God is a Trinity.	Matt. 28:19; 2 Cor. 13:14

16 Old Testament Names for God

1. Elohim, meaning "God," a reference to God's power and might	Gen. 1:1; Ps. 19:1
2. Adonai, meaning "Lord," a reference to the Lordship of God	Mal. 1:6
3. Jehovah (sometimes spelled Yahweh), a reference to God's divine salvation	Gen. 2:4
4. Jehovah-Maccaddeshem, meaning "The Lord thy sanctifier"	Exod. 31:13
5. Jehovah-Rohi, meaning "The Lord my shepherd"	Ps. 23:1
6. Jehovah-Shammah, meaning "The Lord who is present"	Ezek. 48:35
7. Jehovah-Rapha, meaning "The Lord our healer"	Exod. 16:26

8. Jehovah-Tsidkenu, meaning "The Lord our righteousness"	Jer. 23:6
9. Jehovah-Jireh, meaning "The Lord will provide"	Gen. 22:13-14
10. Jehovah-Nissi, meaning "The Lord our banner"	Exod. 17:15
11. Jehovah-Shalom, meaning "The Lord is peace"	Judg. 6:24
12. Jehovah-Sabbaoth, meaning "The Lord of Hosts"	Isa. 6:1-3
13. El-Elyon, meaning "The most high God"	Gen. 14:17-20; Isa. 14:13-14
14. El-Roi, meaning "The strong one who sees"	Gen. 16:12
15. El-Shaddai, meaning "The God of the mountains" or "God almighty"	Gen. 17:1; Ps. 91:1
16. El-Olam, meaning "The everlasting God"	Isa. 40:28-31

15 Things God Sees and Knows

1. He sees all things.	Prov. 15:3
2. He knows the size and scope of the universe.	Ps. 147:4
3. He knows about the animal creation.	Matt. 10:29
4. He knows mankind.	Matt. 10:30
5. He knows our thoughts.	Ps. 139:2b; 44:21
6. He knows our words.	Ps. 139:4
7. He knows our deeds.	Ps. 139:2a
8. He knows our sorrows.	Exod. 3:7
9. He knows our needs.	Matt. 6:32
10. He knows our devotions.	Gen. 18:17-19; 22:11-12; 2 Chron. 16:9
11. He knows our frailties.	Ps. 103:14
12. He knows our foolishness.	Ps. 69:5
13. He knows his own.	John 10:14; 2 Tim. 2:19

14. He knows the past, present, and future. Acts 15:18

15. He knows what might or could have been. Matt. 11:23

50 Facts about the Father

1. He is the Father of all life. Ps. 19:1; 36:9; 148:2-5; John 5:26; Acts 17:24-25

2. He tends and cares for vegetation. Ps. 104:14; 16; Matt. 6:28-30

3. He tends and cares for brute nature. Ps. 104:14, 16, 18, 20-27; Matt. 6:26; 10:29

4. He tends and cares for the weather. Ps. 135:6-7; 147:8, 16, 18; 148:8

5. He tends and cares for the seasons. Gen. 8:22; Acts 14:17

6. He is the Father of our Lord Jesus Christ.

7. The Father sent his Son. John 6:57; 8:18; 20:21; Gal. 4:4; 1 John 4:14; see also John 3:16; 8:16; 12:49

8. The Father commanded the angels to worship his Son. Heb. 1:6; Luke 2:8-15

9. He sealed his Son. John 6:27

10. He honored and honors his Son. John 8:54

11. He bore witness to his Son. John 8:18

12. He loved and loves his Son. John 10:17

13. He glorified his Son. John 12:27-28; 17:1, 5

14. He taught his Son. John 8:28

15. He anointed his Son. Luke 4:16-21; John 3:34

16. He delighted in his Son. Isa. 42:1; Matt. 3:17; 17:5; 2 Pet. 1:17

17. He listened to his Son.	John 11:41-42; 12:27-28; Matt. 26:52-53
18. He offered his Son.	John 18:11; Rom. 8:32; 1 John 4:9-10
19. He was totally satisfied by his Son.	John 8:29
20. He raised his Son.	Gal. 1:1; Eph. 1:20
21. He exalts his Son.	Phil. 2:9-11; Eph. 1:21
22. He makes his Son head of the Church.	Eph. 1:22
23. He commits judgment unto his Son.	John 3:35; 5:22, 27
24. He is the Father of all believers.	
25. He foreknew the believers.	Rom. 8:29; 1 Pet. 1:2
26. He predestinated the believers.	Rom. 8:29; Eph. 1:11; Acts 13:48
27. He elected the believers.	Eph. 1:4; 2 Thess. 2:13; 1 Pet. 1:1-2; 2:9
28. He gave all the elected believers to Christ.	John 6:37, 44; 10:29; 13:3
29. He called the believers.	Rom. 8:30
30. He conforms the believers to the image of Christ.	Rom. 8:29
31. He redeemed the believers.	Eph. 1:7
32. He justified the believers.	Rom. 8:33
33. He indwells the believers.	John 14:23
34. He sealed the believers with the Holy Spirit.	Eph. 1:13; 4:30
35. He keeps the believers.	John 10:29; 17:11
36. He honors the believers.	John 12:26
37. He blesses the believers.	Eph. 1:3
38. He loves the believers.	2 Thess. 2:16; John 14:21
39. He comforts the believers.	2 Cor. 1:3; Rev. 21:4; 2 Thess. 2:16
40. He sanctifies the believers.	Jude 1; John 17:17

41. He bestows peace upon believers. — Rom. 1:7; 1 Cor. 1:3; Gal. 1:3; Eph. 1:2; Phil. 1:2; Col. 1:2; 1 Thess. 1:1; 2 Thess. 1:2; Titus 1:4

42. He is glorified when believers bear fruit. — John 15:8

43. He reveals truth to believers. — Matt. 11:25; 16:17; Luke 10:21; Eph. 1:17

44. He supplies the needs of believers. — Matt. 6:32-33; Eph. 4:19

45. He seeks the worship of believers. — John 4:23

46. He chastens believers. — Heb. 12:5-10

47. He restores the believers. — Ps. 23:3; 51:12; Luke 15:21-24

48. He will someday gather all believers in Christ. — Eph. 1:10

49. He will someday reward all believers. — Matt. 6:1; Heb. 11:6; 2 Tim. 4:8

50. He will someday glorify all believers. — Rom. 8:30

The Trinity and Scriptural Evidences for It

1. The creation of man in God's image. Note that the Bible says, "Let us make man in our image." — Gen. 1:26

2. The expulsion from Eden. Note that the Bible says "The man has become like one of us." — Gen. 3:22

3. The confusion at Babel. Note that the Bible says "Let us go down and confuse their language." — Gen. 11:7

4. The usage of the Hebrew word *echad,* meaning "one," but suggesting more than one person — Gen. 2:24; Deut. 6:4

5. The teachings of King Agur, which suggests a son of God — Prov. 30:4

6. The plural forms used to refer to God — Eccles. 12:1; Isa. 54:5

7. The divine conversations in Isaiah, using a plural form of divine pronoun — Isa. 6:8; 48:16; 63:9-10

8. The divine conversations in the Psalms, which also use plurals — Ps. 2:1-9; 45:6-8; 110:1-5

9. The baptism of Christ, wherein the Father, Son, and Spirit were all present — Matt. 3:16-17

10. The teachings of Jesus about the Father and the Spirit — John 14:16

11. The trinitarian baptismal formula — Matt. 28:19-20

12. The trinitarian apostolic benediction — 2 Cor. 13:14

GODLESS SONS OF GODLY FATHERS

1. Esau, son of Isaac, sold his birthright. — Gen. 25:27-34

2. Nadab and Abihu, sons of Aaron, offered strange fire on the altar of incense. — Lev. 10:1-5

3. Abimelech, son of Gideon, murdered his 70 brothers. — Judg. 9

4. Hophni and Phinehas, sons of Eli, were immoral and dishonest priests. — 1 Sam. 2:12-25

5. Joel and Abijah, sons of Samuel, took bribes and perverted justice. — 1 Sam. 8:1-3

6. Amnon, son of David, raped his half sister. — 2 Sam. 13:1-19

7. Absalom, son of David, led a rebellion against his father. — 2 Sam. 15–18

8. Adonijah, son of David, attempted to steal Solomon's throne. — 1 Kings 1

9. Rehoboam, son of Solomon, caused a tragic civil war. — 1 Kings 12

10. Joram, son of Jehoshaphat, murdered his six brothers.   2 Kings 8:16-24

11. Ahaz, son of Jotham, sacrificed his own children to idols.   2 Kings 16:1-20

12. Manasseh, son of Hezekiah, was Judah's worst king.   2 Kings 21:1-18

13. Jehoahaz, son of Josiah, did evil in the sight of God.   2 Kings 23:31-33

14. Jehoiakim, son of Josiah, burned the scroll from Jeremiah.   Jer. 36:20-26

15. Zedekiah, son of Josiah, persecuted Jeremiah.   2 Kings 24:17– 25:30; Jer. 37:1-21

GODLY SONS OF GODLESS FATHERS

1. Jonathan, son of Saul, risked his life to help David.   1 Sam. 18:1

2. Asa, son of Abijam, was Judah's first righteous king.   1 Kings 15:8-14

3. Hezekiah, son of Ahaz, was Judah's second righteous king.   2 Kings 18:1– 20:21

4. Josiah, son of Amon, led Judah in a great revival.   2 Kings 22:1– 23:30

HANDICAPPED AND DISABLED
See also Diseases and Infirmities, Lepers

Paralysis and Lameness

1. Mephibosheth, the crippled grandson of Saul   2 Sam. 4:4

2. Man at Capernaum, lowered from a roof to be healed — Mark 2:1-12; Luke 5:18-25

3. Centurion's servant whom Jesus healed without even being present — Matt. 8:5-13; Luke 7:1-10

4. Man by pool at Bethesda who had suffered for 38 years when Jesus healed him — John 5:1-8

5. Woman in synagogue who had suffered for 18 years when Jesus healed her — Luke 13:10-13

6. Man at Beautiful Gate whom Peter healed through the power of Christ — Acts 3:2

7. Aeneas, who had suffered eight years when Peter healed him — Acts 9:33-34

8. Man at Lystra whom Paul healed (an act for which Paul was later stoned) — Acts 14:8-10

Withered Hand

1. Man in Galilean synagogue healed by Christ on the Sabbath, which caused the Jews to begin plotting — Matt. 12:10-13; Mark 3:1-5; Luke 6:6-10

Blindness

1. Two men in Galilee who called Jesus the Son of David — Matt. 9:27-31

2. Man at Bethsaida whom Jesus healed after a second touch — Mark 8:22-25

3. Man at Pool of Siloam who had been born blind — John 9:1-7

4. Bartimaeus, healed by Jesus while leaving Jericho — Matt. 20:29-34; Mark 10:46-52; Luke 18:35-42

5. Demon-possessed man in Galilee, whose healing caused the crowd to acknowledge Jesus to be the Son of David — Matt. 12:22; Luke 11:14

Deafness

1. Man from Tyre and Sidon, healed when Jesus spat and put his fingers in the man's ears — Mark 7:32-35

2. Mute boy at base of Mt. Hermon, whom the disciples were unable to heal — Matt. 17:14-18; Mark 9:17-29

3. Mute man in Galilee, whose healing caused the crowd to marvel — Matt. 12:22; Luke 11:14

HEAVEN
See also Prophecies

---

53 Facts about Heaven

1. Heaven is being prepared by Christ himself. — John 14:3

2. It is only for those who have been born again. — John 3:3

3. It is described as a glorious city, likened to pure gold and clear glass. — Rev. 21:11, 18

4. The name of this city is the New Jerusalem. — Rev. 21:2

5. It is in the shape of a cube, with the length, width, and height being equal. — Rev. 21:16

6. Its size is 12,000 furlongs, roughly 1,400 miles long, wide, and high. — Rev. 21:16

7. The city rests upon 12 layers of foundational stones, with each layer being inlaid with a different precious gem. — Rev. 21:19-20

8. Each foundation has one of the names of the 12 apostles on it.　Rev. 21:14

9. The wall around the city is made of pure jasper.　Rev. 21:18

10. The height of the wall is approximately 216 feet.　Rev. 21:17

11. The wall has 12 gates, three on each of the four sides.　Rev. 21:12

12. Each gate is made of solid pearl.　Rev. 21:21

13. Each gate has on it the name of one of the 12 tribes of Israel.　Rev. 21:12

14. An angel stands guard at each gate.　Rev. 21:12

15. The gates will never be shut.　Rev. 21:25

16. The palaces may possibly be made of ivory.　Ps. 45:8

17. The River of Life is there, to insure everlasting life.　Rev. 22:1

18. The Tree of Life is there to insure abundant life.　Rev. 2:7; 22:19

19. It will bear its fruit each month.　Rev. 22:2

20. The throne of God will occupy the central palace.　Rev. 4:2; 22:1

21. It is likened to wheels of burning fire with an emerald rainbow canopy.　Dan. 7:9; Rev. 4:3

22. It is surrounded by 24 small thrones.　Rev. 4:4

23. Near it stands the brazen layer, described as "a sea of glass, like crystal."　Rev. 4:6

24. Beside the throne are four special angels who worship God continually.　Rev. 4:8

25. The golden altar is there, with bowls of incense.　Rev. 5:8; 8:3; 9:13

26. The menorah, or seven-branched lampstand fixture, is there.　Rev. 1:12; 4:5

27. The holy Ark of God may be there.　Rev. 11:19

28. The main street of the city is composed of transparent gold.	Rev. 21:21
29. The city will shine with and be enlightened by God's glory.	John 17:24; Rom. 8:18; Rev. 21:11, 23; 22:5
30. It is a place of holiness.	Rev. 21:27
31. It is a place of beauty.	Ps. 50:2
32. It is a place of unity.	Eph. 1:10
33. It is a place of perfection.	1 Cor. 13:10
34. It is a place of joy.	Ps. 16:11
35. It is a place for all eternity.	John 3:15; Ps. 23:6
36. There may be a tabernacle.	Rev. 15:5; 21:3
37. There will be no temple.	Rev. 21:22
38. There will be no sea.	Rev. 21:1
39. There will be no tears.	Rev. 7:17; 21:4
40. There will be no sickness.	Rev. 22:2
41. There will be no pain.	Rev. 21:4
42. There will be no death.	Isa. 25:8; 1 Cor. 15:26; Rev. 21:4
43. There will be no more thirst or hunger.	Rev. 7:16
44. There will be no more sin.	Rev. 21:27
45. There will be no more judgment upon sin.	Rev. 22:3
46. There will be no need for the sun or moon.	Rev. 21:23
47. There will be no night.	Rev. 21:25; 22:5
48. The city will be the Bridegroom's gift to the bride, Christ's Church.	Rev. 21:2, 10
49. It will be shared by saved Israel.	Heb. 11:10, 16
50. It will be shared by the holy angels.	Dan. 7:10; Heb. 12:22; Rev. 5:11
51. The Father will be there.	Dan. 7:9; Rev. 4:2-3
52. The Son will be there.	Rev. 5:6; 7:17
53. The Holy Spirit will be there.	Rev. 14:13; 22:17

7 Facts about Our Resurrected Bodies in Heaven

1. It will be a recognizable body.	1 Cor. 13:2
2. It will be a body like Christ's body.	1 John 3:2
3. It will be a body that will permit eating.	Luke 24:41-43; John 21:12-13
4. It will be a body in which the spirit predominates.	1 Cor. 15:44, 49
5. It will be a body unlimited by time, gravity, or space.	Luke 24:31; John 20:19, 26
6. It will be an eternal body.	2 Cor. 5:1
7. It will be a glorious body.	Rom. 8:18; 1 Cor. 15:43

3 Activities in Heaven

1. Singing	Isa. 44:23; Heb. 2:12; Rev. 14:3; 15:3
2. Serving	Rev. 7:15; 22:3
3. Learning	1 Cor. 13:9, 10

HELL
See also Prophecies, Satan and Fallen Angels

1. Hell will be a place of unquenchable fire.	Matt. 3:12; 13:41-42; Mark 9:43
2. It will be a place of memory and remorse.	Luke 16:19-31
3. It will be a place of thirst.	Luke 16:24
4. It will be a place of misery and pain.	Rev. 14:10, 11
5. It will be a place of frustration and anger.	Matt. 13:42; 24:51
6. It will be a place of separation.	Rev. 2:11; 20:6, 15

7. It will be a place of undiluted divine wrath.   Hab. 3:2; Rev. 14:10

8. It was originally prepared for Satan and his hosts.   Matt. 25:41

9. It will be a place created for all eternity.   Dan. 12:2; Matt. 25:46; Jude 7

HISTORY IN THE BIBLE

99 Important B.C. Biblical Dates

1. 2165 B.C.—Birth of Abram   Gen. 11:26
2. 2090—Abram enters Canaan   Gen. 12
3. 2066—Destruction of Sodom   Gen. 19
4. 2065—Birth of Isaac   Gen. 21
5. 2045?—Sacrifice of Isaac on Mt. Moriah   Gen. 22
6. 2025—Marriage of Isaac and Rebekah   Gen. 24
7. 2005—Birth of Esau and Jacob   Gen. 25
8. 1990—Death of Abraham   Gen. 25
9. c. 1990?—Life of Job   Job
10. 1928—Jacob deceives his father Isaac and flees to Haran   Gen. 27
11. 1920—Marriage of Jacob to Leah and Rachel   Gen. 29:28
12. 1897—Joseph is sold into Egypt   Gen. 37
13. 1884—Joseph is exalted by Pharaoh   Gen. 41
14. 1875—Jacob and his family enter Egypt.   Gen. 46
15. 1858—Death of Jacob   Gen. 49
16. 1804—Death of Joseph; Israel enjoys prosperity for 75 years   Gen. 50; Exod. 1:1-7

17.	1730—Egyptian oppression begins	Exod. 1:8–12:42
18.	1525—Birth of Moses	Exod. 2:1-4
19.	1485—Moses flees Egypt	Exod. 2:11-15
20.	1445—Moses returns to Egypt	Exod. 4:20
21.	1445—The Exodus	Exod. 12–15
22.	June 15, 1445—Arrival at Mt. Sinai	Exod. 19:1
23.	1444–1405—Wandering in wilderness	Num. 15:1—Deut. 34
24.	October 7, 1405—Death of Moses	Deut. 34:1-7
25.	April 10, 1404—The crossing of the Jordan	Josh. 1:5
26.	1404–1397—The conquering of Canaan	Josh. 6–12
27.	1390—Death of Joshua	Josh. 23–24
28.	1374–1334—Judgeship of Othniel	Judg. 3:7-11
29.	1316–1236—Judgeship of Ehud	Judg. 3:12-14
30.	1216–1176—Judgeship of Deborah and Barak	Judg. 4–5
31.	1169–1129—Judgeship of Gideon	Judg. 6–8
32.	c. 1150?—Life of Ruth	Ruth
33.	c. 1087—Judgeship of Jephthah	Judg. 11–12
34.	c. 1069—Judgeship of Samson	Judg. 13–16
35.	c. 1107—Judgeship of Eli	1 Sam. 1–4
36.	1105—Birth of Samuel	1 Sam. 1:19-20
37.	1043—Saul anointed first king of Israel by Samuel	1 Sam. 10
38.	1025—The anointing of David	1 Sam. 16
39.	1011—Death of Saul	1 Sam. 31
40.	1011—Reign of David over one tribe begins	2 Sam. 2:4
41.	1005—Jerusalem becomes the capital	2 Sam. 2:4
42.	1004—Reign of David over all Israel begins	2 Sam. 5:3
43.	971—Death of David	1 Kings 2:10
44.	971—Reign of Solomon begins	1 Kings 1:39

45. 959—Completion of the temple	1 Kings 6:38
46. 931—Kingdom splits into two kingdoms, Israel and Judah, after Solomon's death	1 Kings 12
47. 874—The reign of Ahab begins in Israel	1 Kings 16–22
48. 860–852—The ministry of Elijah	1 Kings 17–19, 21; 2 Kings 1–2
49. 852–795—The ministry of Elisha	2 Kings 2–9, 13
50. 850—Book of Obadiah	
51. 848—Book of Joel	
52. 785—Book of Jonah	
53. 760—Book of Amos	
54. 758—Book of Hosea	
55. 739—Book of Isaiah	
56. 735—Book of Micah	
57. 721—The capture of the northern kingdom by the Assyrians	2 Kings 17
58. 716—Reign of Hezekiah begins	2 Kings 18–21
59. 701—Jerusalem saved from the Assyrians by the angel of the Lord	2 Kings 19
60. 697—Reign of Manasseh begins	2 Kings 21
61. 650—Book of Nahum	
62. 641—Reign of Josiah begins	2 Kings 22–23
63. 640—Book of Zephaniah	
64. 627—Book of Jeremiah	
65. 612—Fall of Nineveh	
66. 608—Book of Habakkuk	
67. 605—The first siege of Jerusalem; Daniel taken	2 Kings 24
68. 597—The second siege of Jerusalem; Ezekiel taken	2 Kings 24
69. 597—Third siege of Jerusalem	2 Kings 24
70. 587—Fall of Jerusalem to the Babylonians	2 Kings 25

71. 586—The Book of Lamentations

72. 605–536—The ministry of Daniel   Daniel

73. 593–560—The ministry of Ezekiel   Ezekiel

74. October 29, 539—The fall of Babylon   Dan. 5
    to Persia

75. 538—The edict of Cyrus for the Jews'   Ezra 1
    return to Judea

76. 536—First return to Judea under   Ezra 1–6
    Zerubbabel

77. June 535—Work on the temple begun   Ezra 3

78. 520—Ministry of Haggai   Ezra 5:1; Haggai

79. 520—Ministry of Zechariah   Ezra 5:1;
    Zechariah

80. February 18, 516—Work on temple   Ezra 6:15
    completed

81. 478—Esther becomes queen of Persia   Esther 2

82. March 455—Second return to Judea   Ezra 7:10
    under Ezra

83. September 444—The walls of   Neh. 6:15
    Jerusalem are completed.

84. 437—Ministry of Malachi

85. 425—Completion of the Old
    Testament

86. 331–323—Career of Alexander the
    Great

87. 260—Translation of the Old Testament   The Septuagint
    into Greek

88. 175–169—Reign of Antiochus
    Epiphanes, who defiled the temple

89. 166—Revolt of the Maccabees,
    Jewish freedom fighters

90. 164—Roman General Pompey
    conquers Jerusalem

91. 40—Herod the Great appointed king

92. 20—Herod begins enlarging the
    second temple.

93.	5—Birth of John the Baptist	Luke 1:57-60
94.	5—Birth of Jesus Christ	Luke 2:1-20
95.	4—Visit of the wise men	Matt. 2:1-12
96.	4—Flight into Egypt	Matt. 2:13-15
97.	4—Slaughter of the innocent Bethlehem babies	Matt. 2:16
98.	4—Death of Herod	Matt. 2:19
99.	4—Journey from Egypt to Nazareth	Matt. 2:20-23

60 Important A.D. Biblical Dates

1.	8—Temple discussion when Christ was 12	Luke 2:41-52
2.	26—Baptism of Christ	Matt. 3:16-17
3.	28—Choosing of the Twelve	Matt. 10:1-4
4.	29 [Spring]—Death of John the Baptist	Matt. 14:1-12
5.	29 [Fall]—The Feast of Tabernacles message	John 7:14-39
6.	29 [Winter]—Lazarus raised	John 11:1-46
7.	30 [April]—Death and Resurrection of Christ	Matt. 27–28
8.	30 [May]—Ascension of Christ	Acts 1
9.	30 [June]—Pentecost	Acts 2
10.	31—Death of Ananias and Sapphira	Acts 5:1-11
11.	32—Seven deacons selected	Acts 6:1-7
12.	34—Martyrdom of Stephen	Acts 6:8–7:60
13.	35—Conversion of Paul	Acts 9:1-7
14.	37—Paul's first visit in Jerusalem as a believer	Acts 9:26-29; Gal. 1:18
15.	40—Conversion of Cornelius	Acts 10
16.	42—Antioch ministry of Paul and Barnabas	Acts 11:19-30
17.	44—Martyrdom of the apostle James	Acts 12:1-2
18.	47—Beginning of Paul's first missionary journey	Acts 13:1-3

19. 49—Completion of first missionary journey — Acts 14:26

20. 49—Letter to the Galatians

21. 49—Jerusalem Council — Acts 15

22. 50—Beginning of Paul's second missionary journey — Acts 15:40-41

23. 51—First Letter to the Thessalonians

24. 52—Second Letter to the Thessalonians

25. 52—Completion of second missionary journey — Acts 18:22

26. 53—Beginning of Paul's third missionary journey — Acts 18:23

27. 55—First Letter to the Corinthians

28. 56—Second Letter to the Corinthians

29. 57—Letter to the Romans

30. 57—Completion of third missionary journey — Acts 21:15

31. 57—Arrest of Paul in Jerusalem — Acts 21:27

32. 57—Beginning of Paul's imprisonment in Caesarea — Acts 23:33

33. 59—Paul's voyage to Rome — Acts 27:1–28:15

34. 60—Paul's arrival in Rome — Acts 28:16

35. 60—Beginning of Paul's first Roman imprisonment — Acts 28:16

36. 60—Letter to the Ephesians

37. 60—Letter to the Colossians

38. 61—Letter to Philemon

39. 61—Letter to the Philippians

40. 61—Gospel of Luke

41. 61—Book of Acts

42. 61—Letter to the Hebrews

43. 62—Paul released from first Roman imprisonment — Philem. 22

44. 62—Martyrdom of James, the Lord's brother

45. 62—First Letter to Timothy
46. 64—Letter to Titus
47. 64—First Letter of Peter
48. 65—Second Letter of Peter
49. 65—Martyrdom of Peter
50. 65—Gospel of Matthew
51. 65—Gospel of Mark
52. 66—Final Roman imprisonment of   2 Tim. 1:8
      Paul
53. 66—Jewish revolt against Rome
54. 67—Second Letter to Timothy
55. 67—Martyrdom of Paul
56. 70—Destruction of Jerusalem by the
      Romans
57. 85—Letter of Jude
58. 90—Gospel of John
59. 92—First, Second, and Third Letters
      of John
60. 95—Book of Revelation, signifying   Rev. 22:21
      completion of New Testament

12 Stages in Bible History

1. The Creation Stage	Gen. 1–11
2. The Patriarchal Stage	Gen. 12–50; Job
3. The Exodus Stage	Exod.—Deut.
4. The Conquest Stage	Josh.
5. The Judges Stage	Judg.—1 Sam. 1–7
6. The United Kingdom Stage	1 Sam. 8—1 Kings 11; 1 Chron.— 2 Chron. 9; Pss.— Song of Sol.
7. The Chaotic Kingdom Stage	1 Kings 12— 2 Kings; 2 Chron. 10–36; Isa.— Lam.; Hos.— Zeph.
8. The Babylonian Captivity Stage	Dan.; Ezek.

9. The Return Stage	Ezra—Esther; Hag.—Mal.
10. The Gospel Stage	Matt.—John
11. The Early Church Stage	Acts
12. The Epistles Stage	Rom.—Rev.

85 Biblical Phenomena Supported by Archaeological Findings

1. Creation	Gen. 1:1
2. Original monotheism	Gen. 1:1
3. The Garden of Eden	Gen. 2:8-17
4. The fall of man	Gen. 3
5. Earliest civilization	Gen. 4:1-26
6. Pre-Flood longevity	Gen. 5:1-32
7. The universal Flood	Gen. 6–9
8. Mt. Ararat as the site of the landing of Noah's ark	Gen. 8:4
9. The table of nations	Gen. 10
10. The Tower of Babel	Gen. 11:1-9
11. Ur of the Chaldeans	Gen. 11:31
12. Haran	Gen. 12:5
13. The battle route of Chedorlaomer	Gen. 14:1-12
14. The Hittite empire	Gen. 15:20
15. Nahor	Gen. 24:10
16. The employment of camels in patriarchal times	Gen. 24:11
17. The cities of Sodom and Gomorrah	Gen. 19
18. The commonness in inscriptions of biblical names such as Adam, Eve, Lamech, Jabal, Noah, Hagar, Keturah, and Bilhah	Gen. 2:19; 3:20; 4:19-20; 5:29; 16:1; 25:1; 29:29
19. The abundance of food in Gerar in time of famine	Gen. 26:1
20. Joseph and Potiphar's wife	Gen. 39
21. The bricks without straw	Exod. 5:7-19

22. The death of the firstborn in Egypt — Exod. 12

23. The destruction of Pharaoh and his armies in the Red Sea — Exod. 14

24. The parting of the Jordan River — Josh. 3

25. The destruction of Jericho — Josh. 6

26. The altar used by Joshua when Israel crossed into the Promised Land — Josh. 8:30-35

27. The wealth of Gibeon — Josh. 10:2

28. The springs of Kirjath-sepher — Josh. 15:13-19

29. Shiloh, where the tabernacle resided after Israel crossed into the Promised Land — Josh. 18:1

30. The use of the hornet in conquering Palestine — Josh. 24:12

31. The burial of Joshua — Josh. 24:30

32. Cities in the Book of Judges — Judg. 1:21-29

33. The Philistines' use of iron weapons — Judg. 1:19

34. The Deborah and Barak battle — Judg. 4

35. Gideon's hidden grain pit — Judg. 6:11-18

36. The destruction of Gibeah — Judg. 20

37. The taking of the Ark — 1 Sam. 4

38. Saul's house in Gibeah — 1 Sam. 10:26

39. Jonathan's victory over the Philistines — 1 Sam. 14

40. The music of David — 1 Sam. 16:18, 23; 1 Chron. 15:16

41. The pool of Gibeon — 2 Sam. 2:13

42. The capture of Jerusalem — 2 Sam. 5:6-10

43. The wealth of Solomon — 1 Kings 4:26; 9:26; 10:22

44. Solomon's fortresses, built to defend his cities in the Negev — 1 Kings 9:15

45. The invasion of Judah by Pharaoh Shisak of Egypt — 1 Kings 14:25-28; 2 Chron. 12:2-4

46. The reign of northern King Omri — 1 Kings 16:24

47. The rebuilding of Jericho — Josh. 6:26; 1 Kings 16:34

48. The victory of Elijah on Mt. Carmel — 1 Kings 18

49. Ahab's house of ivory — 1 Kings 22:39

50. The pool of Samaria — 1 Kings 22:37-38

51. The war between Israel and Moab — 2 Kings 3

52. The building where Judean King Joash was murdered — 2 Kings 12:20-21

53. The punishment of King Jehu — 2 Kings 10:29-33

54. The official seal of the servant of Jeroboam II — 2 Kings 14:23-29

55. Repentance of Nineveh — Jon. 3

56. The tribute money King Menahem of Israel paid to Assyrian King Pul — 2 Kings 15:19

57. The accomplishments and judgment of King Uzziah — 2 Chron. 26

58. The capture of Israel by Assyrian King Shalmaneser — 2 Kings 17

59. Ahaz's money tribute to King Tiglath-pileser — 2 Kings 16:5-9

60. The seal and tomb of Shebna, Hezekiah's scribe — Isa. 22:15-16

61. A seal bearing the name "Gemariah, the son of Shaphan," who served as official scribe to Judean King Jehoiakim — Jer. 36:9-12

62. The destruction of Lachish by Sennacherib — 2 Chron. 32:9; Isa. 10:29

63. Sennacherib's failure to capture Jerusalem — 2 Kings 18–19; 2 Chron. 32; Isa. 36–37

64. The murder of Sennacherib by his own sons — Isa. 37:37-38

65. The imprisonment of King Manasseh by the Assyrians — 2 Chron. 33:11

66. The discovery of the book of the law in the temple during Josiah's reign — 2 Chron. 34:8-32

67. Hezekiah's water tunnel — 2 Kings 20:20; 2 Chron. 32:30

68. Hezekiah's wall repairs	2 Chron. 32:5
69. The destruction of Lachish by Nebuchadnezzar	Jer. 34:7
70. The captivity of Jehoiachin and the appointment of Zedekiah	2 Kings 24:10-19; 25:27-30
71. The futile hope of Zedekiah in looking to Egypt to aid against Babylon	Jer. 37:1, 5-11
72. The treachery of Ishmael against Gedaliah and his officials	Jer. 41:1-15
73. The great stones buried by Jeremiah in Tahpanhes, Egypt	Jer. 43:8-13
74. The great statue and fiery furnace of Nebuchadnezzar	Dan. 3
75. The pride of Nebuchadnezzar and the greatness of Babylon	Dan. 4
76. The insanity of Nebuchadnezzar	Dan. 4
77. The capture of Babylon and execution of Belshazzar	Dan. 5
78. Daniel and the lions' den	Dan. 6
79. Ahasuerus the Persian king	Esther
80. The edict of King Cyrus	Ezra 1:1-4
81. The wall constructed by Nehemiah	Neh. 1–6
82. The enemies of Nehemiah	Neh. 2, 4, 6
83. The synagogue in Capernaum where Jesus preached	Mark 1:21-25; Luke 7:1-10
84. Simon Peter's home in Capernaum	Mark 1:21, 29
85. The Holy of Holies in the temple of Herod	

70 Most Important Events in the Bible

1. The Creation	Gen. 1
2. Fall of man	Gen. 3:6
3. Universal flood	Gen. 6–8
4. Tower of Babel	Gen. 11:1-9
5. Conversion and call of Abraham	Gen. 12:1-3

6. Giving of Abrahamic Covenant	Gen. 12:7; 13:14-17; 15:1-21
7. The selling of Joseph into Egyptian slavery	Gen. 37
8. The enslavement of Israel in Egypt	Exod. 1
9. The call of Moses	Exod. 3:1-10
10. The ten plagues	Exod. 7–12
11. The Exodus from Egypt	Exod. 12–15
12. The institution of the Sabbath	Exod. 16:29
13. The giving of the Law	Exod. 20:1-17
14. The completion of the tabernacle	Exod. 40:33-34
15. The anointing of Aaron as first high priest	Lev. 8:1-12
16. The Jordan River crossing into Palestine	Josh. 3
17. The victory over Jericho	Josh. 6
18. The marriage of Ruth to Boaz	Ruth 4
19. The anointing of Saul as Israel's first king	1 Sam. 9–10
20. The anointing of David as king	1 Sam. 16:13
21. The capture of Jerusalem and recovery of the Ark by David	2 Sam. 5–6
22. The giving of the Davidic Covenant	2 Sam. 7:8-17
23. The anointing of Solomon	1 King 1:39
24. The completion of Solomon's temple	1 Kings 6:38
25. The splitting of Israel into the two kingdoms, Israel and Judah	1 Kings 12
26. Elijah taken up to heaven	2 Kings 2
27. The deliverance of Joash from murderous Queen Athaliah	2 Chron. 22:10-12
28. The Assyrian conquest of the northern kingdom	2 Kings 17:6
29. The deliverance of Jerusalem from the Assyrians	2 Kings 19:32-35
30. The discovery of the Law of Moses in Josiah's reign	2 Chron. 34

31. The destruction of the temple of Solomon	2 Kings 25:8-9
32. The Babylonian Captivity of the southern kingdom	2 Kings 25:11
33. The return under Cyrus' decree	Ezra 1
34. The completion of the new temple under Zerubbabel	Ezra 6
35. The rescuing of the Jews by Esther	Esther. 4–7
36. Birth of John the Baptist	Luke 1:57-80
37. Birth of Christ	Luke 2:7
38. The flight into Egypt	Matt. 2:13-14
39. The temple visit at age 12	Luke 2:41-50
40. Jesus' baptism	Matt. 3:13-17
41. The temptation	Matt. 4:1-11
42. The temple cleansing	John 2:13-25
43. The choosing of the 12	Matt. 10:1-4
44. The Sermon on the Mount	Matt. 5–7
45. The raising of Lazarus	John 11
46. Death of John the Baptist	Matt. 14; Mark 6
47. Confession of Peter and promise of the Church	Matt. 16
48. The Transfiguration	Matt. 17
49. The triumphal entry into Jerusalem	Matt. 21; Mark 11; Luke 19; John 12
50. Events in the Upper Room	Matt. 26; Mark 14; Luke 22; John 13–14
51. Christ's ordeal in Gethsemane	Matt. 26; Mark 14; Luke 22; John 18
52. His trials	Matt. 26–27; Mark 14–15; Luke 22–23; John 18–19
53. The Crucifixion	Matt. 27:35; Mark 15:24; Luke 23:33; John 19:18
54. The Resurrection	Matt. 28; Mark 16; Luke 24; John 20

55. His ten glorified appearances	Matt. 28; Mark 16; Luke 24; John 20–21
56. Giving the Great Commission	Matt. 28:18-20
57. The Ascension	Acts 1:9-11
58. Pentecost	Acts 2
59. Healing of a lame man by Peter and John	Acts 3:1-11
60. Election of the first deacons	Acts 6:1-8
61. Martyrdom of Stephen	Acts 7:1-60
62. Conversion of Saul	Acts 9:1-20
63. Establishment of the Antioch church	Acts 11:19-26
64. Death of James and deliverance of Peter	Acts 12:1-19
65. Paul's first missionary journey	Acts 13:2–14:28
66. The Jerusalem Council	Acts 15:1-35
67. Paul's second missionary journey	Acts 15:36–18:22
68. Paul's third missionary journey	Acts 18:23–21:16
69. Paul's imprisonment in Rome	Acts 28:30
70. The exile of John to Patmos and the writing of Revelation	Rev. 1:9

THE HOLY SPIRIT
See also God, Jesus Christ

15 Facts about the Holy Spirit

1. He is omnipresent.	Ps. 139:7
2. He is omniscient.	1 Cor. 2:10-11
3. He is omnipotent.	Gen. 1:2
4. He is eternal.	Heb. 9:14
5. He is called God.	Acts 5:3-4

6. He is equal with the Father and with the Son.   Matt. 28:19-20

7. He has a mind.   Rom. 8:27

8. He searches out the human mind.   1 Cor. 2:10

9. He has a will.   1 Cor. 12:11

10. He forbids.   Acts 16:6-7

11. He leads.   Acts 16:10

12. He speaks.   Acts 8:29

13. He loves.   Rom. 15:30

14. He grieves.   Eph. 4:30

15. He prays.   Rom. 8:26

13 Names for the Holy Spirit

1. The Spirit of God   1 Cor. 3:16

2. The Spirit of Christ   Rom. 8:9

3. The eternal Spirit   Heb. 9:14

4. The Spirit of truth   John 16:13

5. The Spirit of grace   Heb. 10:29

6. The Spirit of glory   1 Pet. 4:14

7. The Spirit of life   Rom. 8:2

8. The Spirit of wisdom and revelation   Eph. 1:17

9. The Comforter   John 14:26

10. The Spirit of promise   Acts 1:4-5

11. The Spirit of adoption   Rom. 8:15

12. The Spirit of holiness   Rom. 1:4

13. The Spirit of faith   2 Cor. 4:13

18 Gifts of the Holy Spirit

1. Apostleship   Eph. 4:11; 1 Cor. 12:28

2. Prophecy   Rom. 12:6; 1 Cor. 12:10

3. Miracles   1 Cor. 12:28

4. Healing   1 Cor. 12:9, 28, 30

5. Tongues   1 Cor. 12:10

6. Interpretation of tongues	1 Cor. 12:10
7. Knowledge	1 Cor. 12:8
8. Wisdom	1 Cor. 12:8
9. Discerning of spirits	1 Cor. 12:10
10. Giving	Rom. 12:8
11. Ministering	Rom. 12:7; 1 Cor. 12:28
12. Exhortation	Rom. 12:8; see also Prov. 25:11
13. Showing of mercy	Rom. 12:8
14. Ruling, or administration	Rom. 12:8
15. Faith	Rom. 12:3
16. Teaching	Rom. 12:7
17. Evangelism	2 Tim. 4:5; Acts 8:26-40; 21:8
18. Pastoring-teaching	1 Pet. 5:1-4

57 Ministries of the Holy Spirit

1. Was at work in creating the universe	Gen. 1:2; Ps. 104:30
2. Inspired the writing of the Old Testament	2 Sam. 23:2; Isa. 59:21
3. Inspired the writing of the New Testament	1 Cor. 14:37; 1 Thess. 4:15
4. Came upon Joseph	Gen. 41:38
5. Came upon Moses	Num. 11:17
6. Came upon Joshua	Num. 27:18
7. Came upon Othniel	Judg. 3:10
8. Came upon Gideon	Judg. 6:34
9. Came upon Jephthah	Judg. 11:29
10. Came upon Samson	Judg. 14:6, 19; 15:14-15
11. Came upon Saul	1 Sam. 10:10
12. Came upon David	1 Sam. 16:13; Ps. 51:11
13. Came upon Elijah	1 Kings 18:12; 2 Kings 2:16

14. Came upon Elisha	2 Kings 2:15
15. Came upon Azariah the prophet	2 Chron. 15:1
16. Came upon Zechariah the high priest	2 Chron. 24:20
17. Came upon Israel's elders	Num. 11:25
18. Led Israel through the wilderness	Neh. 9:20
19. Will minister to Israel during the Great Tribulation	Joel 2:28-32
20. Will minister to Israel during the Millennium	Zech. 12:10; Ezek. 37:13-14; 39:29
21. Restrains the power of Satan	Isa. 59:19; 2 Thess. 2:7-14
22. Provided the Savior with his earthly body	Luke 1:35; Matt. 1:18-20
23. Anointed the Savior	Matt. 3:16; Luke 4:18; Acts 10:38; Heb. 1:9
24. Directed the Savior to be tempted by Satan	Matt. 4:1
25. Empowered the Savior	Matt. 12:28
26. Caused the Savior to sorrow	John 11:33
27. Caused the Savior to rejoice	Luke 10:21
28. Led the Savior to Calvary	Heb. 9:14
29. Raised the body of the Savior	Rom. 8:11; 1 Pet. 3:18
30. Convicts the unsaved person of sin, righteousness, and judgment	John 16:7-11
31. Gave birth to the church	Acts 2:1-4; Eph. 2:19-22
32. Desires to inspire the worship service of the church	Phil. 3:3
33. Desires to direct its missionary work	Acts 8:29; 13:2, 4; 16:6-7, 10
34. Desires to aid in its singing services	Eph. 5:18-19
35. Appoints its preachers	Acts 20:28
36. Anoints its preachers	1 Cor. 2:4
37. Warns its members	1 Tim. 4:1

38. Desires to determine its decisions	Acts 15:28
39. Desires to direct its evangelistic attempts	Rev. 22:17
40. Alone is able to condone or condemn its ministry	Rev. 2:7, 11, 17, 29
41. Regenerates the believing sinner	Titus 3:5; John 3:3-7; 1 Pet. 1:23
42. Baptizes the believer	Rom. 6:3-4; 1 Cor. 12:13; Gal. 3:27; Eph. 4:4-5; Col. 2:12
43. Indwells the believer	John 14:16, 20; 1 Cor. 2:12; 3:16; 7:37-39; Rom. 8:9; 1 John 3:24
44. Seals the believer	2 Cor. 1:22; Eph. 1:13; 4:30; 2 Cor. 5:5; Eph. 1:14
45. Fills the believer	Acts 2:4
46. Conforms him to the image of Christ	2 Cor. 3:18
47. Strengthens his new nature	Eph. 3:16; 1 Pet. 2:2; Jude 1:20
48. Reveals biblical truth to him	1 Cor. 2:10
49. Assures him concerning salvation and service	Rom. 8:16; 1 John 3:24
50. Gives him liberty	Rom. 8:2; 2 Cor. 3:17
51. Fills his mouth with appropriate things	Mark 13:11
52. Prays for him	Rom. 8:26
53. Guides him	John 16:13; Rom. 8:14
54. Teaches him	1 John 2:27
55. Empowers him for witnessing	Acts 1:8
56. Imparts the love of Christ to him and through him	Rom. 5:5
57. Will someday raise the bodies of all departed believers	Rom. 8:11

HYMNS AND SONGS

1. The song of Moses after he led Israel through the Red Sea — Exod. 15:1-19

2. The song of Moses just prior to his death — Deut. 32:1-4

3. The song of Israel as they dug some wells en route to the Promised Land — Num. 21:17-18

4. The song of Deborah and Barak, after their victory over Sisera — Judg. 5:1-31

5. The song of Hannah at the dedication of her son, Samuel — 1 Sam. 2:1-10

6. The song sung by the Israelite women to celebrate David's victory over Goliath — 1 Sam. 18:6-7

7. The song of the Levitical choir that sang at the temple dedication — 2 Chron. 5:12-14

8. The song of Jehoshaphat's marching choir which led his soldiers into battle against Judah's enemies — 2 Chron. 20:20-23

9. The song of this Levitical choir at the great restoration ceremony of the temple during Hezekiah's reign — 2 Chron. 29:25-30

10. The song of Mary (the "Magnificat") after learning of the future virgin birth — Luke 1:46-55

11. The song of Zacharias (the "Benedictus") at the circumcision of his son, John the Baptist — Luke 1:68-79

12. The song sung by the disciples in the Upper Room — Matt. 26:30

13. The song of Paul and Silas while in a Philippian jail at midnight — Acts 16:25

14. The songs of praise God desires believers to sing — Eph. 5:19; Col. 3:16

15. The new song sung by all believers to glorify Christ in heaven — Rev. 5:9-10

16. The song of the 144,000 — Rev. 14:1-3

17. The song of the tribulational
    overcomers   Rev. 15:2-4

IDOLS AND FALSE GODS

1. Asherah, or Ashtaroth, the chief   Judg. 6:24-32
   goddess of Tyre, referred to as the
   lady of the sea. Gideon destroyed a
   statue of this consort of Baal, that had
   been worshiped by his own father.

2. Ashtoreth, a Canaanite goddess,   1 Sam. 7:3-4
   another consort of Baal. The prophet
   Samuel led Israel in a great revival
   that resulted in the people giving up
   the sexual practices associated with
   the worship of Ashtoreth.

3. Baal, the chief deity of Canaan. The   1 Kings 18:17-40;
   struggle between Baal and Jehovah   2 Kings 10:28;
   came to a dramatic head on Mount   11:18
   Carmel under Elijah. Jehu later dealt a
   severe blow to Baalism.

4. Beelzebub, the prince of the demons,   Matt. 10:25; 12:24
   according to Jesus. The name literally
   means "lord of the flies."

5. Dagon, the chief Philistine agriculture   1 Sam. 5:1-7;
   god and father of Baal. The Ark of   Judg. 16:23-30
   the Covenant destroyed an idol of
   Dagon in its own temple. Later,
   Samson would destroy the temple of
   Dagon.

6. Diana, or Artemis, a grotesque,   Acts 19:27, 35
   many-breasted Asiatic goddess,
   believed to be the nursing mother of
   other gods, men, animals, and even

plants. Paul encountered Diana while in Ephesus. She is not the same as the Diana of Roman mythology.

7. Jupiter, the chief Roman god, another name for the Greek god Zeus. The people of Lystra called Barnabas "Jupiter," perhaps because of his impressive appearance. — Acts 14:12-13

8. Mercury, the Roman god of commerce, speed, and eloquence, and the son of Jupiter. As a messenger of the gods he had wings on his feet. Paul was mistaken for Mercury at Lystra because of his speaking abilities. — Acts 14:12

9. Merodach, also called Marduk, the chief god of the Babylonian pantheon and Nebuchadnezzar's favorite god

10. Molech, the god of the Ammonites and the most horrible idol in the Scriptures. Children were sacrificed to this Semitic deity. Solomon built an altar to Molech at Tophet in the Valley of Hinnom. Later both King Ahaz and his godless grandson Manasseh sacrificed their children to this blood-demanding idol. — 1 Kings 11:7; 2 Chron. 28:1-4; 33:6

11. Nanna, the moon god of Ur, worshiped by Abraham before his salvation — Josh. 24:2

12. Nebo, the Babylonian god of wisdom and literature — Isa. 46:1

13. Nishroch, the Assyrian god of Sennacherib. The king was murdered in the temple of his idol after returning from the death angel defeat at Jerusalem. — 2 Kings 19:37

14. Rimmon, the Syrian god of Naaman the leper — 2 Kings 5:15-19

15. Tammuz, the husband and brother of Ishtar (Asherah), goddess of fertility — Ezek. 8:14
16. Rachel's household gods — Gen. 31:19
17. The golden calf at Sinai — Exod. 32
18. The two golden images made by King Jeroboam and set up at the shrines of Dan and Bethel — 1 Kings 12:28-31
19. The golden image in the plain of Dura — Dan. 2
20. The unknown god on Mars Hill — Acts 17
21. The statue of the Beast — Rev. 13:14

JERUSALEM

14 Names for Jerusalem

1. The city of David — 2 Sam. 6:12
2. The city of the great king — Matt. 5:35
3. The holy city — Isa. 48:2; 52:1; Matt. 4:5
4. Salem — Gen. 14:18
5. The city of God — Ps. 46:4; 48:1; 87:3
6. The city of the Lord of hosts — Ps. 48:8
7. The city of righteousness — Isa. 1:26
8. The city of truth — Zech. 8:3
9. The city of the Lord — Isa. 60:14
10. The perfection of beauty — Lam. 2:15
11. The joy of the whole earth — Lam. 2:15
12. The Lord our righteousness — Jer. 23:6; 33:16
13. The Lord is there — Ezek. 48:35
14. Ariel, the hearth of God — Isa. 29:1

History and Significance

1. It was the place where Abraham fellowshiped with its mysterious king-priest Melchizedek.

   Gen. 14:18

2. Joshua later defeated its wicked king Adonizedek during Israel's southern campaign invasion of Palestine.

   Josh. 10:1

3. It was taken temporarily by the tribe of Judah around 1425 B.C.

   Judg. 1:8

4. It was the location of a vile sexual crime committed by the perverted Jebusites who controlled it around 1405 B.C.

   Judg. 19:22-30

5. It was captured by David around 1050 B.C. and made the capital of his kingdom.

   2 Sam. 5:6-12; 6:1-19

6. It was temporarily taken by Absalom around 1020 B.C.

   2 Sam. 16:15

7. Solomon built the temple around 1005 B.C.

   1 Kings 6

8. It was plundered by Shishak, king of Egypt, during Rehoboam's reign around 925 B.C.

   1 Kings 14:25-28; 2 Chron. 12:2-12

9. It was plundered by the Philistines and the Arabians during Jehoram's reign around 890 B.C.

   2 Chron. 21:16-17

10. It was plundered by the Syrians during the reign of Joash around 850 B.C.

    2 Chron. 24:23-24

11. It was plundered by northern Israel during Amaziah's reign around 800 B.C.

    2 Chron. 25:23

12. It was surrounded by Sennacherib's Assyrian army during Hezekiah's reign around 710 B.C.

    2 Chron. 32

13. Manasseh, its wicked king, was briefly captured by the Assyrians around 690 B.C.

    2 Chron. 33

14. It was taken briefly by Pharaoh-Neco
    after King Josiah's death around 630
    B.C.

    2 Kings 23:28-37

15. It was besieged by Nebuchadnezzar
    during the reign of Jehoiachin around
    598 B.C.

    2 Kings 24:10-16

16. It was destroyed and the temple
    burned by Nebuchadnezzar during the
    reign of Zedekiah, Judah's last king,
    around 588 B.C.

    2 Kings 25

17. It began to be reconstructed after the
    decree of Cyrus around 536 B.C.

    Ezra 1

18. The temple was dedicated by
    Zerubbabel around 516 B.C.

    Ezra 3:8-13

19. The walls of the city were completed
    under Nehemiah around 445 B.C.

    Neh. 6:15

20. Alexander the Great visited the city in
    332 B.C.

21. Jerusalem was captured by Ptolemy
    Soter in 320 B.C.

22. It was annexed to Egypt in 302.

23. The walls were destroyed and its
    temple desecrated by Antiochus
    Epiphanes in 170 B.C.

24. The temple was cleansed and
    rededicated by Mattathias of the
    Hasmonean dynasty, 167–164 B.C.

25. Jerusalem was captured by the Roman
    general Pompey in 63 B.C.

26. The walls were rebuilt by Antipater
    (Herod the Great's father) in 44 B.C.

27. In 20 B.C., Herod the Great began his
    world-famous project of enlarging and
    rebuilding the temple begun by
    Zerubbabel. It was built of large
    blocks of white stone and its facade
    was plated with gold, so that at a
    distance it resembled a mountain

    See John 2:20

covered with snow. It cost many millions and took 46 years to complete.

28. Jesus was dedicated. — Luke 2:1-38

29. He attended the Passover when he was 12. — Luke 2:41-50

30. He cleansed the temple. — John 2:13-17

31. He spoke to Nicodemus. — John 3:1-16

32. He healed a 38-year-old invalid. — John 5:8

33. He preached on the Holy Spirit during the Feast of the Tabernacles. — John 7:10-39

34. He forgave an adulterous woman. — John 8:1-11

35. He preached on the Devil and his children. — John 8:33-59

36. He healed a man born blind. — John 9:7

37. He preached a sermon on the Good Shepherd. — John 10:1-18

38. He made his triumphal entry. — John 12:12-15

39. He cursed the fig tree. — Matt. 21:19

40. He utterly condemned the wicked Pharisees. — Matt. 23:1-36

41. He preached the Mount Olivet discourse. — Matt. 24–25

42. He wept over the city. — Luke 19:41; Matt. 23:37-39

43. He conducted the service in the Upper Room. — John 13–14

44. He preached on the vine and branches. — John 15–16

45. He prayed his great high priestly prayer. — John 17

46. He was arrested in Gethsemane. — Matt. 26:47-56

47. He restored a severed ear. — Matt. 26:51

48. He was condemned to death. — Matt. 27:26

49. He was crucified. — Matt. 27:27-50

50. He was buried. — Matt. 27:57-60

51. He rose from the dead.	Matt. 28:1-10
52. He visited the Upper Room for the first time after his resurrection.	Luke 24:36-43; John 20:19-23
53. He visited the Upper Room for the second time.	John 20:24-29
54. He visited the Upper Room for the third and final time.	Mark 16:14-18; Luke 24:44-49
55. The disciples conducted a prayer meeting in the Upper Room.	Acts 1:12-26
56. Peter preached his first sermon at Pentecost.	Acts 2:14-41
57. The lame man was healed by Peter and John.	Acts 3:1-11
58. Peter preached his second sermon.	Acts 3:12-26
59. The disciples experienced their first persecution.	Acts 4:1-3
60. Peter preached his third sermon.	Acts 4:5-12
61. The disciples conducted a mighty prayer meeting.	Acts 4:23-31
62. Ananias and Sapphira were judged and died.	Acts 5:1-11
63. The disciples experienced their second persecution.	Acts 5:17-28, 40-42
64. The first deacons were chosen.	Acts 6:1-7
65. Stephen became the first martyr for Jesus after the Ascension; the disciples' third persecution began.	Acts 6:8–7:60
66. The disciples experienced their fourth persecution.	Acts 8:1-3
67. Saul returned to Jerusalem after his mighty conversion and was vouched for by Barnabas.	Acts 9:26-28
68. A famine hit the city.	Acts 11:27-30
69. The disciples experienced their fifth persecution.	Acts 12:1-19
70. The council on circumcision was held.	Acts 15

71. Paul was arrested.   Acts 21:17–23:22
72. The temple and city of Jerusalem were   Matt. 24:2
destroyed by Titus the Roman general
on September 8, A.D. 70.

JESUS CHRIST
See also God, The Holy Spirit, Miracles, Prophecies

117 Scriptural Names for Christ

1. Adam (the last Adam)	1 Cor. 15:45
2. Advocate	1 John 2:1
3. Almighty	Rev. 1:8
4. Alpha	Rev. 1:8; 21:6
5. Amen	Rev. 3:14
6. Angel of the Lord	Gen. 16:9-14; Judg. 6:11-14
7. Anointed	Ps. 2:2
8. Apostle	Heb. 3:1
9. Author	Heb. 12:2
10. Babe	Luke 2:16
11. Beginning of creation	Rev. 3:14
12. Begotten of the Father	John 1:14
13. Beloved	Eph. 1:6
14. Bishop	1 Pet. 2:25
15. Blessed	1 Tim. 6:15
16. Branch	Zech. 3:8
17. Brazen serpent	John 3:14
18. Bread of life	John 6:35
19. Bridegroom	Matt. 9:15
20. Bright morning star	Rev. 22:16
21. Captain	Josh. 5:4

22. Carpenter	Matt. 13:55; Mark 6:3
23. Chief Shepherd	1 Pet. 5:4
24. Child	Isa. 9:6
25. Christ	Matt. 1:16; 2:4
26. Commander	Isa. 55:4
27. Consolation of Israel	Luke 2:25.
28. Cornerstone	Eph. 2:20
29. Dayspring from on high	Luke 1:78
30. Day star	2 Pet. 1:19
31. Deliverer	Rom. 11:26
32. Desire of nations	Hag. 2:7
33. Door	John 10:9
34. Door of the sheepfold	John 10:7
35. Emmanuel	Matt. 1:23
36. Everlasting Father	Isa. 9:6
37. Express image of God	Heb. 1:3
38. Faithful witness	Rev. 1:5; 3:14; 19:11
39. First fruits	1 Cor. 15:23
40. Forerunner	Heb. 6:20
41. Foundation	Isa. 28:16
42. Fountain	Zech. 13:1
43. Friend of sinners	Matt. 11:19
44. Gift of God	2 Cor. 9:15
45. Glory of God	Isa. 60:1
46. God	John 1:1; Rom. 9:5; 1 Tim. 3:16
47. Good Samaritan	Luke 10:33
48. Good Shepherd	John 10:11, 14
49. Governor	Matt. 2:6
50. Great Shepherd	Heb. 13:20
51. Guide	Ps. 48:14
52. Head of the Church	Col. 1:18

53. Heir of all things	Heb. 1:2
54. High Priest	Heb. 3:1; 7:1
55. Holy child	Acts 4:30
56. Holy One of God	Mark 1:24
57. Holy One of Israel	Isa. 41:14
58. Horn of salvation	Ps. 18:2
59. Jehovah	Isa. 26:4; 40:3
60. Jesus	Matt. 1:21
61. Judge	Mic. 5:1; Acts 10:42
62. King of Israel	Matt. 27:42; John 1:49
63. Lamb of God	John 1:29, 36
64. Lawgiver	Isa. 33:22
65. Light of the world	John 9:5
66. Lion of the tribe of Judah	Rev. 5:5
67. Lord of lords	Rev. 19:16
68. Man	Acts 17:31; 1 Tim. 2:5
69. Master	Matt. 8:19
70. Mediator	1 Tim. 2:5
71. Messiah	Dan. 9:25; John 1:41
72. Mighty God	Isa. 9:6; 63:1
73. Minister	Heb. 8:2
74. Nazarene	Mark 1:24
75. Only begotten Son	John 1:18
76. Passover	1 Cor. 5:7
77. Physician	Matt. 9:12
78. Potentate	1 Tim. 6:15
79. Power of God	1 Cor. 1:24
80. Prince	Acts 3:15; 5:31
81. Prophet	Acts 3:22
82. Propitiation	1 John 2:2; 4:10
83. Purifier	Mal. 3:3

84. Priest	Heb. 4:14
85. Rabbi	John 3:2; 20:16
86. Ransom	1 Tim. 2:6
87. Reaper	Rev. 14:15
88. Redeemer	Isa. 59:20; 60:16
89. Refiner	Mal. 3:3
90. Refuge	Isa. 25:4
91. Resurrection	John 11:25
92. Righteousness	Jer. 23:6; 33:16
93. Rock	Deut. 32:15
94. Rod	Isa. 11:1
95. Root of David	Rev. 22:16
96. Rose of Sharon	Song of Sol. 2:1
97. Sacrifice	Eph. 5:2
98. Savior	Luke 1:47; 2:11
99. Second Adam	1 Cor. 15:47
100. Seed of Abraham	Gal. 3:16, 19
101. Seed of David	2 Tim. 2:8
102. Seed of the woman	Gen. 3:15
103. Servant	Isa. 42:1; 49:5-7
104. Shepherd	Ps. 23:1
105. Shiloh	Gen. 49:10
106. Son of David	Matt. 15:22; 20:30; 21:9
107. Son of God	Luke 1:35; Matt. 16:16
108. Son of Man (his favorite name for himself)	Matt. 18:11
109. Son of Mary	Mark 6:3
110. Son of the Most High	Luke 1:32
111. Stone	Matt. 21:42; Mark 12:10; Acts 4:11; Rom. 9:32-33; Eph. 2:20; 1 Pet. 2:6-7

112. Sun of Righteousness	Mal. 4:2
113. Teacher (Master)	Matt. 26:18; John 3:2
114. True vine	John 15:1
115. Way	John 14:6
116. Wonderful	Isa. 9:6
117. Word	John 1:1; Rev. 19:13

8 Divine Announcements Concerning Christ's Birth

1. To Zacharias	Luke 1:17, 76
2. To Mary	Luke 1:31, 35
3. To Elisabeth	Luke 1:41-43
4. To Joseph	Matt. 1:20-21
5. To the shepherds	Luke 2:10-12
6. To the wise men	Matt. 2:1-2
7. To Simeon	Luke 2:25-32
8. To Anna	Luke 2:38

14 Reasons for the Virgin Birth

1. To reveal the invisible God	John 1:18; 14:9
2. To fulfill prophecy	Gen. 3:15
3. To guarantee the Davidic covenant	2 Sam. 7:8-17; Luke 1:31-33
4. To make a sacrifice for our sins	Heb. 2:9; 10:4-5, 10, 12; 1 John 3:5; Mark 10:45
5. To reconcile man to God	2 Cor. 5:19; Heb. 2:17; 1 Tim. 2:5-6
6. To provide an example for believers	1 Pet. 2:21; 1 John 2:6
7. To provide the believer with a high priest	Heb. 2:17; 3:1
8. To destroy the devil and his works	Heb. 2:14; 1 John 3:8
9. To escape the historical curse upon Adam's seed	Rom. 5:12
10. To heal the brokenhearted	Luke 4:18

11. To set at liberty the bruised	Luke 4:18
12. To proclaim the acceptable year of the Lord	Luke 4:18
13. To give abundant life	John 3:36; 10:10
14. To glorify the Father	John 13:31; 14:13; 17:4

25 Proofs of the Humanity of Christ

1. He had a human parentage.	Luke 1:31; Gal. 4:4
2. He had a human body.	Matt. 26:12
3. He looked like a man.	John 4:9
4. He possessed flesh and blood.	Heb. 2:14
5. He grew.	Luke 2:40
6. He asked questions.	Luke 2:46
7. He increased in wisdom.	Luke 2:52
8. He prayed.	Mark 1:35; Luke 11:1
9. He was tempted.	Matt. 4:1; Heb. 2:18; 4:15
10. He learned obedience.	Heb. 5:8
11. He hungered.	Matt. 4:2; 21:18
12. He thirsted.	John 4:7; 19:28
13. He was weary.	John 4:6
14. He slept.	Matt. 8:24
15. He loved.	Mark 10:21
16. He had compassion.	Matt. 9:36
17. He was angered and grieved.	Mark 3:5
18. He wept.	John 11:35; Luke 19:41
19. He experienced joy.	Heb. 12:2; Luke 10:21
20. He was troubled.	Mark 14:33-34; John 11:33; 12:27; 13:21
21. He sweat drops as of blood.	Luke 22:44
22. He suffered.	1 Pet. 4:1

23. He bled.	John 19:34
24. He died.	Matt. 27:50; 1 Cor. 15:3
25. He was buried.	Matt. 27:59-60

37 Proofs of the Deity of Christ

1. He was omnipotent over disease.	Matt. 8:1-4; Luke 4:39
2. He was omnipotent over demons.	Matt. 8:16-17, 28-32; Luke 4:35
3. He was omnipotent over men.	Matt. 9:9; John 17:2
4. He was omnipotent over nature.	Matt. 8:26
5. He was omnipotent over sin.	Matt. 9:1-8
6. He was omnipotent over traditions.	Matt. 9:10-17
7. He was omnipotent over death.	Luke 7:14-15; 8:54-56; John 11:4
8. He was omniscient, knowing the whereabouts of Nathanael.	John 1:48
9. He was omniscient, knowing the plot of Judas.	John 6:70
10. He was omniscient, knowing the hearts of the Pharisees.	Matt. 12:25; Luke 5:22; 6:8; 7:39-40
11. He knew the thoughts of the scribes.	Matt. 9:3-4
12. He knew the sincerity of one scribe.	Mark 12:34
13. He knew the history of the Samaritan woman.	John 4:24
14. He knew the problems of his disciples.	Luke 9:46-47
15. He was omnipresent.	Matt. 18:20; 28:20; John 3:13; 14:20
16. He was worshiped as God by the angels.	Heb. 1:6
17. He was worshiped as God by the shepherds.	Luke 2:15
18. He was worshiped as God by the wise men.	Matt. 2:2, 11

19. He was worshiped as God by a leper.	Matt. 8:2
20. He was worshiped as God by a ruler.	Matt. 9:18
21. He was worshiped as God by a Canaanite woman.	Matt. 15:25
22. He was worshiped as God by a mother.	Matt. 20:20
23. He was worshiped as God by a maniac.	Mark 5:6
24. He was worshiped as God by a man born blind.	John 9:38
25. He was worshiped as God by Thomas.	John 20:28
26. He was worshiped as God by some Greeks.	John 12:20-21
27. He was worshiped as God by his apostles.	Matt. 14:33; 28:9
28. He forgave sins.	Mark 2:5, 10-11
29. He judges.	John 5:22
30. He saves.	Matt. 18:11; John 10:28
31. Stephen called him God.	Acts 7:59
32. The eunuch called him God.	Acts 8:37
33. Paul called him God.	Gal. 2:20; Col. 1:15-17; 2:9; 1 Tim. 3:16; Titus 2:13
34. Peter called him God.	1 Pet. 3:22; 2 Pet. 1:17
35. Jude called him God.	Jude 25
36. James called him God.	James 2:1
37. John called him God.	1 John 5:20; Rev. 1:18; 19:16

10 Witnesses for the Sinlessness of Christ

1. Paul	2 Cor. 5:21
2. Peter	1 Pet. 2:22
3. The author of Hebrews	Heb. 4:15
4. John the apostle	1 John 3:5

5. Pilate	John 19:4
6. Pilate's wife	Matt. 27:19
7. Judas Iscariot	Matt. 27:4
8. The dying thief	Luke 23:41
9. The Roman centurion	Luke 23:47
10. Christ himself	John 14:30

9 Examples of Christ's Humility

1. He left heaven's glory.	John 17:5; 2 Cor. 8:9
2. He made himself of no reputation.	Phil. 2:7
3. He abstained from his omnipresence for a period.	John 11:14-15
4. He abstained from his omniscience for a period.	Mark 13:32; Luke 8:45-46
5. He abstained from his omnipotence for a period.	John 5:19-20
6. He was made in the likeness of men.	John 1:14; Rom. 1:3; Gal. 4:4; Heb. 2:14, 17
7. He humbled himself—that is, he submitted to authority.	1 Pet. 2:21-24
8. He became obedient unto death.	Matt. 26:39; John 10:18; Heb. 5:8; 12:2
9. He died on a cross.	Ps. 22; Isa. 53; Gal. 3:13

17 Post-Resurrection Appearances of Christ

1. First appearance: to Mary Magdalene as she remained at the site of the tomb	John 20:11-17
2. Second appearance: to the other women who were also returning to the tomb	Matt. 28:9-10
3. Third appearance: to Peter	Luke 24:34; 1 Cor. 15:5
4. Fourth appearance: to the disciples as they walked on the road to Emmaus	Mark 16:12-13; Luke 24:13-31

5. Fifth appearance: to the ten disciples	Mark 16:14; Luke 24:36-51; John 20:19-23
6. Sixth appearance: to the 11 disciples a week after his resurrection	John 20:26-29
7. Seventh appearance: to seven disciples by the Sea of Galilee	John 21:1-23
8. Eighth appearance: to 500	1 Cor. 15:6
9. Ninth appearance: to James, the Lord's brother	1 Cor. 15:7
10. Tenth appearance: to 11 disciples on the mountain in Galilee	Matt. 28:16-20
11. Eleventh appearance: at the time of the Ascension	Luke 24:44-53; Acts 1:3-9
12. Twelfth appearance: to Stephen just prior to his martyrdom	Acts 7:55-56
13. Thirteenth appearance: to Paul on the road to Damascus	Acts 9:3-6; cf. 22:6-11; 26:13-18
14. Fourteenth appearance: to Paul in Arabia	Gal. 1:12-17
15. Fifteenth appearance: to Paul in the temple	Acts 9:26-27; 22:17-21
16. Sixteenth appearance: to Paul while he was in prison in Caesarea	Acts 23:11
17. Seventeenth appearance: to the apostle John	Rev. 1:12-20

14 Results of Christ's Resurrection

1. It guarantees our justification.	Rom. 4:24
2. It guarantees present-day power and strength.	Eph. 1:18–2:10
3. It guarantees fruitful labor.	1 Cor. 15:58
4. It guarantees our own resurrection.	2 Cor. 4:14
5. It will exchange bodily corruption for incorruption.	1 Cor. 15:42
6. It will exchange dishonor for glory.	1 Cor. 15:43

7. It will exchange our physical weaknesses for power. 1 Cor. 15:43

8. It will exchange a material body for a spiritual body. 1 Cor. 15:44

9. It emphasizes the deity of Christ. Acts 10:40; Rom. 1:4

10. It is the springboard of Christ's exaltation. Acts 5:30-31; Phil. 2:9-11

11. It marks the beginning of his lordship over the Church. Eph. 1:19-23

12. It warns the sinner of the coming Judgment Day. Acts 17:31

13. It forever seals the doom of Satan. Heb. 2:14; Rev. 20:10

14. It transfers the worship day from Saturday to Sunday. Acts 20:7; 1 Cor. 16:2

16 Signs Suggesting the Return of Christ

1. Increase of wars and rumors of wars Mark 13:7

2. Extreme materialism 2 Tim. 3:1-2

3. Lawlessness 2 Tim. 3:2-4

4. Population explosion Gen. 6:1; Luke 17:26

5. An increase in speed and knowledge Dan. 12:4

6. Unification of the world's systems Rev. 13:4-8; Ps. 2:1-3

7. Intense demonic activity 1 Tim. 4:1-3

8. A departure from the Christian faith 2 Thess. 2:3; 1 Tim. 4:1; 2 Tim. 4:3-4; 2 Pet. 3:3-4

9. Abnormal sexual activities Luke 17:26, 28; 2 Pet. 2:5-8

10. The abortion movement. (Especially note the three words, "without natural affection," which can be accurately applied to mothers who murder their unborn children.) 2 Tim. 3:1-3

11. Revival of the old Roman Empire, or Western civilization	Dan. 2:41; 7:7-8; Rev. 13:1; 17:12
12. A universal numbering system	Rev. 13:16-18
13. Developments in Russia	Ezek. 38–39
14. Hatred and ridicule of the Bible	2 Pet. 3:2-4; Jude 17-18
15. The restoration of the nation Israel	Matt. 25:32-34
16. Interest in rebuilding the third temple	2 Thess. 2:3-4; Rev. 11:1

6 Reasons for Christ's Second Coming

1. To defeat the Antichrist and the world's nations assembled at Armageddon	Rev. 19:17-21
2. To regather, regenerate, and restore faithful Israel	Isa. 43:5-6; Jer. 24:6; Ezek. 11:17; 36:28; Amos 9:14-15; Mic. 7:18-19; Matt. 24:31
3. To judge and punish faithless Israel	Ezek. 11:21; 20:38
4. To separate the sheep from the goats	Matt. 25:31-46
5. To resurrect Old Testament and tribulational saints	Job 19:25-26; Ps. 49:15; Isa. 25:8; 26:19; Dan. 12:2; Hos. 13:14; John 5:28-29; Heb. 11:35; Rev. 20:4-5
6. To judge fallen angels	1 Cor. 6:3

39 Descriptions of Christ in the 39 Old Testament Books

1. Seed of the woman; Shiloh	Gen. 3:15; 49:10
2. Passover Lamb	Exod. 12:3
3. Anointed high priest	Lev. 8:7-9
4. Star of Jacob; brazen serpent	Num. 21:8; 24:17
5. Prophet like Moses; the great rock	Deut. 18:15; 32:4
6. Captain of the Lord's hosts	Josh. 5:14
7. Messenger of the Lord	Judg. 2:1

8. Kinsman-redeemer	Ruth 2:1
9. Great judge	1 Sam. 2:10
10. Seed of David	2 Sam. 7:13
11. Lord God of Israel	1 Kings 8:15, 26
12. God of the cherubim	2 Kings 19:15
13. God of our salvation	1 Chron. 16:35
14. God of our fathers	2 Chron. 20:6
15. Lord of heaven and earth	Ezra 1:2
16. Covenant-keeping God	Neh. 1:5
17. The God of providence	Esther
18. Risen and returning redeemer	Job 19:25
19. The anointed Son; the Holy One; the good shepherd; the king of glory	Ps. 2:7, 12; 16:10; 23:1; 24:7-10
20. The wisdom of God	Prov. 8
21. The one above the sun	Eccles.
22. Chief among ten thousand; altogether lovely	Song of Sol. 5:10, 16
23. Virgin-born Immanuel; wonderful, counselor, the mighty God, the everlasting Father, the prince of peace; the man of sorrows	Isa. 7:14; 9:6; 52:13; 53:3
24. The Lord our righteousness	Jer. 23:6; 33:16
25. The faithful and compassionate God	Lam. 3:22-23, 31-33
26. The Lord is there	Ezek.
27. Stone, Son of God, Son of Man	Dan. 2:34; 3:25; 7:13
28. King of the resurrection	Hos. 13:9, 14
29. God of the battle and giver of the Spirit	Joel 2:11, 28-32; 3:2, 9-17
30. God of hosts and the plumbline	Amos 4:13; 7:9
31. Destroyer of the proud	Obad. 8, 15
32. The risen prophet; God of second chance; the longsuffering one	Jon. 2:10; 3:1; 4:9-11
33. God of Jacob; the Bethlehem-born; the pardoning God	Mic. 4:1-5; 5:2; 7:18-19

34. The avenging God; the bringer of good tidings	Nah. 1:2, 15
35. The everlasting, pure, glorious, and anointed one	Hab. 1:12-13; 2:14; 3:13
36. The king of Israel	Zeph. 3:15
37. Desire of all nations	Hag. 2:7
38. Branch; builder of temple; king of triumphal entry; pierced one; king of the earth	Zech. 3:8; 6:12-13; 9:9; 12:10; 14:9
39. The sun of righteousness	Mal. 4:2

27 Descriptions of Christ in the 27 New Testament Books

1. King of the Jews	Matt. 2:2; 27:37
2. Servant	Mark 9:35; 10:43-44
3. Perfect man	Luke 2:40, 52; 9:22, 56, 58; 22:48
4. Eternal God	John 1:1-5; 20:28, 31
5. Ascended Lord	Acts 1:9
6. The Lord our righteousness	Rom. 10:4
7. Our resurrection	1 Cor. 15
8. God of all comfort	2 Cor. 1:3
9. Redeemer from the law	Gal. 4:4-5
10. Head of the Church; giver of gifts	Eph. 1:22, 2:20; 3:23–4:7-8
11. Supplier of every need; obedient servant	Phil. 1:19; 4:19; 2:5-8
12. Fullness of the Godhead	Col. 1:19; 2:9
13. The coming Christ	1 Thess. 4:13-18; 5:2
14. The consuming Christ	2 Thess. 2:8
15. Savior of sinners	1 Tim. 2:15; 3:16; 1:15
16. Righteous and rewarding Judge; author of Scripture	2 Tim. 4:8; 3:16-17

17. Our great God and savior — Titus 1:3; 2:10, 13; 3:4

18. Payer of our debt — Philem.

19. Appointed heir of all things; one greater than the prophets or angels — Heb. 1:2, 4; 3:3

20. Ever-present God; great physician; the coming one — James 4:6-8; 5:15; 5:7-8

21. Unblemished lamb; great example; chief shepherd; Lord of glory — 1 Pet. 1:19; 2:21-24; 5:4; 3:22

22. The beloved Son — 2 Pet. 1:17

23. Word of life; advocate; propitiation; Son of God — 1 John 1:1; 2:1; 3:8; 4:15; 5:5

24. Son of the Father — 2 John 1:3

25. The truth — 3 John 1:4, 8

26. Preserver and only wise God — Jude 1-25

27. The Alpha and Omega; the lion of Judah; king of kings — Revelation 1:8; 5:5, 19:16

JOURNEYS

1. Noah's descendants, from Mount Ararat to Babel — Gen. 11:1-9

2. Abraham, from Ur of the Chaldees to Canaan — Gen. 12:1-9

3. Abraham, from Canaan to Egypt — Gen. 12:10-20

4. Abraham, from Hebron to Mount Moriah — Gen. 22

5. Rebekah, from Haran to Canaan — Gen. 24

6. Jacob, from Hebron to Bethel to Haran — Gen. 28–29

7. Jacob, from Haran to Bethel — Gen. 32–35

8. Joseph, from Canaan to Egypt — Gen. 37

9. Jacob and his family, from Canaan to Egypt	Gen. 42–46
10. Moses, from Egypt to Midian	Exod. 2:15
11. Moses, from Midian back to Egypt	Exod. 3–4
12. Israel, from Egypt to Canaan	Exod.—Josh.
13. Ruth, from Moab to Bethlehem	Ruth 1
14. Saul, from Gibeah to Ramah	1 Sam. 9
15. Samuel, from Ramah to Bethlehem	1 Sam. 16
16. David, from Philistia to Hebron	2 Sam. 2:1
17. David, from Hebron to Jerusalem	2 Sam. 5:7
18. David, from Jerusalem to the eastern wilderness	2 Sam. 15:23
19. Solomon, from Jerusalem to Gibeon	1 Kings 3:4-5
20. The queen of Sheba, from Africa (or Arabia) to Jerusalem	1 Kings 10
21. Rehoboam, from Jerusalem to Shechem	1 Kings 12:1
22. Elijah, from the brook at Cherith to Mount Carmel	1 Kings 17–18
23. Elijah, from Mount Carmel to Mount Horeb	1 Kings 19
24. Naaman, from Syria to Samaria	2 Kings 5
25. The captives of Judah, from Palestine to Babylon	2 Kings 24-25; Ps. 137; Dan. 1
26. The captives of Judah, from Babylon to Jerusalem	Ezra 1; Ps. 126
27. Nehemiah, from Babylon to Jerusalem	Neh. 1–2
28. Jesus, from the glory of heaven to this sinful earth	Luke 2:7; Phil. 2:5-8; Gal. 4:4
29. Joseph and Mary, from Nazareth to Bethlehem	Luke 2:4
30. The wise men, from Persia to Bethlehem	Matt. 2:1-12
31. Joseph, Mary, and Jesus, from Bethlehem to Egypt	Matt. 2:13-14

32.	Joseph, Mary, and Jesus, from Egypt to Nazareth	Matt. 2:23
33.	Jesus, from this sinful earth to the glory of heaven	Acts 1
34.	Philip, from Jerusalem to Samaria	Acts 8:5
35.	Philip, from Samaria to the Gaza desert	Acts 8:26
36.	Paul, from Jerusalem to Damascus	Acts 9
37.	Peter, from Joppa to Caesarea	Acts 10
38.	Barnabas, from Jerusalem to Antioch	Acts 11:19-26
39.	Paul and Barnabas, from Antioch to their first missionary trip	Acts 13–14
40.	Paul and Silas, from Antioch to the second journey	Acts 15:36–18:22
41.	Paul, from Antioch to his third journey	Acts 18:23–21:15
42.	Paul, from Jerusalem to Rome	Acts 21:16–28:31

JUDGES

1.	Othniel, who captured a strong Canaanite city	Judg. 1:12-13; 3:8-11
2.	Ehud, who killed Eglon, king of Moab, and defeated the cruel Moabites in battle	Judg. 3:12-20
3.	Shamgar, who killed 600 Philistines with an oxgoad	Judg. 3:31
4.	Deborah, prophetess who urged Barak to lead an army that defeated Sisera's troops	Judg. 4–5
5.	Gideon, who defeated 135,000 Midianites with only 300 men	Judg. 6–8

6. Tola, who delivered Israel from her enemies for 23 years	Judg. 10:1
7. Jair, who, with his sons delivered 30 Israelite cities from their enemies	Judg. 10:3-5
8. Jephthah, who defeated the Ammonites after making a vow	Judg. 10:6–12:17
9. Ibzan, who delivered Israel from her enemies for seven years	Judg. 12:8-10
10. Elon, who delivered Israel from her enemies for ten years	Judg. 12:11-12
11. Abdon, who delivered Israel from her enemies for eight years	Judg. 12:13-15
12. Samson, who killed 1000 Philistines with the jawbone of an ass and later tore down the Philistines' temple while blinded	Judg. 13–16

JUDGMENTS FROM GOD
See also Executed by God, Prophecies

Past Judgments

1. The Garden of Eden judgment	Gen. 3:14-19; Rom. 5:12; 1 Cor. 15:22
2. The Flood judgment	Gen. 6:5-7; 2 Pet. 3:1-6
3. The Israelite judgment at the hands of the Assyrians	2 Kings 17
4. The Israelite judgment at the hands of the Babylonians	2 Kings 24–25
5. The Calvary judgment	Matt. 27:33-37; Isa. 53:1-10; Ps. 22:1; Heb. 2:9; 1 Pet. 2:21-25; 3:18

6. The Jewish judgment at the hands of the Romans	Matt. 24:2; Luke 19:41-44
7. The Lord's judgment upon local churches	Rev. 2–3

Present-day Judgments

1. The Lord's judgment upon individual believers when the believer judges himself	1 Cor. 11:31; 1 John 1:9
2. The Lord's judgment upon individual believers when the Father has to step in and judge	Acts 5:1-11; 1 Cor. 11:30; Heb. 12:3-13; 1 Pet. 4:17; 1 John 5:16

Future Judgments

1. The judgment seat of Christ	Rom. 14:10; 1 Cor. 3:9-15; 2 Cor. 5:10; Rev. 22:12
2. The tribulational judgment upon man's religious systems	Rev. 17
3. The tribulational judgment upon man's economic and political systems	Rev. 18
4. The tribulational judgment upon man's military systems	Rev. 19:11-21
5. The tribulational judgment upon man himself	Rev. 6, 8–9, 16
6. The lamp and talent judgment on Israel	Matt. 24:45-51; 25:1-30; Ezek. 20:33-38
7. The sheep and goat judgment on the Gentiles	Matt. 25:31-46
8. The judgment upon the Antichrist and false prophet	Rev. 19:20
9. The judgment upon Satan in the bottomless pit for 1000 years	Rev. 20:1-3
10. The judgment upon Satan in the lake of fire forever	Rev. 20:10

11. The fallen angel judgment	1 Cor. 6:3; 2 Pet. 2:4; Jude 6
12. The Great White Throne judgment	Rev. 20:11-15

KINGS AND RULERS

Amalekite

Agag, the wicked king spared by Saul and put to death by Samuel	1 Sam. 15:8-9, 32-33

Ammonite

1. The king of Ammon defeated by Jephthah	Judg. 11:12-28
2. Nahash, the first king defeated by Saul	1 Sam. 11:1-11
3. Hanun, the king who humiliated David's peace delegation	2 Sam. 10:1-2
4. Baalis, the king who hired Ishmael to assassinate Gedaliah	Jer. 40:14

Assyrian

1. Tiglath-pileser III (Pul), who carried off the tribes beyond Jordan	2 Kings 15:29; 16:7, 10
2. Shalmaneser V, who destroyed Samaria and captured and imprisoned Hoshea	2 Kings 17:1-6; 18:9-11
3. Sargon II, who finished the sacking of Samaria	Isa. 20
4. Sennacherib, whose armies were destroyed near Jerusalem by the death angel	2 Kings 18–19
5. Esarhaddon, who may have been the ruler that imprisoned Manasseh	2 Chron. 33

6. Ashurbanipal, who settled foreigners in Samaria — Ezra 4:10

Babylonian

1. Merodach-baladan, whose ambassadors were shown the wealth of Judah by Hezekiah — 2 Kings 20:12; Isa. 39:1

2. Evil-merodach, who released the imprisoned Jehoiachin in Babylon — 2 Kings 25:27

3. Nebuchadnezzar, who captured and destroyed Jerusalem and was ruler while Daniel was in Babylon — 2 Kings 25; Dan. 1–4

4. Belshazzar, who saw the divine handwriting on the wall — Dan. 5

Canaanite

1. Bera, the king of Sodom — Gen. 14:2-24

2. The king of Jericho, the ruler when the walls fell down — Josh. 2:2

3. Adonizedek, evil king of Jerusalem who formed a military alliance against Israel — Josh. 10:1-27

4. Jabin, king of Hazor and the last enemy Joshua defeated — Josh. 11:1-11

5. Jabin, king of Hazor, whose commander, Sisera, was killed by Jael after his forces were defeated by Barak — Judg. 4:2

Edomite

1. The king of Edom who refused Israel passage — Num. 20:14-21

2. Herod the Great, who may have been partly Edomite

Egyptian

1. Unknown pharaoh to whom Abraham lied concerning Sarah — Gen. 12:18-20

2. Unknown pharaoh who made Joseph second ruler in Egypt — Gen. 41:38-45

3. Thutmose I, possibly the king who "knew not Joseph" — Exod. 1:8

4. Thutmose III, possibly the king who attempted to kill Moses — Exod. 2:15

5. Amenhotep II, possibly the king during the ten plagues and the Exodus — Exod. 5:1

6. Unknown pharaoh who gave Solomon his daughter as a wife — 1 Kings 3:1

7. Shishak, who besieged Jerusalem in the days of Rehoboam — 1 Kings 14:25-26

8. Necho, the king who killed Josiah in battle and was later defeated by the Babylonians — 2 Kings 23:29-30

9. Hophra, defeated by the Babylonians at the Battle of Carchemish — Jer. 44:30; 46:1-26

Herodian

1. Herod the Great, ruler over Judah at the time of Jesus' birth — Matt. 2:1-20

2. Herod Archelaus, oldest son of Herod the Great; king when Joseph, Mary, and Jesus left Egypt — Matt. 2:22

3. Herod Philip, another son of Herod the Great and first husband of Herodias, who left him for Antipas, his brother — Matt. 14:3

4. Herod Antipas, youngest son of Herod the Great and the king who killed John the Baptist — Matt. 14:1-11

5. Herod Agrippa I, grandson of Herod the Great and killer of the apostle James, whom an angel of the Lord killed for accepting the people's worship — Acts 12

6. Herod Agrippa II, great-grandson of Herod the Great and the king Paul spoke to about becoming a Christian — Acts 25:13–26:32

Moabite

1. Balak, the king who hired Balaam to curse Israel — Num. 22–24
2. Eglon, the fat king assassinated by Ehud — Judg. 3:12-30
3. Mesha, the king who sacrificed his own son — 2 Kings 3:4-27

Persian and Mede

1. Cyrus the Great, who issued the return decree for the Jews — 2 Chron. 36:22-23; Ezra 1; Isa. 44:28
2. Darius the Mede, conqueror of Babylon while Daniel was there — Dan. 6
3. Darius the Great, who allowed the temple work to continue — Ezra 6:1-12
4. Ahasuerus, husband of Esther — Esther 1
5. Artaxerxes, who befriended both Ezra and Nehemiah — Ezra 7:1; Neh. 2:1
6. Darius III, whose armies were destroyed by Alexander the Great — Dan. 8

Philistine

1. Abimelech, the king to whom Abraham lied about Sarah — Gen. 20
2. Abimelech, the king to whom Isaac lied about Rebekah — Gen. 26
3. Achish, a king in Gath to whom David fled — 1 Sam. 21:10-14; 27–29

Roman

1. Augustus Caesar, emperor when Jesus was born — Luke 2:1
2. Tiberius Caesar, emperor during Jesus' earthly ministry — Luke 3:1; 20:22-25

3. Claudius Caesar, emperor during the ministry of Paul	Acts 11:28; 18:2
4. Nero Caesar, emperor Paul appealed to and, later, the one who probably executed both Peter and Paul	Acts 25:10-12

Syrian

1. Ben-hadad I, defeated twice by Ahab	1 Kings 20:1-34
2. Ben-hadad II, who sent Naaman to Israel for healing	2 Kings 5:5-6
3. Hazael, anointed by Elisha, and later the assassin of Ben-hadad II	1 Kings 19:15; 2 Kings 8:7-15, 28-29
4. Rezin, allied with Pekah in unsuccessful siege against Jerusalem	2 Kings 16:5-9

Tyrian

1. Hiram, who furnished the wood for the temple	1 Kings 5:1-18
2. Prince of Tyre, denounced by Ezekiel	Ezek. 28:1-10

The United Kingdom of Israel

1. Saul, Israel's first king, rejected by God	1 Sam. 9–10
2. David, Saul's successor, Israel's best-loved king	1 Sam. 16–31; 2 Sam. 1–24
3. Solomon, David's son, Israel's wisest and richest king	1 Kings 1–11

Israel (The Northern Kingdom)

1. Jeroboam, who perverted the worship of God	1 Kings 11:26–14:20
2. Nadab, son of Jeroboam, killed by the rebel Baasha	1 Kings 15:25-28
3. Baasha, who built a wall to cut off trade with Jerusalem	1 Kings 15:27–16:7

4. Elah, son of Baasha, killed while drunk by Zimri — 1 Kings 16:6-14

5. Zimri, who committed suicide after ruling for seven days — 1 Kings 16:9-20

6. Omri, builder of Samaria, the northern capital — 1 Kings 16:15-28

7. Ahab, son of Omri, wicked husband of Jezebel, condemned by Elijah and killed in battle — 1 Kings 16:28–22:40

8. Ahaziah, wicked oldest son of Ahab — 1 Kings 22:40–2 Kings 1:18

9. Jehoram, youngest son of Ahab, who sent Naaman to the prophet Elisha to be healed — 2 Kings 3:1–9:25

10. Jehu, known for his chariot riding and extermination of Ahab's dynasty — 2 Kings 9:1–10:36

11. Jehoahaz, Jehu's son, who saw his army almost wiped out by the Syrians — 2 Kings 13:1-9

12. Jehoash, Jehoahaz's son, who waged a successful war against Judah and visited Elisha on his deathbed — 2 Kings 13:10–14:16

13. Jeroboam II, Jehoahaz's son, who reigned during the time of Jonah the prophet — 2 Kings 14:23-29

14. Zechariah, Jeroboam's son and the last of Jehu's dynasty, killed by Shallum — 2 Kings 14:19–15:12

15. Shallum, who reigned for only a month and was killed by Menahem — 2 Kings 15:10–15

16. Menahem, one of the most brutal kings ruling over the ten tribes — 2 Kings 15:14-22

17. Pekahiah, son of Menahem, killed by his army commander, Pekah — 2 Kings 15:22-26

18. Pekah, killed by Hoshea — 2 Kings 15:27-31

19. Hoshea, dethroned and imprisoned by the Assyrians — 2 Kings 15:30–17:1-6

Judah (The Southern Kingdom)

1. Rehoboam, Solomon's son, whose stupidity and arrogance sparked the civil war — 1 Kings 11:43–12:24; 14:21-31

2. Abijam, Rehoboam's son, helped by God to defeat Jeroboam in battle — 1 Kings 14:31–15:8

3. Asa, Abijam's son, Judah's first godly king — 1 Kings 15:8-14

4. Jehoshaphat, Asa's son, godly king who built a merchant fleet and made an alliance with Ahab — 1 Kings 22:41-50

5. Jehoram, Jehoshaphat's son, married to Athaliah, the wicked daughter of Ahab and Jezebel — 2 Kings 8:16-24

6. Ahaziah, son of Jehoram and Athaliah, killed by Jehu — 2 Kings 8:24–9:29

7. Athaliah, queen, daughter of Ahab, who assumed the throne on the death of Ahaziah and slaughtered all the royal seed but one — 2 Kings 11:1-20

8. Joash, son of Ahaziah, hidden as a boy from Athaliah and ruler after she was executed — 2 Kings 11:1–12:21

9. Amaziah, son of Joash, defeated by Jehoash, king of the ten tribes and slain in a conspiracy — 2 Kings 14:1-20

10. Uzziah (Azariah), son of Amaziah, struck with leprosy for his sin in the temple — 2 Kings 15:1-7

11. Jotham, son of Uzziah, who built the temple's upper gate and fortified Jerusalem — 2 Kings 15:32-38

12. Ahaz, son of Jotham, godless king who sacrificed his son to a pagan god — 2 Kings 16:1-20

13. Hezekiah, son of Ahaz, reformer, friend of Isaiah, and king when Jerusalem was saved by the death angel — 2 Kings 18–20

14. Manasseh, son of Hezekiah and Judah's worst king, though later converted — 2 Kings 21:1-18

15. Amon, son of Manasseh, executed by his own household servants — 2 Kings 21:19-26

16. Josiah, son of Amon, ruler when the Book of the Law was found in the temple, leader of a national reform, slain in battle against Egypt — 2 Kings 22:1–23:30

17. Jehoahaz, son of Josiah and ruler after his death in battle; deposed after only 90 days by Pharaoh-Neco and taken to Egypt, where he died — 2 Kings 23:31-33

18. Jehoiakim, Josiah's son who persecuted Jeremiah and burned the prophet's scroll; carried to Babylon by Nebuchadnezzar — 2 Kings 23:34–24:5; Jer. 36

19. Jehoiachin, Jehoiakim's son, who incurred a special judgment from God and was carried to Babylon with Nebuchadnezzar — 2 Kings 24:6-16

20. Zedekiah, uncle of Jehoiachin, blinded and taken into exile in Babylon while Jerusalem and the temple were destroyed — 2 Kings 24:17–25:30

Queens

1. Michal, daughter of Saul and David's first wife — 1 Sam. 18:20-28; 2 Sam. 6:20-23

2. Rizpah, Saul's wife who attempted to protect the bodies of her seven sons until David had them buried — 2 Sam. 21:8-14

3. Bathsheba, originally the wife of Uriah, then David's wife and mother of Solomon — 2 Sam. 11–12

4. Queen of Sheba, an African or Arabian queen who visited Solomon — 1 Kings 10:1-13

5. Maacah, idol-worshiping mother of King Asa — 1 Kings 15:10; 2 Chron. 15:16

6. Jezebel, wicked and idolatrous wife of King Ahab — 1 Kings 16:31

7. Athaliah, wicked daughter of Ahab and Jezebel — 2 Kings 11

8. Nehushta, mother of Jehoiachin, who was taken to Babylon — 2 Kings 24:8-16

9. The Babylonian queen mother, who advised Belshazzar to call for Daniel — Dan. 5:10-12

10. Vashti, the disobedient Persian queen deposed by King Ahasuerus — Esther 1

11. Esther, the Jewish maiden who became wife of Ahasuerus — Esther 2–10

12. Herodias, Herod Antipas's vicious wife who plotted John the Baptist's death — Matt. 14:1-12

13. Candace, Ethiopian queen who allowed her servant, the eunuch, to visit Judea — Acts 8:27–28

14. Bernice, the sister and wife of King Agrippa II — Acts 25:13, 23; 26:30

KISSES

1. The kiss of deceit, given by Jacob to Isaac — Gen. 27:26-27

2. The kiss of introduction, given by Jacob to Rachel — Gen. 29:11

3. The kiss of reconciliation, given by Esau to Jacob — Gen. 33:4

4. The kiss of forgiveness, given by Joseph to his brothers — Gen. 45:14-15

5. The kiss of farewell, given by Jacob to his two grandchildren — Gen. 48:10

6. The kiss of two brothers, Aaron and Moses — Exod. 4:27

7. The kiss of return, given by Moses to Jethro — Exod. 18:7

8. The kiss of sorrow, given by Naomi to Ruth and Orpah — Ruth 1:9

9. The kiss of coronation, given by Samuel to Saul — 1 Sam. 10:1

10. The kiss of friendship, given by David to Jonathan — 1 Sam. 20:41

11. The kiss of a subdued welcome, given by David to Absalom — 2 Sam. 14:33

12. The kiss of politics, given by Absalom to the citizens of Israel — 2 Sam. 15:5

13. The kiss of murder, given by Joab to Amasa, killed while Joab kissed him — 2 Sam. 20:9

14. The kiss of salvation, given by the believer to Christ — Ps. 2:12

15. The kiss of righteousness and peace — Ps. 85:10

16. The kiss of lovers — Song of Sol. 1:2

17. The kiss of repentance, given by a harlot to the feet of Christ — Luke 7:45

18. The kiss of restoration, given by a father to his prodigal son — Luke 15:20

19. The kiss of betrayal, given by Judas Iscariot to Christ — Matt. 26:49

20. The kiss of church leaders, given by the Ephesian elders to Paul — Acts 20:37

LAMPS, LIGHTS, AND TORCHES

1. The burning lamp of the Abrahamic covenant — Gen. 15:17

2. The golden lamp of the tabernacle   Exod. 25:37
3. The lamps of Gideon   Judg. 7:16
4. The lamp of Samuel and Eli   1 Sam. 3:3
5. The golden lamp of the temple   1 Kings 7:49
6. The lamps of the ten virgins   Matt. 25:1

LAST WORDS

1. Jacob's   Gen. 49:10
2. Joseph's   Gen. 50:24
3. Moses'   Deut. 33:27-29
4. Caleb's   Josh. 14:7-12
5. Joshua's   Josh. 23:14; 24:15
6. Samson's   Judg. 16:28
7. Eli's   1 Sam. 4:15-18
8. Saul's   1 Sam. 31:4
9. David's   2 Sam. 23:1-4; 1 Kings 2:1-9
10. Elijah's   2 Kings 2:8-11
11. Elisha's   2 Kings 13:14-19
12. Belshazzar's   Dan. 5:13-16
13. Daniel's   Dan. 12:8
14. Simeon's   Luke 2:25-35
15. Jesus'   Matt. 28:18-20; Acts 1:8
16. Stephen's   Acts 7:59-60
17. Paul's   2 Tim. 4:6-8
18. James's   James 5:19-20
19. Peter's   2 Pet. 3:13-18
20. Jude's   Jude 24-25
21. John's   Rev. 22:18-21

LEPERS

1. Miriam, Moses' sister, stricken with leprosy because of her criticism of Moses — Num. 12

2. Naaman, captain of the Syrian army, healed by bathing in the Jordan as instructed by Elisha — 2 Kings 5:1-14

3. Gehazi, Elisha's servant, stricken because of his greed — 2 Kings 5:20-27

4. Four lepers who brought some good news to the starving city of Samaria — 2 Kings 7:3

5. Uzziah, the Judean king who attempted to act a priest and was stricken with leprosy — 2 Chron. 26:16-21

6. Simon of Bethany, healed by Jesus — Matt. 26:6-13; Mark 14:3

7. Galilean leper who asked Christ to make him whole — Matt. 8:2-4; Mark 1:40-45; Luke 5:12-15

8. Ten lepers healed by Jesus, only one of whom returned to thank him — Luke 17:12-19

LETTERS

1. David's letter to Joab concerning Uriah — 2 Sam. 11:14-15

2. The king of Syria's letter to the king of Israel concerning Naaman — 2 Kings 5:5-7

3. Jezebel's letter to the rulers of Jezreel concerning Naboth — 1 Kings 21:8

4. Jehu's letter to the rulers of Jezreel concerning Ahab's 70 sons — 2 Kings 10:1-2

5. Sennacherib's letter to Hezekiah concerning surrender — 2 Kings 19:14

6. Hezekiah's letter to the Israelite leaders concerning the Passover — 2 Chron. 30:1

7. Elijah's letter to King Jehoram predicting judgment upon his sinful reign — 2 Chron. 21:12

8. The letter sent by the enemies of Zerubbabel to the Persian king attempting to smear Zerubbabel — Ezra 4:6-16

9. The Persian king's letter to Judah's enemies, giving them permission to stop the Jews' work on the temple — Ezra 4:17-22

10. Darius's letter granting permission to continue the temple construction — Ezra 6:6-12

11. Artaxerxes' letter to the manager of the royal forest, ordering him to provide Nehemiah with building material for Jerusalem's walls — Neh. 2:8

12. Mordecai's letter to the Jews concerning the new Feast of Purim — Esther 9:20

13. Sanballat's letter to Nehemiah, attempting to discourage him — Neh. 6:5

14. The Jewish high priest's letter to the religious leaders in Damascus concerning the Christian problem — Acts 9:2

15. James's letter to the Christian churches concerning the Jerusalem council's decision on circumcision — Acts 15:23

16. The Ephesian Christians' letter of recommendation to the Corinthian believers concerning Apollos — Acts 18:27

17. Claudius Lysias's letter to Felix concerning the apostle Paul — Acts 23:25

18. Paul's letter to Philemon concerning Onesimus — Philem.

19. Jesus' letter to his seven churches in
    Asia concerning their spiritual
    condition   Rev. 1–3

LIES

1. Satan's lie to Eve	Gen. 3:4
2. Abraham's lie to Pharaoh	Gen. 12:13
3. Abraham's lie to Abimelech	Gen. 20:2
4. Sarah's lie to God	Gen. 18:15
5. Jacob's lie to Isaac	Gen. 27:19
6. Isaac's lie to Abimelech	Gen. 26:7
7. Laban's lie to Jacob	Gen. 29:18-24
8. Jacob's sons' lie to Jacob	Gen. 37:32
9. Potiphar's wife's lie to her husband	Gen. 39:17
10. Rahab's lie to the Jericho searching party	Josh. 2:4
11. Saul's lie to David	1 Sam. 18:17
12. Michal's lie to her father Saul	1 Sam. 19:13-17
13. Ananias and Sapphira's lie to Peter	Acts 5:1

LOTS

1. To determine which sacrificial animal would be the scapegoat in the tabernacle	Lev. 16:8
2. To determine the land area for Israel's 12 tribes	Num. 26:55; Josh. 18:10

3. To determine the Levitical work load and responsibility in the temple during Nehemiah's time — Neh. 10:34

4. To determine who would live in Jerusalem during Nehemiah's time — Neh. 11:1

5. To determine who should be thrown overboard in a storm — Jon. 1:7

6. To determine who would receive the Savior's seamless coat — Matt. 27:35

7. To determine who would replace Judas Iscariot as an apostle — Acts 1:26

MARRIAGES
See also Brides, Couples, Polygamists

1. Adam to Eve — Gen. 2:21-25
2. Lamech to Adah and Zillah — Gen. 4:19
3. Isaac to Rebekah — Gen. 24:63-67
4. Esau to Judith — Gen. 26:34-35
5. Abraham to Keturah — Gen. 25:1
6. Jacob to Leah and Rachel — Gen. 29:18-23
7. Joseph to Asenath — Gen. 41:45
8. Moses to Zipporah — Exod. 2:21
9. Samson to a Philistine girl — Judg. 14
10. Boaz to Ruth — Ruth 4:13
11. David to Michal — 1 Sam. 18:20, 28
12. David to Abigail — 1 Sam. 25:39
13. David to Bathsheba — 2 Sam. 11:27
14. Solomon to Pharaoh's daughter — 1 Kings 3:1
15. Ahab to Jezebel — 1 Kings 16:31
16. Ahasuerus to Esther — Esther 2:17

17. Hosea to Gomer	Hos. 1:2-3
18. Joseph to Mary	Matt. 1:24
19. Herod to Herodias	Matt. 14:3-4
20. A Cana couple	John 2
21. Christ to the Church	Rev. 19:7-8

MARTYRS

1. Isaiah, traditionally said to have been sawn asunder by Manasseh	Heb. 11:37
2. Zechariah, stoned by his own countrymen for boldly rebuking their sin	2 Chron. 24:20-21
3. Uriah, murdered by wicked King Jehoiakim	Jer. 26:20-23
4. Stephen, the church's first martyr, stoned by the Jews	Acts 7:59
5. James, the first of the 12 apostles to be martyred	Acts 12:1-2
6. Paul, believed to have been beheaded by Emperor Nero	2 Tim. 4:6
7. Peter, believed to have been crucified upside down by Nero	John 21:18-19; 2 Pet. 1:14
8. Antipas, martyred in the city of Pergamos	Rev. 2:13
9. Two tribulational witnesses martyred by the Beast	Rev. 11:7

MEASUREMENTS, WEIGHTS, MONEY

1. Bath, equal to 6 gallons — 1 Kings 7:26
2. Bekah, equal to ¼ ounce — Exod. 38:26
3. Bushel, equal to a peck — Matt. 5:15; Mark 4:21; Luke 11:33
4. Cab, equal to 2 quarts — 2 Kings 6:25
5. Cubit, equal to 18 inches — Gen. 6:15; 1 Sam. 17:4; Esther 5:14; Dan. 3:1
6. Cor, equal to 6½ bushels of dry measure, or 61 gallons of liquid — Ezek. 45:14
7. Daric (dram), equal to $5 — Neh. 7:70; Ezra 2:69
8. Day's journey, equal to around 20 miles — Luke 2:44
9. Denarius (penny), equal to a day's wages — Matt. 20:2; 22:19; Luke 10:35
10. Didrachmon (didrachma), equal to 32 cents; also equivalent to a Jewish half-shekel of silver — Matt. 17:24
11. Drachme (drachma), equal to 16 cents — Luke 15:8-9
12. Ephah, equal to a bushel, or 6 gallons of grain — Ruth 2:17; 1 Sam. 17:17
13. Farthing, equal to ¼ cent — Matt. 10:29; Mark 12:42
14. Fathom, equal to 6 feet — Acts 27:28
15. Finger span (digit), equal to ¾ inch — Jer. 52:21
16. Firkin (metretes), equal to 9 gallons — John 2:6
17. Furlong, equal to ⅛ mile — Luke 24:13; John 6:19; Rev. 14:20; 21:16
18. Gerah, equal to 1/40 ounce — Exod. 30:13
19. Handbreadth, equal to 3 inches — 1 Kings 7:26; Ps. 39:5
20. Hin, equal to 6 quarts — Exod. 29:40

21. Homer, equal to 90 gallons, or 11 bushels — Num. 11:32; Hosea 3:2

22. Log, equal to a pint — Lev. 14:10

23. Measure, equal to a peck — Gen. 18:6; Matt. 13:33

24. Maneh, equal to 2 pounds — Ezek. 45:12

25. Mile, equal to 4,880 feet — Matt. 5:41

26. Mina (translated "pound" here), equal to $16 — 1 Kings 10:17

27. Mite, equal to ⅛ cent — Mark 12:42

28. Omer, equal to 7 pints — Exod. 16:22

29. Pace, equal to a yard — 2 Sam. 6:13

30. Pound
    a. where the Greek word is *mina,* equal to $16 — Luke 19:13
    b. referring to silver, equal to $40 — Nehemiah 7:71
    c. referring to gold, equal to $600 — 1 Kings 10:17

31. Quadrans, equal to ¼ cent — Matt. 5:26; Mark 12:42

32. Reed, equal to 11 feet — Ezek. 42:16; Rev. 21:15

33. Sabbath day's journey, equal to ½ mile — Acts 1:12

34. Seah, equal to a gallon and 5 pints — Gen. 18:6; 1 Sam. 25:18

35. Shekel
    a. when used as a unit of weight, equal to ½ ounce — 1 Sam. 17:5, 7
    b. when used as a unit of silver, equal to 64 cents — Josh. 7:21; 2 Kings 7:1; Jer. 32:9

36. Span, equal to 9 inches — Exod. 28:16

37. Stater (tetradrachma), equal to 64 cents — Matt. 17:27

38. Talent
    a. equal to $1,000 — Matthew 18:24; 25:15

b. equal to $2,500   2 Kings 5:5; Esther 3:9

c. equal to $30,000   1 Kings 10:10, 14

Note: All equivalents of biblical measurements, weights, and currency can only be estimates.

MEMORIALS
See also Signs

1. The rainbow, a reminder that God would never again destroy the world by a flood	Gen. 9:13-16
2. The Passover, a reminder that the blood of a lamb saved sinners from judgment	Exod. 12:11-14
3. Some brazen censors, a reminder that no one except Aaron's seed must attempt to offer incense	Num. 16:39-40
4. The Sabbath, a reminder of a completed creation	Deut. 5:15
5. Twelve stones, a reminder of God's mighty power in bringing Israel across the Jordan into Canaan	Josh. 4:7
6. The manna in the Ark of the Covenant, a reminder of God's supernatural provision in the desert	Exod. 16:32
7. Purim, a reminder of salvation from wicked Haman	Esther 9:28
8. The Feast of Tabernacles, a reminder of Israel's deliverance from Egypt	Lev. 23:39-43
9. The anointing of Jesus' head and feet by Mary, the sister of Lazarus, a reminder of Mary's devotion to Christ	Matt. 26:6-13; John 12:1-7
10. The Lord's Supper, a reminder of the broken body and shed blood of Christ	Luke 22:19

MILITARY MEN
See also Wars and Battles

General Commanders

1. Joshua, Israel's first commander-in-chief   Exod. 17:8-10

2. Sisera, Canaanite commander defeated by Barak and Deborah and killed by Jael   Judg. 4

3. Abner, commander of King Saul's troops   1 Sam. 14:50

4. Joab, commander of King David's troops   1 Chron. 18:14-15

5. Amasa, commander of Absalom's troops during the rebellion against David   2 Sam. 17:25

6. Naaman, a leper and commander of the Syrian troops   2 Kings 5:1

7. Rabshakeh, commander of the Assyrian troops when the angel struck them down   2 Kings 18:17–19:37

8. Nebuzaradan, commander of Nebuchadnezzar's troops   2 Kings 25:8

9. Claudius Lysias, Roman commander who sent Paul from Jerusalem to Felix, the Roman governor in Caesarea   Acts 23:12-33

Regular Soldiers

1. Potiphar, Egyptian soldier who employed Joseph as his servant and then imprisoned him on false charges   Gen. 39:1

2. Caleb, the loyal scout who, along with Joshua, gave a positive report about the land   Josh. 14:6-13; Num. 13:25–14:9

3. Abishai, one of David's chief soldiers who personally killed 300 enemy soldiers in a battle — 1 Chron. 11:20

4. Benaiah, one of David's captains — 2 Sam. 8:18

5. Uriah, Hittite soldier whom David had murdered so he might marry his wife, Bathsheba — 2 Sam. 11

6. Ittai, a Gittite who supported David during the rebellion by Absalom — 2 Sam. 15:19-23

7. Irajah, a soldier of Judah who arrested Jeremiah, falsely accusing him of treason — Jer. 37:13

Centurions

1. The centurion at Capernaum, who asked and received from Jesus healing for his dying servant — Luke 7:1-10

2. The centurion at Calvary, who recognized Jesus as the Son of God — Matt. 27:54

3. Cornelius, led to Christ by Peter at Caesarea — Acts 10

4. The centurion at Antonia fortress, who rescued Paul from the Jews in Jerusalem — Acts 21:32; 22:25

5. Julius, who treated Paul kindly during his fateful ship voyage to Rome — Acts 27:1-44

MIRACLES
See also Angels, God, Jesus Christ

Performed by the Full Godhead

1. Creation — Gen. 1–2; Prov. 8; Ps. 104; Heb. 11:3

2. Enoch's translation	Gen. 5:19-24; Heb. 11:5; Jude 14-15
3. The Flood	Gen. 6–8; Matt. 24:37-39; Heb. 11:7; 1 Pet. 3:20; 2 Pet. 2:5
4. Confusion of tongues at Babel	Gen. 11; Isa. 13:1
5. Plaguing of Pharaoh	Gen. 12:10-20
6. The burning lamp and smoking furnace	Gen. 15:17-18
7. Sarah's conception	Gen. 17:15-19; 18:10-14; 21:1-8
8. Destruction of Sodom and Gomorrah	Gen. 19; Matt. 10:15; 2 Pet. 2:6; Jude 7
9. Lot's wife turned into a pillar of salt	Gen. 19:24-28; Luke 17:28, 32
10. Plaguing Abimelech	Gen. 20:1-7, 17-18
11. Hagar's well	Gen. 21:14-21
12. The burning bush	Exod. 3:1-14; Deut. 33:16; Mark 12:26; Luke 20:37; Acts 7:30-31
13. Moses' rod	Exod. 4:1-5; 7:8-13; 2 Tim. 3:8
14. Moses' leprous hand	Exod. 4:6-12
15. The Exodus	Deut. 8:4; 29:5; Neh. 9:21
16. Balaam's speaking donkey	Num. 22:20-35; 2 Pet. 2:15; Jude 11
17. The death and burial of Moses	Deut. 32
18. The fall of the idol Dagon	1 Sam. 5:1-5
19. The Philistines' tumors	1 Sam. 5:6-12; 6:17-18; Deut. 28:27; Ps. 78:66
20. Judgment on the men of Bethshemesh	1 Sam. 6:19
21. Judgment upon Uzzah	2 Sam. 6:7

22. Judgment upon Israel for David's sin	1 Sam. 24:10-16
23. Judgment upon the disobedient man of God	1 Kings 13:24
24. Judgment upon Jeroboam	2 Chron. 13:20
25. Feeding Elijah with ravens	1 Kings 17:2-6
26. Speaking through nature to Elijah	1 Kings 19:9-18
27. Taking Elijah to heaven in a fiery chariot	2 Kings 2:9-11
28. Reviving a dead man through Elisha's bones	2 Kings 13:21
29. Judging Uzziah with leprosy	2 Kings 15:1-8; 2 Chron. 26:15-21
30. Healing Hezekiah	2 Kings 20:1-11; 2 Chron. 32:24; Isa. 38
31. The handwriting on the wall in Belshazzar's palace	Dan. 5:5, 25
32. Sending a storm to Jonah's ship	Jon. 1:1-16
33. Preparing a fish to swallow Jonah	Jon. 1:17–2:10
34. Preparing a gourd to shade Jonah	Jon. 4:6
35. Preparing a worm to eat the gourd	Jon. 4:7
36. Preparing an east wind for Jonah	Jon. 4:8-10
37. Allowing Elisabeth to bear a son	Luke 1:6-13, 57
38. The Virgin Birth of Jesus	Matt. 1:18-24; Luke 1:26-37; 2:6-7
39. The star in the east that guided the wise men	Matt. 2:1-10
40. The Transfiguration of Jesus	Matt. 17:1-13; Mark 9:1-13; Luke 9:28-36; 2 Pet. 1:16-18
41. The Calvary miracles	
a. Darkness	Matt. 27:45; Luke 23:44
b. Earthquake	Matt. 27:51
c. Rent veil in the temple	Matt. 27:51; Mark 15:38; Luke 23:45

d. Restoration of bodies	Matt. 27:52-53
42. The Resurrection	Matt. 28; Mark 16; Luke 24; John 20
43. The Ascension	Luke 24:50-52; Acts 1:4-11
44. Pentecost	Acts 2:1-4
45. Shaking of the place after the prayer meeting	Acts 4:31
46. Judgment upon Ananias and Sapphira	Acts 5:1-11
47. Allowing Stephen to view the third heaven	Acts 7:55-56
48. Blinding Saul	Acts 9:8
49. Coming upon the Gentiles	Acts 10:44-46
50. Freeing Paul and Silas from prison	Acts 16:19-40

Performed by Christ

1. Changing water into wine	John 2:7-8
2. Healing the nobleman's son	John 4:50
3. Healing the Capernaum demoniac	Mark 1:25; Luke 4:35
4. Healing Peter's mother-in-law	Matt. 8:15; Mark 1:31; Luke 4:39
5. Catching a great number of fish	Luke 5:5-6
6. Healing a leper	Matt. 8:3; Mark 1:41
7. Healing a paralytic	Matt. 9:2; Mark 2:5; Luke 5:20
8. Healing a man with withered hand	Matt. 12:13; Mark 3:5; Luke 6:10
9. Healing a centurion's servant	Matt. 8:13; Luke 7:10
10. Raising a widow's son	Luke 7:14
11. Calming the stormy sea	Matt. 8:26; Mark 4:39; Luke 8:24
12. Healing the Gadarene demoniac	Matt. 8:32; Mark 5:8; Luke 8:33
13. Healing a woman with internal bleeding	Matt. 9:22; Mark 5:29; Luke 8:44

14. Raising Jairus's daughter	Matt. 9:25; Mark 5:41; Luke 8:54
15. Healing two blind men	Matt. 9:29
16. Healing a dumb demoniac	Matt. 9:33
17. Healing of an invalid	John 5:8
18. Feeding the 5,000	Matt. 14:19; Mark 6:41; Luke 9:16; John 6:11
19. Walking on the sea	Matt. 14:25; Mark 6:48; John 6:19
20. Healing a demoniac girl	Matt. 15:28; Mark 7:29
21. Healing a deaf·man with a speech impediment	Mark 7:34-35
22. Feeding the 4,000	Matt. 15:36; Mark 8:6
23. Healing a blind man at Bethsaida	Mark 8:25
24. Healing a man born blind	John 9:7
25. Healing a demoniac boy	Matt. 17:18; Mark 9:25; Luke 9:42
26. Catching a fish with a coin in its mouth	Matt. 17:27
27. Healing a blind and dumb demoniac	Matt. 12:22; Luke 11:14
28. Healing a woman with an 18-year infirmity	Luke 13:10-17
29. Healing a man with dropsy	Luke 14:4
30. Healing ten lepers	Luke 17:11-19
31. Raising Lazarus	John 11:43-44
32. Healing a blind man of Jericho	Luke 18:42
33. Healing blind Bartimaeus	Mark 10:46
34. Withering the unfruitful fig tree	Matt. 21:19; Mark 11:14
35. Restoring a severed ear	Matt. 26:51; Mark 14:47; Luke 22:50-51; John 18:10
36. Catching a great number of fish after the Resurrection	John 21:6

Performed by Angels

1. Blinding the Sodomites	Gen. 19:9-11
2. Giving of the Law	Acts 7:53; Gal. 3:19; Heb. 2:2
3. The rock and fire miracle	Judg. 6:19-24
4. Rescuing Moses' dead body from Satan	Jude 9
5. Feeding of Elijah	1 Kings 19:5-7
6. Destroying the Assyrian army	2 Kings 19:35
7. Preserving three Hebrew men in a fire	Dan. 3:25
8. Preserving Daniel in a den of lions	Dan. 6:1-24
9. Rolling away the stone at Jesus' resurrection	Matt. 28:2
10. Opening prison doors for disciples	Acts 5:19-23
11. Freeing Peter from prison	Acts 12:1-17
12. Death of Herod	Acts 12:23
13. Future regathering of Israel	Matt. 24:31
14. Pouring out of the wrath of God	Rev. 6–19

Performed by Joseph

1. Interpreting the dreams of two jail mates	Gen. 40:1-23
2. Interpreting the dream of Pharaoh	Gen. 41:14-32

Performed by Moses and Aaron

1. Turning the Nile into blood	Exod. 4:9; 7:14-24; Ps. 78:44; 105:29
2. The plague of frogs	Exod. 8:1-6; Ps. 78:45; 105:30
3. The plague of lice	Exod. 8:16-19; Ps. 105:31
4. The plague of flies	Exod. 8:20-31; Ps. 78:45; 105:31
5. The plague of murrain upon the beasts	Exod. 9:1-7
6. The plague of boils	Exod. 9:8-11

7. The plague of hail	Exod. 9:13-25; Ps. 78:47-48; 105:32-33
8. The plague of locusts	Exod. 10:1-20; Ps. 78:46; 105:34-35
9. The plague of darkness	Exod. 10:21-29; Ps. 105:28
10. The plague of death of the firstborn	Exod. 11–12; Ps. 78:51; 105:36; 135:8; 136:10
11. The cloud and the fire	Exod. 13:21-22; 40:34-38; Ps. 78:14; 105:39; Neh. 9:12, 19; 1 Cor. 10:1-2, 6, 11
12. The Red Sea parting	Exod. 14:21-31; Ps. 78:53; 106:9, 11, 22; Heb. 11:29
13. The healing of Marah's bitter waters	Exod. 15:22-27; Num. 33:8
14. The giving of manna	Exod. 15:6-15; Num. 11:1-9; Josh. 5:11, 12; Neh. 9:15; 20; Ps. 78:20; 105:40
15. The giving of quail	Exod. 16:8, 11-15; Num. 11:31-34; Ps. 78:26-30; 105:39-42
16. Bringing water from the smitten rock	Exod. 17:1-9; Ps. 78:16-17; 105:41
17. The victory over the Amalekites	Exod. 17:8-16; Num. 13:29; 14:25; Deut. 25:17-19; Ps. 83:7
18. The miracles at Sinai	Exod. 19:16-25; Deut. 4:5; 5:7-22; 9:8-11; Ps. 68:8; Heb. 12:18-21
19. The punishment of Nadab and Abihu	Lev. 10:1-7; Num. 3:1-4; 26:61; 1 Chron. 24:2

20. The fire at Taberah | Num. 11:1-3; Deut. 9:22; Ps. 78:21

21. Miriam's leprosy | Num. 12; 20:1; Lev. 13:46; Deut. 24:8-9

22. Judgment upon Korah | Num. 16; 26:9-11; Ps. 106:17

23. The budding of Aaron's rod | Num. 17; Heb. 9:4

24. The brazen serpent healing the people | Num. 21:4-9; 2 Kings 18:4; John 3:14; 1 Cor. 10:9

25. The miracle water | Num. 21:13-18

Performed by Joshua

1. The parting of the Jordan | Josh. 3:7-17; Ps. 114:3

2. The falling down of Jericho's walls | Josh. 6

3. The victory at Gibeon | Josh. 10:12-15; Isa. 28:21

Performed by Gideon

1. The fleece | Judg. 6:25-40

2. The victory over Midian | Judg. 7

Performed by Samson

1. The slain lion | Judg. 14:5-10

2. The foxes' tails | Judg. 15:1-6

3. The hip and thigh slaughter | Judg. 15:7-8

4. Escaping from bonds | Judg. 15:9-14

5. Slaying 1000 Philistines | Judg. 15:15-20

6. The uprooting of doors | Judg. 16:1-3

7. The miracles of his own hair | Judg. 16:4-22

8. The destruction of Dagon's temple | Judg. 16:23-31

Performed by David

1. Overcoming a lion and a bear   1 Sam. 17:34-37
2. Defeating Goliath   1 Sam. 17

Performed by Elijah

1. The three-year drought   1 Kings 17:1; James 5:17
2. The unfailing barrel and cruse   1 Kings 17:13-16; Luke 4:25-26
3. Raising of the widow's son   1 Kings 17:17-24
4. Praying down fire on Mount Carmel   1 Kings 18:1-39
5. Causing it to rain   1 Kings 18:1-2, 41-46
6. Destruction of King Ahaziah's soldiers   2 Kings 1:1-16
7. Parting of the Jordan   2 Kings 2:8

Performed by Elisha

1. Parting of the Jordan   2 Kings 2:14
2. Solving Jericho's water problem   2 Kings 2:19-22
3. Judgment of young hecklers from Bethel   2 Kings 2:23-24
4. Flooding ditches for the Israelite army in Edom   2 Kings 3:16-20
5. Creating oil for a widow   2 Kings 4:1-7
6. Raising of the Shunammite's son   2 Kings 4:32-37
7. Healing of the poisonous stew   2 Kings 4:38-41
8. Multiplying food   2 Kings 4:42-44
9. Healing Naaman the leper   2 Kings 5:1-19
10. Judgment upon Gehazi   2 Kings 5:26-27
11. Causing an axe head to float   2 Kings 6:1-7
12. Allowing his servant to see protecting angels   2 Kings 6:17
13. Judging Syrians with blindness   2 Kings 6:18
14. Delivering starving Samaria   2 Kings 7

Performed by Daniel

1	Interpreting Nebuchadnezzar's dreams	Dan. 2:19-45; 4:4-27
2.	Interpreting the handwriting on the wall	Dan. 5:13-28

Performed by Peter

1.	Healing a lame man	Acts 3:6-8
2.	Healing many	Acts 5:15
3.	Healing Aeneas	Acts 9:32-34
4.	Raising Dorcas from the dead	Acts 9:36-41

Performed by Paul

1.	The blinding of Elymas	Acts 13:10-11
2.	Healing of a cripple	Acts 14:8-10
3.	Miracles in Ephesus	Acts 19:11-12
4.	Raising Eutychus	Acts 20:1-12
5.	Miracles at Malta	Acts 28:1-10

MISSIONARIES AND EVANGELISTS
See also Pastors

1.	Noah, who warned people about the flood	2 Pet. 2:5
2.	Jonah, reluctant Hebrew prophet sent to warn Nineveh concerning divine judgment	Book of Jonah
3.	John the Baptist, great Nazarite New Testament evangelist and forerunner of Christ	Matt. 3:1-6
4.	Philip, one of the original seven deacons, who later led the Ethiopian eunuch to Christ	Acts 8:5; 21:8; 26:38

5. Paul, history's greatest missionary and evangelist and author of much of the New Testament
   Acts 13–28; 1 Tim. 1:12

6. Barnabas, Paul's companion during the first missionary journey
   Acts 9:26-31; 11:19-31; 13–14

7. John Mark, nephew of Barnabas, author of Gospel of Mark, and traveling companion of Paul, though he failed Paul during the first missionary journey
   Acts 12:25; 13:5; 15:36-40; 2 Tim. 4:11

8. Silas, Paul's companion during the second missionary journey
   Acts 15:40–17:15

9. Timothy, Paul's companion during the second journey
   Acts 16:1-5; 1 Tim. 1:3

10. Luke, Paul's traveling companion and author of Luke and Acts
    Luke 1:1-4; Col. 4:14; 2 Tim. 4:11

11. Epaphras, an evangelist from Colosse trained by Paul
    Col. 1:7; 4:12-13

12. Apollos, powerful teacher from Alexandria
    Acts 18:24-28

13. Titus, Paul's companion, appointed to oversee the church in Crete
    Titus 1:5

MOUNTAINS

1. Ararat, where the ark of Noah landed in Turkey
   Gen. 8:4

2. Carmel, where Elijah challenged the priests of Baal; located straight west of the Sea of Galilee and overlooking the Mediterranean Sea
   1 Kings 18:19

3. Ebal, where the curses of Israel (if the people disobeyed) were pronounced; located in Samaria
   Deut. 11:29; 27:9-13

4. Gerizim, where the blessings of Israel (for obedience) were pronounced, and where the Samaritans later built their temple; located opposite Mount Ebal — Deut. 11:29; John 4:20-21

5. Gilboa, where Saul was defeated by the Philistines and killed along with Jonathan, his son; located on the eastern side of the Plain of Esdraelon — 1 Sam. 31:1-6

6. Gilead, where Jacob and Laban made their covenant; located southeast of the Galilean Sea — Gen. 31:20-49

7. Harmon, where Jesus was transfigured; located southwest of Nazareth — Matt. 17

8. Hor, where Aaron died; located northeast of Kadesh-barnea — Num. 20:25-29

9. Horeb, the sacred mountain chain of which Sinai was the summit; located in the peninsula between the Gulf of Aqabah and the Suez

   a. Here Moses received his commission at the burning bush. — Exod. 3:1

   b. Here he brought water out of the rock. — Exod. 17:6

   c. Here the people waited as Moses spent forty days on Mount Sinai. — Exod. 32–33

   d. Here Elijah fled from Jezebel. — 1 Kings 19:8

10. Lebanon, where the cedar and cypress timber was cut for Solomon's temple; a snowclad mountain range extending in a northeasterly direction for a hundred miles along the Syrian coast — 1 Kings 5:6-14

11. Moriah, where Abraham almost sacrificed Isaac, and where Solomon built the temple — Gen. 22:2; 2 Chron. 3:1

12. Nebo, the summit point of Mount Pisgah, where Moses viewed the Promised Land; located east of the Jordan River — Deut. 3:27; 34:1-4

13. Olives, just east of Jerusalem
    a. David crossed this during his flight from Absalom.   2 Sam. 15:30
    b. Here Jesus wept over Jerusalem.   Luke 19:41
    c. Here Jesus preached his final discourse.   Matt. 24–25
14. Pisgah, where Balaam attempted to curse Israel, and where Moses was buried; located east of the Jordan River   Num. 22–24; Deut. 34:5-6
15. Sinai, the summit of Mount Horeb where Moses received the Ten Commandments   Exod. 20:1-17
16. Tabor, where Deborah and Barak descended to defeat Sisera; located in Galilee, east of Nazareth   Judg. 4:6-15

MURDERERS
See also Plots, Troublemakers

1. Cain killed Abel out of envy.   Gen. 4:8
2. Lamech killed a young man out of pride and revenge.   Gen. 4:23
3. Simeon and Levi killed Hamor and Shechem for revenge.   Gen. 34:26
4. Moses killed an Egyptian who was persecuting a laborer.   Exod. 2:12
5. Ehud killed Eglon of Moab.   Judg. 3:21
6. Jael killed Sisera.   Judg. 4:17-21
7. Joab killed Abner to eliminate competition.   2 Sam. 3:27
8. Rechab and Baanah killed Ish-bosheth to get in David's good graces.   2 Sam. 4:6

9. David had Uriah killed to conceal his adultery with Bathsheba.   2 Sam. 12:9

10. Absalom killed Amnon to avenge the rape of Tamar.   2 Sam. 13:28-29

11. Joab killed Absalom for revenge.   2 Sam. 18:14

12. Joab killed Amasa, the troublemaker.   2 Sam. 20:10

13. Zimri killed Elah to steal his throne.   1 Kings 16:10

14. Jezebel had Naboth killed to obtain his land for Ahab.   1 Kings 21:13

15. Hazael killed Ben-hadad to steal his throne.   2 Kings 8:7, 15

16. Jehu killed Jehoram to fulfill a prophecy and rid the country of Ahab's dynasty.   2 Kings 9:24

17. Jehu killed Ahaziah because he was with Jehoram.   2 Kings 9:27

18. Jehu killed Jezebel to fulfill a prophecy.   2 Kings 9:30-37

19. Servants killed Joash because of his cruel ways.   2 Kings 12:20-21

20. Shallum killed Zechariah to take his throne.   2 Kings 15:10

21. Menahem killed Shallum to take his throne.   2 Kings 15:14

22. Pekah killed Pekahiah to take his throne.   2 Kings 15:25

23. Hoshea killed Pekah to take his throne.   2 Kings 15:30

24. Servants killed Amon because of his cruelty.   2 Kings 21:23

25. Ishmael killed Gedaliah as an act of anarchy.   2 Kings 25:25

26. Israel killed Zechariah the high priest because of his fearless preaching against sin.   2 Chron. 24:20-21

27. Nebuchadnezzar killed Zedekiah's sons to punish him for his rebellion.   Jer. 39:6

28. Herod killed some Bethlehem babies in an attempt to kill Christ. — Matt. 2:16

29. Herodias had John the Baptist killed because of his preaching against her adultery. — Mark 6:25, 27

30. The Savior of the world was killed:

   a. by the Jews — Acts 5:30; 1 Thess. 2:15

   b. by Judas — Mark 14:10-11

   c. by Pilate — Matt. 27:24-26

   d. by the Roman soldiers — Matt. 27:27-31

   e. by sinners — Isa. 53:4-9

   f. by the Father — Isa. 53:10

31. The Jewish elders killed Stephen. — Acts 7:58-59

32. Herod killed James because of his preaching. — Acts 12:2

33. Sinners in Pergamos killed Antipas because of his testimony. — Rev. 2:13

34. The Antichrist will kill the two witnesses. — Rev. 11:7

MUSICAL INSTRUMENTS

1. Castanets—the name comes from the word which means chestnut. In ancient times two chestnuts were attached to the fingers and beat together to make music. — Ps. 150:5

2. Cornet—a hollow, curved horn, originally made from an animal's horn and later from metal. — Ps. 98:6; Dan. 3:5, 7, 10, 15

3. Cymbals—two concave plates of brass which were clanged together or beat — 2 Sam. 6:5; Ps. 150:5; 1 Cor. 13:1

4. Drum (also referred to as a timbrel, tambour, and tambourine)—a wooden hoop with skins pulled across the frame.

Exod. 15:20; Judg. 11:34; Ps. 68:25; 81:2; 1 Chron. 13:8

5. Dulcimer—a resonance box with strings stretched across it, played with small hammers.

Daniel 3:5, 10, 15

6. Flute—a straight pipe with holes.

Judg. 5:16; Dan. 3:5

7. Harp—the first musical instrument mentioned in the Bible. It was made of wood and had ten strings.

Gen. 4:21; 1 Sam. 16:16

8. Lyre—an instrument with five or more strings stretched across a rectangular frame. The strings were made from the small intestines of sheep. It was similar to the harp.

1 Sam. 16:23

9. Organ—not the large keyboard instrument, but a simple reed instrument made of wood, ivory, or bone, perhaps to be identified with the oboe.

Gen. 4:21; Job 21:12; Ps. 150:4

10. Psaltery—similar to, but not the same as, the harp. The psaltery was thought by some to have been a bottle-shaped string instrument.

1 Sam. 10:5; 2 Chron. 5:12; Ps. 71:22

11. Sackbut—a portable, harplike instrument which was tied to the player's waist and held upright as he walked and played. It was considered a luxury in oriental musical instruments.

Dan. 3:5, 7, 10, 15

12. Trumpet—usually made from the horn of a ram or goat, but, on one occasion, from silver.

Num. 10:1-10; Judg. 7:16-23; Matt. 24:31; 1 Cor. 15:52; 1 Thess. 4:16; Rev. 8:2

13. Zither (psaltery)—ten-stringed instrument, similar to the harp.

Ps. 33:2; 144:9

MUSICIANS

1. Heman, grandson of Samuel, author of Psalm 88, and one of four chief musicians in time of David — 1 Chron. 6:33; 15:17; 16:41-42

2. Asaph, one of four chief musicians in time of David and probable author of Psalms 50, 73–83 — 1 Chron. 6:39; 15:17; 16:5, 7, 37, 41

3. Jeduthun, one of four chief musicians in time of David — 1 Chron. 16:41-42

4. Ethan, author of Psalm 89 and one of four chief musicians in time of David — 1 Chron. 16:41

5. Benaiah and Jahaziel, trumpeters in time of David — 1 Chron. 16:6

6. Chenaniah, song leader in time of David — 1 Chron. 15:22

NATIONS AND PEOPLES

1. Akkadians lived in the northern part of Mesopotamia. — Gen. 10:10

2. Ammonites lived east of the Dead Sea. — Judg. 11:5

3. Amorites lived in the central part of Mesopotamia. — 1 Sam. 7:14

4. Arabians lived in the northern part of the Arabian peninsula. — 2 Chron. 17:11; 21:16; Gal. 1:17

5. Assyrians lived in the northern part of Mesopotamia. — 2 Kings 18:9

6. Babylonians lived in the southern part of Mesopotamia. — 2 Kings 25:1

7. Canaanites lived in Palestine and southern Syria. — Gen. 12:6

8. Chaldeans lived in southern Mesopotamia. — Dan. 3:8

9. Cilicians, called the Kue people in the Old Testament, lived near Tarsus, Paul's native city. — 1 Kings 10:28-29

10. Cretans lived on the island of Crete near Greece. — Acts 2:11; Titus 1:12

11. Cypriots lived on the island of Cyprus. — Acts 13:4

12. Edomites lived south of the Dead Sea. — Num. 20:14

13. Egyptians lived in Egypt. — Gen. 12:10

14. Elamites lived east of Babylon. — Acts 2:9

15. Ethiopians lived south of Egypt. — Acts 8:27

16. Greeks lived on the Greek islands and peninsulas. — John 12:20

17. Hittites lived in central Asia Minor. — Gen. 15:20

18. Hurrians, also known as the Horites and the Hivites, lived in northern Asia Minor. — Exod. 34:11; Josh. 9:1

19. Lydians, also called Ludim, lived in western Asia Minor. — Jer. 46:9

20. Medes lived in northwest Persia. — Dan. 5:28-31

21. Midianites lived in the central part of the Sinai Peninsula. — Exod. 3:1

22. Moabites lived northeast of the Dead Sea. — Ruth 1:1

23. Persians lived east of Mesopotamia. — Neh. 1:1

24. Philistines lived on the southern coast of Palestine. — Judg. 13:1

25. Phoenicians lived on the northern coasts of Palestine. — Acts 11:19

26. Sumerians lived in the southern part of Babylon. — Gen. 11:1

27. Syrians lived east of the Sea of Galilee. — 2 Kings 5:1

NUMBERS

1. One, the primary number, signifying absolute singleness — Exod. 4:4-6; Deut. 6:4; Eph. 4:4-6

2. Two, the number of witness and support
   a. Two great lights of creation — Gen. 1:16
   b. Two angels at Sodom — Gen. 19:1
   c. Two cherubim on the Ark of the Covenant — Exod. 25:22
   d. The Ten Commandments written on two stones — Exod. 31:18
   e. Two witnesses to establish a truth — Deut. 17:6; Matt. 26:60
   f. The good report of the two spies at Kadesh — Num. 14:6
   g. Two spies at Jericho — Josh. 2:1
   h. Two better than one — Eccl. 4:9
   i. Jesus' disciples sent out two by two — Luke 10:1
   j. Two angels attendant at the Resurrection — Luke 24:4
   k. Two angels present at the Ascension — Acts 1:10
   l. God's two immutable things — Heb. 6:18
   m. The two tribulational witnesses — Rev. 11:3

3. Three, the number of unity, of accomplishment, and of the universe
   a. The unity of the human race traced to Noah's three sons — Gen. 6:10
   b. Three days involved in the crossing of the Jordan — Josh. 1:11
   c. Israel's three yearly feasts — Exod. 23:14, 17
   d. Gideon's mighty victory accomplished through three bands of soldiers — Judg. 7:22

e. Three days of preparation for a   Ezra 10:9
revival in Ezra's time

f. Three days involved in the decision   Neh. 2:11
to build the walls of Jerusalem in
Nehemiah's time

g. Esther's heart prepared for three   Esther 4:16
days before meeting with the king

h. Jonah in the fish's belly for three   Jon. 1:17
days

i. Christ in the heart of the earth for   John 2:19
three days

j. His earthly ministry of three years   Luke 13:7

k. The Trinity—Father, Son, Holy
Spirit

l . The tabernacle and the temple—
outer court, inner court, Holy of
Holies

m. The offices of Christ—prophet,
priest, king

n. Salvation—justification,
sanctification, glorification

4. Four, an earth-related number

a. Four directions—north, south, east,
west

b. Four seasons—summer, winter,
fall, spring

c. Four great earthly kingdoms   Dan. 7:3

d. Four kinds of spiritual soil   Matt. 13

e. Four horsemen of the Tribulation   Rev. 6

f. Fourfold earthly ministry of
Christ—Matthew describes him as
a king, Mark as a servant, Luke as
the perfect man, John as the mighty
God.

5. Five, the number of grace

a. Five Levitical offerings   Lev. 1–5

b. Five Israelites to chase 100 enemies   Lev. 26:8

     c. Five wise virgins   Matt. 25:2

     d. Five barley loaves used by Jesus to   Matt. 14:17
        feed the 5,000

  6. Six, the number of man

     a. Creation in six days   Gen. 1:31

     b. Six cities of refuge   Num. 35:6

     c. Israel marched around Jericho six   Josh. 6:3
        times.

     d. Goliath was 6 cubits and a span tall   1 Sam. 17:4
        (over 9 feet tall).

     e. The number of the Antichrist is   Rev. 13:18
        666.

     f. Nebuchadnezzar's statue was 60   Dan. 3:1
        cubits by 6 cubits (90 feet high and
        6 feet wide).

  7. Seven, the number of God, or divine
     perfection

     a. God rested on the seventh day.   Gen. 2:2

     b. His word is as silver purified by   Ps. 12:6
        fire seven times.

     c. Seventy weeks (or years) are   Dan. 9:24
        determined upon Israel.

     d. Jesus taught Peter to forgive 70   Matt. 18:22
        times 7.

     e. There are seven miracles in the
        Gospel of John.

     f. There were seven sayings on the
        cross.

     g. John wrote to seven churches.   Rev. 1:4

     h. He saw seven golden candlesticks. Rev. 1:12

     i. There are seven stars in Christ's   Rev. 1:16
       hand.

     j. The Father holds a seven-sealed   Rev. 5:1
       book.

     k. Seven angels pronounce judgment Rev. 8:2
       in the Tribulation.

8. Eight, the new beginning number

   a. Eight were saved from the Flood.   Gen. 7:13, 23

   b. Circumcision was to be performed   Gen. 17:12
     on the eighth day.

   c. Thomas saw Jesus eight days after   John 20:26
     the Resurrection.

9. Nine, the fullness of blessing number

   a. The fruit of the Spirit is ninefold.   Gal. 5:22-23

   b. Sarah was 90 at the birth of Isaac   Gen. 17:17

   c. There are 18 gifts of the Spirit   Rom. 12; 1 Cor. 12; Eph. 4

10. Ten, the human government number

   a. The revived Roman Empire will   Dan. 7:24; Rev. 17:12
     consist of ten nations.

   b. The northern kingdom had ten   1 Kings 11:31-35
     tribes.

   c. A local government of ten men   Ruth 4:2
     decided the fate of Ruth.

11. Twelve, the divine government number

   a. There were 12 tribes of Israel.   Rev. 7

   b. There were 12 apostles.   Matt. 10

   c. There will be 12 gates and   Rev. 21
     foundations in the New Jerusalem.

12. Thirty, associated with sorrow and mourning

   a. Israel mourned after Aaron's death   Num. 20:29
     for 30 days.

   b. Israel mourned for Moses 30 days.   Deut. 34:8

13. Forty, the number of testing and trial

   a. It rained 40 days during the Flood.   Gen. 7:4

   b. Moses spent 40 years in the desert.   Exod. 3

   c. Israel spied out the land for 40   Num. 13:25
     days.

   d. Moses spent 40 days on Mount   Exod. 24:18
     Sinai.

e. Israel wandered 40 years in the desert.   Num. 14:33

f. Goliath taunted Israel for 40 days.   1 Sam. 17:16

g. Jonah preached repentance to Nineveh for 40 days.   Jon. 3:4

h. Jesus spent 40 days in the wilderness before being tempted.   Matt. 4:2

i. There were 40 days between the resurrection and ascension of Christ.   Acts 1:3

14. Fifty, associated with celebration and ceremony

a. The Feast of Weeks was 50 days after the Passover.   Lev. 23:15-16

b. The fiftieth year was to be a jubilee to Israel.   Lev. 25:10

c. Absalom appointed 50 men to run before him.   2 Sam. 15:1

d. Adonijah did the same.   1 Kings 1:5

e. Pentecost occurred 50 days after Christ's resurrection.   Acts 2

15. Seventy, associated with human committees and judgment

a. Moses appointed 70 elders.   Num. 11:16

b. Tyre was to be judged for 70 years.   Isa. 23:15

c. Israel spent 70 years in Babylon.   Jer. 29:10

d. God would accomplish his total plan upon Israel in 70 times 7 years.   Dan. 9:24

e. Jesus appointed 70 disciples.   Luke 10:1

f. The Sanhedrin was made up of 70 men.

OCCUPATIONS

1.	Baker	Gen. 40:1
2.	Barber	Ezek. 5:1
3.	Boat builder	1 Kings 9:26
4.	Brazier	Gen. 4:22
5.	Brickmaker	Gen. 11:3
6.	Butler	Gen. 40:2
7.	Carpenter	2 Sam. 5:11
8.	Caulker	Ezek. 27:9
9.	Confectioner	1 Sam. 8:13
10.	Cook	1 Sam. 8:13
11.	Coppersmith	2 Tim. 4:14
12.	Draftsmen	Ezek. 4:1
13.	Druggist	Exod. 30:25, 35
14.	Dyer	Exod. 25:5
15.	Embalmer	Gen. 50:3
16.	Embroiderer	Exod. 28:39
17.	Engraver	Exod. 28:11
18.	Fisherman	Matt. 4:18
19.	Fuller	2 Kings 18:17
20.	Gardener	Jer. 29:5
21.	Goldsmith	2 Chron. 2:7
22.	Jeweler	Exod. 28:17-21
23.	Mason	2 Kings 12:12
24.	Military men	Acts 10:1
25.	Molder	Exod. 32:4
26.	Musician	2 Sam. 6:5
27.	Needleworker	Exod. 26:36
28.	Painter	Jer. 22:14
29.	Porter	2 Sam. 18:26
30.	Potter	Isa. 64:8

31. Refiner   Mal. 3:3
32. Seamstress   Ezek. 13:18
33. Silversmith   Acts 19:24
34. Smelter   Job 28:1-2
35. Smith   1 Sam. 13:19
36. Spinner   Exod. 35:25
37. Stonecutter   Exod. 31:5
38. Tailor   Exod. 39:1
39. Tanner   Acts 9:43
40. Tax collector   Matt. 9:9
41. Tentmaker   Acts 18:3
42. Weaver   Exod. 28:32
43. Worker in metal   Exod. 31:3-4

OFFERINGS
See also Altars

1. Burnt   Exod. 29:18
2. Drink   Lev. 23:13
3. Heave   Lev. 7:14
4. Meal   Lev. 2:1
5. Peace   Lev. 7:11
6. Sin   Lev. 4:3
7. Trespass   Lev. 5:6
8. Wave   Lev. 7:30

ORDAINED BEFORE BIRTH FOR SPECIAL SERVICE
See also Called by God to Special Service

1. Isaac, ordained to be in the bloodline leading to Christ — Gen. 15:4; 17:19-21; 18:10, 14

2. Jacob, ordained to be in the bloodline leading to Christ — Gen. 25:23; Rom. 9:9-12

3. Samson, ordained to deliver Israel from the Philistines and serve God as a Nazarite — Judg. 13:2-5

4. Samuel, ordained to serve God as a Nazarite — 1 Sam. 1:11-28

5. David, ordained to rule over Israel — Ps. 139:13-18

6. Cyrus, ordained to set the Jewish remnant in Babylon and Persia free — Isa. 44:28; 45:1; Ezra 1:2-4

7. Josiah, ordained to destroy the false altar of King Jeroboam — 1 Kings 13:2

8. Jeremiah, ordained to be God's prophet to the nations — Jer. 1:5

9. John the Baptist, ordained to be Christ's forerunner — Luke 1:13-17

10. Paul, ordained to be God's minister to the Gentiles — Gal. 1:15

PALACES

1. Artaxerxes' — Neh. 1:1; 2:1
2. Solomon's — 1 Kings 7:1
3. Ahasuerus's — Esther 1:2
4. Belshazzar's — Dan. 5:5
5. Darius's — Dan. 6:18

6. The high priest's   Matt. 26:3, 58, 69
7. Caesar's   Phil. 1:13

PARABLES
See also Allegories, Fables, Symbols and Emblems

A parable is a placing beside or comparison of earthly truths with heavenly truths. It is an earthly story, often historical in nature, but not necessarily so, with a heavenly meaning.

Old Testament Parables

1. Mount Moriah	Gen. 22; Heb. 11:17-19
2. The tabernacle	Exod. 25–31; Heb. 9:1-10
3. The trees	Judg. 9:7-15
4. The ewe lamb	2 Sam. 12:1-4
5. The two sons	2 Sam. 14:1-24
6. The wounded prophet	1 Kings 20:35-43
7. The shepherdless flock	1 Kings 22:13-28
8. The thistle and the cedar	2 Kings 14:8-14
9. The nature of wisdom	Job 28
10. The vine out of Egypt	Ps. 80
11. The little city	Eccl. 9:14-18
12. The master's crib	Isa. 1:2-9
13. The Lord's vineyard	Isa. 5:1-7
14. The almond rod and the boiling pot	Jer. 1:11-19
15. The marred girdle	Jer. 13:1-11
16. The wine bottle	Jer. 13:12-14
17. The potter and the clay	Jer. 18:1-10
18. The broken bottle	Jer. 19:1-13
19. The two baskets of figs	Jer. 24:1-10

20.	The cup of fury	Jer. 25:15-38
21.	The bonds and yokes	Jer. 27–28
22.	The hidden stones	Jer. 43:8-13
23.	The living creatures	Ezek. 1:1-28
24.	The eaten scroll	Ezek. 2–3
25.	The tile	Ezek. 4:1-17
26.	The shaved head and beard	Ezek. 5:1-17
27.	The temple wickedness	Ezek. 8:1-18
28.	The writer's inkhorn	Ezek. 9–10
29.	The cauldron and the flesh	Ezek. 11:1-25
30.	The great escape	Ezek. 12:1-28
31.	The vine branch	Ezek. 15:1-8
32.	The harlot wife	Ezek. 16
33.	The great eagle	Ezek. 17:1-24
34.	The lioness and her whelps	Ezek. 19:1-9
35.	The plucked up vine	Ezek. 19:10-14
36.	The two sisters	Ezek. 23:1-49
37.	The boiling cauldron	Ezek. 24:1-4
38.	The prophet's dead wife	Ezek. 24:15-24
39.	The cedar in Lebanon	Ezek. 31
40.	The unfaithful shepherds	Ezek. 34
41.	The valley of dry bones	Ezek. 37:1-14
42.	The two sticks	Ezek. 37:15-28
43.	The rising waters	Ezek. 47:1-12
44.	The great image	Dan. 2:31-45
45.	The great tree	Dan. 4
46.	The four beasts	Dan. 7
47.	The ram and the goat	Dan. 8:1-25
48.	The harlot wife	Hos. 1–3
49.	The horse and myrtle trees	Zech. 1:8-17
50.	The horns and smiths	Zech. 1:18-21
51.	The measuring line	Zech. 2:1-13
52.	The parable of Joshua the priest	Zech. 3:1-10

53. The golden candlestick	Zech. 4:1-6
54. The flying scroll	Zech. 5:1-4
55. The woman and the basket	Zech. 5:5-11
56. The four war chariots	Zech. 6:1-8
57. The crowns	Zech. 6:9-15
58. The parable of beauty and bands	Zech. 11:1-17

Jesus' Parables

1. Two houses in a hurricane	Matt. 7:24-27; Luke 6:47-49
2. Forgiving the 50 and the 500	Luke 7:41-42
3. Subduing a strong man	Mark 3:22-30
4. The sower, the seed, and the soil	Matt. 13:1-9, 18-23; Mark 4:1-20; Luke 8:4-15
5. Satan's tares in the Savior's field	Matt. 13:24-30, 36-43
6. From scattering to sickling	Mark 4:26-29
7. The mighty mustard seed	Matt. 13:31, 32; Mark 4:30-32; Luke 13:18-19
8. The cook's leaven and the kingdom of heaven	Mark 13:33; Luke 13:20-21
9. Finding a fortune in a field	Matt. 13:44
10. The pearl of great price	Matt. 13:45-46
11. Sorting out a sea catch	Matt. 13:47-50
12. A trained man and his treasure	Matt. 13:52
13. A rent cloth and a ruptured container	Matt. 9:16-17; Mark 2:21-22; Luke 5:36-39
14. A generation of gripers	Matt. 11:16-19; Luke 7:31-35
15. The forgiven who wouldn't forgive	Matt. 18:23-35
16. The Good Samaritan	Luke 10:25-37
17. Seven spirits and a swept house	Matt. 12:43-45; Luke 11:24-26
18. A fool in a fix	Luke 12:16-21

19. Keep the home fires burning — Luke 12:32-40

20. A sinning servant and a returning ruler — Matt. 24:45-51; Luke 12:42-48

21. A fruitless fig tree — Luke 13:6-9

22. Choosing the least at a wedding feast — Luke 14:7-11

23. Two fools and a henpecked husband — Luke 14:15-24

24. A missing sheep, misplaced silver, and a miserable son — Luke 15:1-32

25. The stewings of a steward — Luke 16:1-13

26. The rich man and Lazarus — Luke 16:19-31

27. When our best is but the least — Luke 17:7-10

28. A widow and a weary judge — Luke 18:1-8

29. A haughty Pharisee and a humble publican — Luke 18:9-14

30. The workers in the vineyard — Matt. 20:1-16

31. Three stewards and their silver — Luke 19:11-27

32. Two sons who changed their minds — Matt. 21:28-32

33. The vicious vinekeepers — Matt. 21:33-46; Mark 12:1-12; Luke 20:9-19

34. A wedding guest with no wedding garment — Matt. 22:1-14

35. The fig tree and the future — Matt. 24:32-35; Mark 13:28-31; Luke 21:29-33

36. Five lamps that went out — Matt. 25:1-13

37. Three stewards and their talents — Matt. 25:14-30

38. Separating the sheep from the goats — Matt. 25:31-46

Other New Testament Parables

1. The great sheet — Acts 10:9-22

2. The parable of rewards — 1 Cor. 3:12-15

3. The olive tree — Rom. 11:13-25

4. The two women, sons, and mountains — Gal. 4:19-31

5. The whole armor of God — Eph. 6:11-17

6. The Promised Land — Heb. 3:7–4:16

7. The two mountains	Heb. 12:18-24
8. The tongue	James 3
9. The sevenfold lampstand	Rev. 1:9–3:22
10. The seven-sealed book	Rev. 5:1-14
11. The four horsemen	Rev. 6:1-8
12. The persecuted woman	Rev. 12:1-17
13. The seven-headed, ten-horned dragon	Rev. 12:3-4; 13:1
14. The bloody harlot	Rev. 17
15. The arrogant queen	Rev. 18
16. The pure bride	Rev. 19:1-10

PARADOXES

General

1. Of finding one's life, yet eventually losing it	Matt. 10:39; John 12:25
2. Of losing one's life, yet eventually finding it	Matt. 10:39
3. Of being unknown, yet being well known	2 Cor. 6:9
4. Of dying, yet possessing life	2 Cor. 6:9
5. Of dying, yet being able to give life	John 12:24
6. Of being sorrowful, yet always rejoicing	2 Cor. 6:10
7. Of being poor, yet making many rich	2 Cor. 6:10
8. Of having nothing, yet possessing all things	2 Cor. 6:10
9. Of hearing words that cannot be expressed	2 Cor. 12:4
10. Of being strong when one is weak	2 Cor. 12:10

11. Of knowing the love of Christ that surpasses knowledge   Eph. 3:19

12. Of seeing the unseen   2 Cor. 4:18

Concerning Christ

The very life and ministry of Jesus Christ was itself a divine paradox.

1. He hungered, yet fed multitudes.   Matt. 4:2; John 6

2. He thirsted, yet is the Water of life.   John 19:28; 4:14

3. He grew weary, yet is our rest.   John 4:6; Matt. 11:29-30

4. He paid tribute, yet is the King of kings.   Matt. 17:27; Rev. 19:16

5. He prayed, yet hears our prayers.   Mark 14:32-42; John 14:13-14

6. He wept, yet dries our tears.   John 11:35; Rev. 21:4

7. He was sold for 30 pieces of silver, yet redeems the world.   Matt. 26:15; 1 Pet. 1:18-19

8. He was led as a sheep to the slaughter, and yet is the Good Shepherd.   Isa. 53:7; John 10:11

9. He was put to death, yet raises the dead.   John 5:25; 19:33

PASTORAL DUTIES

1. To administer the ordinances   Matt. 28:19-20

2. To be a man of prayer   1 Tim. 2:1

3. To warn his flock   1 Tim. 4:1, 6

4. To study the Word   2 Tim. 2:15

5. To preach the Word   2 Tim. 4:2; Acts 6:2-4

6. To exhort and rebuke   1 Thess. 5:12; Titus 2:15

7. To watch over souls, his own and those of others
   Acts 20:28-31; Col. 4:17; 1 Tim. 4:6; 6:11; Heb. 13:17

8. To feed and lead his flock
   Acts 20:28; 1 Pet. 5:2

9. To be an example to all
   1 Cor. 11:1; 4:16; Phil. 3:17; 2 Thess. 3:9; 1 Tim. 4:12; Heb. 13:7; 1 Pet. 5:3

PASTORS
See also Churches, Missionaries and Evangelists

1. James, half brother of Christ, pastor of the church in Jerusalem, and author of the Letter of James
   Acts 12:17; 15:13-21; 21:18

2. Apollos, eloquent Alexandrian Jew who pastored the church in Corinth for a time
   Acts 18:24-28; 1 Cor. 3:6; Titus 3:13

3. Timothy, Paul's faithful companion who pastored in Ephesus
   1 Tim. 4:6-16

4. Titus, Paul's young friend who pastored a church on Crete
   Titus 1:5

5. John, the beloved apostle who authored five New Testament books and pastored the church at Ephesus
   1 John

PHARISEES

1. The Pharisee with whom Jesus dined, who criticized Jesus for allowing an immoral woman to wash his feet — Luke 7:36, 40

2. Another Pharisee with whom Jesus dined, who criticized the Savior for not observing the rite of cleansing before eating — Luke 11:37

3. Another Pharisee with whom Jesus dined, whose home was the scene for Jesus healing a man with dropsy — Luke 14:1

4. Hypocritical Pharisee whom Jesus contrasted with the humble publican — Luke 18:10-14

5. Nicodemus, the sincere Pharisee who came to Jesus by night — John 3:1-20

6. Gamaliel, famous Jewish teacher who cautioned the Sanhedrin against persecuting the apostles — Acts 5:34-40

7. Paul, Scripture's greatest theologian and missionary — Acts 23:6

PLAGUES

Upon Nations

1. Egypt
   a. Waters turned to blood — Exod. 7:20
   b. Frogs — Exod. 8:6
   c. Lice — Exod. 8:17
   d. Beetles, flies — Exod. 8:24
   e. Cattle disease — Exod. 9:3

f. Boils	Exod. 9:10
g. Hail	Exod. 9:24
h. Locusts	Exod. 10:13
i. Darkness	Exod. 10:22
j. Death of the firstborn	Exod. 12:29

2. Israel

a. Death by the sword, due to idolatry	Exod. 32:27
b. Death by fire, due to complaining	Num. 11:1
c. Death by an unnamed plague, due to lust	Num. 11:31-35
d. Death for unbelief	Num. 14:37
e. Death by an earthquake for rebellion	Num. 16:32
f. Death by poisonous serpents for rebellion	Num. 21:6
g. Death for immorality	Num. 25:9
h. Death for looking into the Ark of God	1 Sam. 6:19
i. Death due to David's census	2 Sam. 24:15

3. Philistia—a plague of tumors, for capturing the Ark of God	1 Sam. 5:8-9
4. Syria—a plague of blindness for attacking Israel	2 Kings 6:18

5. All nations during the Tribulation

a. White horse plague—conquest	Rev. 6:2
b. Red horse plague—war	Rev. 6:3-4
c. Black horse plague—famine	Rev. 6:5-6
d. Pale horse plague—death	Rev. 6:7-8
e. Sixth seal plague—earthquake	Rev. 6:12
f. First trumpet plague—destruction of one-third of vegetation	Rev. 8:7
g. Second trumpet plague—one-third of salt waters turned to blood	Rev. 8:8
h. Third trumpet plague—one-third of fresh waters turned bitter	Rev. 8:10-11

i. Fourth trumpet plague—one-third of moon, sun, stars darkened — Rev. 8:12

j. Fifth trumpet plague—men plagued with scorpion stings for five months — Rev. 9:12

k. Sixth trumpet plague—one-third of earth's population slain — Rev. 9:14

l. First vial plague—sores upon men — Rev. 16:2

m. Second vial plague—all sea life destroyed — Rev. 16:3

n. Third vial plague—all rivers turned to blood — Rev. 16:4

o. Fourth vial plague—men scorched by the sun — Rev. 16:8-9

p. Fifth vial plague—darkness upon the empire of the Antichrist — Rev. 16:10

q. Sixth vial plague—drying up of the Euphrates River — Rev. 16:12

r. Seventh vial plague—destruction of political and economic Babylon — Rev. 16:17-21; 18

Upon Individuals

1. Upon Pharaoh for attempting to marry Sarah — Gen. 12:17

2. Upon Abimelech for attempting to marry Sarah — Gen. 20:18

3. Upon Moses to show him God's power — Exod. 4:6-7

4. Upon Nadab and Abihu for offering strange fire — Lev. 10:1-2

5. Upon Miriam for criticizing Moses — Num. 12:1-10

6. Upon Saul for his disobedience — 1 Sam. 16:14

7. Upon Nabal for his hatred of David — 1 Sam. 25:38

8. Upon Jeroboam for his false religion — 1 Kings 13:4

9. Upon Gehazi for lying — 2 Kings 5:20-27

10. Upon Uzziah for attempting to assume priestly duties — 2 Chron. 26:16-21

11. Upon Herod for receiving worship from men — Acts 12:20-25

12. Upon Bar-Jesus for opposing Paul — Acts 13:6-11

PLANTS
See also Foods, Trees

---

1. Aloe, a succulent plant with thick, fleshy leaves and a tall stem with many bell-shaped flowers. Used for purifying the bodies of the dead. — Ps. 45:8; Prov. 7:17; John 19:38-40

2. Anise — Matt. 23:23

3. Balm, an evergreen shrub with white blossoms and applelike fruit. Gum resin from its bark was used for medicinal purposes. — Gen. 37:25; Jer. 8:22

4. Barley, a staple cereal — Ruth 1:22; 2 Kings 7:1, 16, 18; John 6:1-13

5. Briar — Judg. 8:7, 16

6. Bulrush, a tall plant whose stems were used for paper making — Exod. 2:3

7. Calamus, a plant belonging to the reed and cane family. Strong-smelling oil was taken from its root. — Song of Sol. 4:14; Ezek. 27:19

8. Coriander. It has leaves like parsley, white or pinkish flowers, and a rounded gray seed that contains a valuable oil used for flavoring or perfume. — Exod. 16:31; Num. 11:6-9

9. Cumin, a small delicate plant used for medicinal purposes and spice for food — Isa. 28:27; Matt. 23:23

10. Flax, a plant used to make linen

Exod. 9:31; 26:1; 28:6; Josh. 2:6; Prov. 31:13

11. Gall, a plant perhaps related to the opium poppy

Ps. 69:21; Matt. 27:34

12. Garlic, used as food flavoring

Num. 11:5

13. Gourd, a large (8 to 10 feet high) bush with rich green or bronze leaves and bright red fruit. Its oil was used for fuel for lamps.

2 Kings 4:39; Jon. 4:6-10

14. Grass

Ps. 23:2; 103:15

15. Henna, a shrub that produces white scented flowers, used to color the hair or fingernails in reddish and yellowish hues

Song of Sol. 1:14; 4:13

16. Hyssop

   a. Old Testament hyssop. This was a plant of the mint family, with small leaves and bunches of golden flowers. It was used for sprinkling blood, for cleansing lepers, and for other rites of purification.

Exod. 12:22; Lev. 14:4; Ps. 51:7

   b. New Testament hyssop. A tall, yellow-green plant with strong stems and ribbonlike leaves.

John 19:29

17. Leeks, a favorite vegetable in Palestine resembling an onion, also used for medicinal purposes

Num. 11:5

18. Lentil. It has the appearance of a pea and is used as a cereal or for making bread.

Gen. 25:34; 2 Sam. 17:28; 23:11; Ezek. 4:9

19. Lilies, a beautiful purple flower

Matt. 6:28

20. Mandrake, a leafy plant of the nightshade family

Gen. 30:14-16

21. Mint, a small leaf plant used for medicinal, flavoring, and perfume purposes

Matt. 23:23

22. Mustard, a yellow-flowered plant whose leaves were used as a vegetable

Matt. 13:13-32; 17:20

23. Myrrh, the resin, or drippings of a thorny bush with thin bark — Matt. 2:11

24. Pomegranate, a wild shrub with dark green, shiny leaves, and bright red, waxlike flowers, having dark red fruit about the size of an orange. It was used as a medicine and for food. — Exod. 28:31-34

25. Reed, a tall plant with purple blossoms, used as a measuring device and to make pens for writing purposes — Ezek. 40:3; Isa. 18:2

26. Rose. The famous Rose of Sharon was a beautiful tuliplike flower with bright red blossoms. — Isa. 35:1; Song of Sol. 2:1

27. Rue, a five-foot-tall plant with clusters of bright yellow flowers, used as a disinfectant, as flavoring, and for medicinal remedies — Luke 11:42

28. Rush, a flowery plant used to make baskets, chair seats, and other items — Job 8:11; Isa. 35:7

29. Scarlet, a large evergreen shrub, whose shoots are the breeding ground of an insect from which a scarlet dye is taken. The bark of the tree yields a black dye. — Lev. 14:51

30. Spikenard, a small plant with hairy stems producing a costly, sweet-smelling ointment — Song of Sol. 1:12; 4:14; Mark 14:3-6

31. Tares, one of the most destructive weeds of the Holy Land. The seeds often contain a poisonous fungus which when eaten produces dizziness, nausea, and sometimes even death. — Job 31:40; Matt. 13:24-30, 36-43

32. Thistle, a tall weed with yellow flowers and a spiny stem — Gen. 3:18; Hos. 10:8; Matt. 7:16; Heb. 6:8

33. Thorns — Matt. 7:16

34. Vine — Isa. 5:2-7; John 15:1-8

35. Wheat — Gen. 41:1-7

36. Wormwood, a plant having a strong, bitter taste, used as a symbol of bitterness, sorrow, and calamity

Deut. 29:18;
Jer. 23:15;
Rev. 8:10-11

PLOTS
See also Traitors

1. Cain's plot against Abel. Out of envy he lured him into a field and killed him.

Gen. 4:8

2. Jacob's and Rachel's plot against Esau and Isaac. They deceived Isaac into believing that Jacob was Esau so as to secure the blessing for Jacob.

Gen. 27

3. Simeon's and Levi's plot against Shechem. They tricked Shechem and his tribe into circumcising themselves and then, while they were recovering, killed them. This was done in revenge for seducing Dinah.

Gen. 34

4. Joseph's brothers's plot against Joseph. Out of envy they sold him into Egyptian slavery and then told their father a wild animal had eaten him.

Gen. 37:18

5. Tamar's plot against Judah. She disguised herself as a common harlot and then lured Judah into her tent for sexual purposes, so she could have a child.

Gen. 38

6. Potiphar's wife's plot against Joseph. She accused Joseph of rape after he refused her sexual advances.

Gen. 39:13-19

7. Korah's plot against Moses. He wanted an equal (if not superior) place of leadership to that of Moses.   Num. 16:1-3

8. The Gibeonites' plot against Joshua. They dressed in old and ragged clothes to deceive Joshua into believing they had come as citizens from a far-off country.   Josh. 9

9. Delilah's plot against Samson. She demanded he prove his love to her by telling her the secret of his great strength. This was done so she could hand him over to the Philistines.   Judg. 16:4-20

10. Saul's plot against David. Thinking David would be killed, Saul offered the hand of his daughter Michal in marriage to David if he would singlehandedly kill 100 Philistines and bring back their foreskins.   1 Sam. 18

11. Absalom's plot against David. Under the pretense of fulfilling a vow to God, Absalom received permission to visit Hebron. He actually went there to organize and announce his rebellion.   2 Sam. 15

12. Adonijah's plot against Solomon. He invited some leading Israelites (including a general and chief priest) to a feast, planning to use the occasion to stage his rebellion against Solomon.   1 Kings 1

13. Jezebel's plot against Naboth. Jezebel sent a letter ordering Naboth to be falsely accused of blasphemy and murdered so Ahab could possess Naboth's vineyard.   1 Kings 21

14. Certain Chaldeans' plot against three Hebrew young men. Their good names and loyalty were slandered before King Nebuchadnezzar.   Dan. 3

15. Certain Chaldeans' plot against   Dan. 6
    Daniel. They caused a law to be made
    whereby no one could pray to any god
    except King Darius.

16. Sanballat's plot against Nehemiah.   Neh. 4, 6
    Sanballat opposed Nehemiah's work
    by ridiculing it and finally by
    threatening it. He wanted to keep the
    wall of Jerusalem from going up.

17. Haman's plot against the Persian   Esther 3
    Jews. Because of his hatred for
    Mordecai, Haman persuaded the king
    to issue a decree that all Jews be put
    to death on a given date.

18. Satan's plot against Job, to take away   Job 1–2
    Job's family, wealth, and health

19. Herod's plot against Christ, to kill the   Matt. 2
    infant Christ by the sword. He wanted
    to rid the country of a king that might
    threaten his own rule.

20. Satan's plot against Jesus. He wanted   Matt. 4
    to cause Jesus to sin by turning stones
    into bread, by defying gravity, and by
    worshiping Satan.

21. Herodias's plot against John. She   Matt. 14
    wanted to take revenge on John for
    his fearless preaching against her
    adultery, so she asked her daughter to
    request John's head on a platter after
    Herod offered her anything she
    wished.

22. The Jewish leaders' plot against Jesus   John 11:47-57

23. The Jewish leaders' plot to kill   John 12:10-11
    Lazarus. They hoped to dispose of the
    evidence for the greatest of Jesus'
    miracles—the raising of a dead man
    four days in the grave.

24. Judas Iscariot's plot against Jesus   Matt. 26:14-16

25. The synagogue leaders's plot to kill   Acts 6:8-15
    Stephen. They wanted to kill him so
    that his message of judgment might be
    silenced.

26. Saul's plot to imprison Christians   Acts 8:3; 9:1-2

27. The Damascus Jews' plot against   Acts 9:22-25
    Paul. They wanted this Pharisee-
    turned-Christian to be silenced, so
    they planned to kill him as he left
    Damascus through the city gate.

28. The Jerusalem Jews' plots against   Acts 9:26-29;
    Paul   21:31; 22:17-21;
                                         23:6-14; 24:1;
                                         25:1-3

29. Herod's plot against believers. He   Acts 12
    killed James and placed Peter on
    death row to please the unbelieving
    Jews.

30. Asian Jews' plot against Paul
    a. At Antioch in Pisidia   Acts 13:14, 45, 50
    b. At Iconium   Acts 14:1-2
    c. At Lystra   Acts 14:6-7, 19

31. Greek Jews' plots against Paul
    a. At Thessalonica   Acts 17:1, 5
    b. At Berea   Acts 17:13
    c. At Corinth   Acts 18:1, 12
    d. At Macedonia   Acts 20:3

32. Demetrius's plot against Paul. He   Acts 19:24-27
    accused Paul of blasphemy against the
    goddess Diana because the spread of
    the gospel was causing the merchants
    of the Diana movement to lose
    money.

POLITICAL AND RELIGIOUS GROUPS

1. The Diaspora—the Jews scattered abroad because of the Assyrian and Babylonian captivities — Acts 2:5, 9-11

2. Epicureanism—a hedonistic philosophy developed by Epicurus (341–270 B.C.) — see Acts 17:18

3. The Galileans—Jewish followers of a rebel named Judas of Galilee — Luke 13:1

4. The Hellenists—Greek-speaking Jews — Acts 6:1

5. The Herodians—a political dynasty from the family of Herod, deriving authority from the Roman government — Mark 3:6; 8:15; 12:13-17

6. The Levites—the descendants of Levi who had charge of the temple — John 1:19; Luke 10:32

7. The Libertines—a group of ex-slaves who apparently had their own synagogues in Jerusalem — Acts 6:9

8. The Nazarites—men taking a special religious vow as prescribed in Numbers 6 — Judg. 13:3-7; Luke 1:15

9. The Pharisees—the separatists, legalists, and guardians of both the written and oral law — Matt. 12:1-2; 23

10. The proselytes—Gentile converts to Judaism — Matt. 23:15; Acts 2:10; 13:43

11. The publicans—the state-appointed tax collectors of Roman revenue, widely disliked — Luke 3:13; 19:8; Matt. 9:9

12. The Sadducees—the aristocrats among the Jews, who denied belief in angels and the afterlife and believed only in the Torah — Mark 12:18; Luke 20:27

13. The Samaritans—the hated half-Jew, half-Gentile people living between the provinces of Judea and Galilee — John 4:9; 8:48; Matt. 10:5; Luke 10:33; 17:16

14. The Sanhedrin—the religious and legal Jewish Supreme Court — Matt. 26:65-66; 27:1-2

15. The scribes (also called lawyers)—the students, interpreters, and teachers of the Old Testament law — Matt. 16:21; 21:15; 23:2; 26:3

16. The Stoics—a group founded by the philosopher Zeno (c. 300 B.C.), who believed life's goal was to rise above all things and to show no emotion in either pain or pleasure — Acts 17:18

17. The Zealots—a group of Jewish patriots, fanatical defenders of theocracy and haters of the Romans — Luke 6:15; Acts 1:13

POLYGAMISTS
See also Marriages

1. Lamech, descendant of Cain who had two wives — Gen. 4:19

2. Abraham, who had a wife and a concubine — Gen. 16:1-3

3. Esau, son of Isaac who had three wives — Gen. 26:34; 28:9

4. Jacob, son of Isaac who had four wives — Gen. 29:15-35; 30:4, 9

5. Gideon, Israelite judge who had many wives — Judg. 8:30

6. Elkanah, father of Samuel and husband of Hannah and Peninnah — 1 Sam. 1:1-2

7. Saul, who had a wife and a concubine — 1 Sam. 14:50; 2 Sam. 3:7

8. David, who had eight wives — 1 Sam. 18:27; 25:42-43; 2 Sam. 3:2-5; 11:27; 12:8

9. Solomon, who had 700 wives and 300 concubines   1 Kings 11:3

10. Ahab, wicked Israelite northern king and husband of Jezebel and several other wives   1 Kings 20:7

11. Rehoboam, Solomon's son who had 18 wives and 60 concubines   2 Chron. 11:21

12. Abijah, king of Judah who had 14 wives   2 Chron. 13:21

13. Joash, king of Judah who had two wives   2 Chron. 24:1-3

PRAYERS

Petition

1. For an heir
   a. Prayer of Abraham   Gen. 15:2-3
   b. Prayer of Isaac   Gen. 25:21-23
   c. Prayer of Hannah   1 Sam. 1:9-13
   d. Prayer of Zacharias   Luke 1:13

2. For a city
   a. Abraham's prayer for Sodom   Gen. 18:23-33
   b. Hezekiah's prayer for Jerusalem   2 Kings 19:14-19
   c. The citizens' prayer for Nineveh   Jon. 3

3. The prayer of Abraham's servant for a bride for Isaac   Gen. 24:12-14

4. For deliverance from danger
   a. Jacob's prayer that God would save him from Esau   Gen. 32:9-12
   b. David's prayer that God would save him from Saul   Pss. 31, 57, 142

   c. The sailors' prayer that God would   Jon. 1:14
      spare their lives

   d. The disciples' prayer that Jesus   Matt. 8:24-25
      would save them from drowning

   e. Peter's prayer that Jesus would save   Matt. 14:28-31
      him from drowning

   f. The Jerusalem church's prayer that   Acts 12:5
      God would deliver Peter from
      prison

5. Moses' prayer for plagues on the   Exod. 8–12
   Egyptians

6. For waters to part

   a. Moses' prayer for the Red Sea to   Exod. 14:21
      part its waters

   b. Joshua's prayer for the Jordan   Josh. 4:15-18
      River to part its waters

7. Moses' prayer for a glimpse of God's   Exod. 33:18
   glory

8. Moses' prayer for a new leader   Num. 27:15-17

9. The apostles' prayer for someone to   Acts 1:24-25
   take Judas Iscariot's place

10. Moses' prayer for a visit to Canaan   Deut. 3:23-25

11. Moses' prayer for Aaron after his sin   Deut. 9:20
    in making the gold calf

12. Joshua's prayer for extended daylight   Josh. 10:12

13. Gideon's prayer for a sign   Judg. 6:36-40

14. Samson's prayer for strength   Judg. 16:28-31

15. For forgiveness

   a. David's prayer to be forgiven for   2 Sam. 24:10
      numbering the people

   b. David's prayer to be forgiven for   Ps. 32, 51
      his immorality with Bathsheba

   c. Manasseh's prayer to be forgiven   2 Chron. 33:11-13
      and reinstated as king

   d. Job's prayer to be forgiven for   Job 40:3-4; 42:6
      pride

e. The Prodigal Son's prayer to be forgiven for backsliding — Luke 15:17-19

16. Solomon's prayer for wisdom — 1 Kings 3:5-9
17. For rain
    a. Elijah's prayer for rain — 1 Kings 18:42-43
    b. Joel's prayer for rain — Joel 1:19-20
18. For fire
    a. David's prayer for fire — 1 Chron. 21:26
    b. Elijah's prayer for fire — 1 Kings 18:36-37
19. Elisha's prayer for spiritual vision for his servant — 2 Kings 6:17
20. Hezekiah's prayer for a lengthened life — 2 Kings 20:1-3
21. Jabez's prayer for prosperity in his work — 1 Chron. 4:10
22. For false friends
    a. Job's prayer — Job 42:7-10
    b. Paul's prayer — 2 Tim. 4:16
23. David's prayer for personal guidance in war matters — 1 Sam. 17:45; 30:8; 2 Sam. 2:1; 5:19
24. Prayer by Daniel and his three friends for interpretation of a dream — Dan. 2:18
25. For new birth information — Acts 10:1-6
26. The rich man's prayer for relief in hell — Luke 16:22-31
27. The disciples' prayer for boldness in witnessing — Acts 4:24-30
28. Stephen's prayer for his murderers — Acts 7:59-60
29. For the ministry of the Holy Spirit
    a. The disciples' prayer for the Holy Spirit to come upon the Samaritans — Acts 8:14-15
    b. Peter's prayer for the Holy Spirit to come upon the Greeks — Acts 11:5
    c. Paul's prayer for the Holy Spirit to come upon the Ephesians — Acts 19:6
30. Paul's prayer at his conversion — Acts 9:5-6

31. Prayer by Antioch elders for outgoing missionaries Paul and Silas — Acts 13:3

32. Paul's prayer for a prosperous journey — Rom. 1:9-11

33. Paul's prayer for the removal of a handicap — 2 Cor. 12:7-10

34. Martyred souls' prayer for justice to be meted out — Rev. 6:10

35. Paul's prayer for a successful ministry for Timothy — 2 Tim. 1:3-6

36. Prayer by wicked men for rocks and mountains to fall upon them — Rev. 6:16-17

37. John's prayer for Jesus' return — Rev. 22:20

38. For healing
   a. Abraham's prayer for Abimelech — Gen. 20:17-18
   b. David's prayer for his sick child — 2 Sam. 12:16
   c. A man of God's prayer for Jeroboam — 1 Kings 13:6
   d. A leper's prayer for himself — Matt. 8:2
   e. A centurion's prayer for his servant — Matt. 8:5-9
   f. A maniac's prayer for himself — Mark 5:6
   g. Jairus's prayer for his daughter — Matt. 9:18
   h. A diseased woman's prayer for herself — Matt. 9:20-21
   i. Two blind men's prayer for themselves — Matt. 9:27
   j. A Canaanite mother's prayer for her daughter — Matt. 15:21-28
   k. A father's prayer for his son — Matt. 17:14-16
   l. Bartimaeus's prayer for himself — Mark 10:46-47
   m. A deaf and dumb man's prayer for himself — Mark 7:32-34
   n. Ten lepers' prayer for themselves — Luke 17:12-16
   o. A nobleman's prayer for his son — John 4:46-50
   p. Mary and Martha's prayer for their sick brother — John 11:30

q. Paul's prayer for Publius's father-in-law — Acts 28:8

39. For resurrection
    a. Elijah's prayer for a dead son — 1 Kings 17:20-21
    b. Elisha's prayer for a dead son — 2 Kings 4:33-35
    c. Peter's prayer for Dorcas — Acts 9:36-43

40. For the welfare of Israel
    a. Jacob's prayer that God would bless the twelve tribes — Gen. 48–49
    b. Israel's prayer that God would deliver them from Egypt — Exod. 2:23
    c. Moses' prayer that God would spare them — Exod. 32:31-32; Num. 11:1-2; 21:7-9
    d. Moses' prayer that God would protect them — Num. 10:35-36
    e. Israel's prayer that God would lead them — Judg. 1:1

41. For the forgiveness of Israel
    a. Israel's prayer for themselves — Judg. 10:10
    b. Moses' prayer — Num. 14:13-19
    c. David's prayer — Ps. 85
    d. Jeremiah's prayer — Jer. 14:20-22
    e. Daniel's prayer — Dan. 9
    f. Ezra's prayer — Ezra 9:5; 10:4
    g. Nehemiah's prayer — Neh. 1:4-11
    h. Habakkuk's prayer — Hab. 3

42. For sanctifying Israel's tabernacle — 1 Kings 8:22-54

43. For the salvation of Israel — Rom. 10:1

44. For the welfare of the church
    a. Paul's prayer for Rome — Rom. 1:8-10
    b. Paul's prayer for Ephesus — Eph. 1:15-20; 3:13-21
    c. Paul's prayer for Philippi — Phil. 1:2-7
    d. Paul's prayer for Colosse — Col. 1:1-14

e. Paul's prayer for Thessalonica	1 Thess. 1:2-3; 3:9-13; 2 Thess. 1:3, 11-12; 2:13, 16-17
f. The prayer for Jerusalem	Heb. 13:20-21
g. Peter's prayer for Pontus, Galatia, Cappadocia, Asia, Bithynia	1 Pet. 5:10-11

Praise and Thanksgiving

1. Israel's praise for the Red Sea deliverance	Exod. 15
2. Hannah's praise for the birth of Samuel	1 Sam. 2:1-10
3. David's praise for God's goodness	Pss. 100, 103, 106–107
4. David's praise for God's word	Ps. 119
5. Ezra's praise for deliverance from Babylon	Ezra 7:27
6. Mary's praise for being chosen to give birth to the Messiah	Luke 1:46-55
7. The angels' praise for the birth of Jesus	Luke 2:13-14
8. Simeon and Anna's praise for the child Jesus	Luke 2:25-38
9. Paul's praise for God's wisdom	Rom. 11:33-36
10. Paul and Silas's praise for being allowed to suffer for God	Acts 5:41; 16:25
11. The hosts of heaven thanking God for his wonderful redemption	Rev. 5:8-14; 7:9-12
12. The elders thanking God for finally taking matters in hand	Rev. 11:16-18
13. Crowds in heaven thanking God for judging the great harlot	Rev. 19:1-10

Complaint

1. Moses' complaint about returning to Egypt	Exod. 3–5

2. Moses' complaint about leading Israel into Canaan   Num. 11:11-15

3. Joshua's complaint that Israel had just suffered defeat at the hands of Ai   Josh. 7:6-9

4. Elijah's complaint that Jezebel was trying to kill him   1 Kings 19:4

5. Job's complaint that he was suffering terribly   Job 3:3-12; 10:18-22

6. Jeremiah's complaint that God had deceived him   Jer. 4:10; 20:7-13

7. Jonah's complaint that God had spared Nineveh   Jon. 4

8. Habakkuk's complaint that he could not understand the affliction of the godly and the apparent prosperity of the wicked   Hab. 1

9. David's complaint about his persecution by Saul   Pss. 42; 43; 102:1-11

10 Elements in the Lord's Prayer

1. A personal relationship with God—"Our Father"
2. Faith—"which art in heaven"
3. Worship—"hallowed be thy name"
4. Expectation—"thy kingdom come"
5. Submission—"thy will be done in earth, as it is in heaven"
6. Petition—"give us this day our daily bread"
7. Confession—"and forgive us our debts"
8. Compassion—"as we forgive our debtors"
9. Dependence—"and lead us not into temptation, but deliver us from evil"
10. Acknowledgment—"for thine is the kingdom, and the power, and the glory forever"

PRAYING
See also The Christian Life, Commands to Believers
---

17 Reasons for Prayer

1. God's repeated command to do so	1 Sam. 12:23; Rom. 12:12; Col. 4:2: 1 Thess. 5:17; 1 Tim. 2:8
2. The example of Christ	Heb. 5:7
3. The example of the early church	Acts 1:14; 2:42; 6:4; 12:5
4. The example of Paul	Acts 9:10-11; 16:25; 20:36; 21:5; Rom. 10:1
5. Prayer defeats the Devil.	Luke 22:32; 1 Pet. 4:7
6. Prayer saves the sinner.	Luke 18:13
7. Prayer restores the backslider.	James 5:16
8. Prayer strengthens the saint.	Jude 20
9. Prayer sends forth laborers.	Matt. 9:38; Acts 13:2-3
10. Prayer heals the sick.	James 5:13-15
11. Prayer glorifies God's name.	Rev. 5:8; 8:2-4
12. Prayer accomplishes the impossible.	Matt. 21:22; Mark 9:29; Acts 12:5-7; James 5:17-18
13. Prayer gives good things.	Ps. 102:17; Matt. 7:7-11
14. Prayer imparts wisdom.	James 1:5
15. Prayer bestows peace.	Phil. 4:5-7
16. Prayer keeps one from sin.	Matt. 26:41
17. Prayer reveals the will of God.	Luke 11:9-10

8 Qualifications for Prayer

1. Prayer should be humble.	Ps. 10:17; Luke 18:13-14
2. Prayer should be bold.	1 John 5:13-15

3. Prayer should be in faith.	Heb. 11:6
4. Prayer should be sincere.	Ps. 145:18
5. Prayer should be simple.	Matt. 6:7
6. Prayer should be persistent.	Luke 18:7; Col. 4:2
7. Prayer should be definite.	Ps. 27:4; Acts 12:5
8. Prayer should be in accord with God's will.	1 John 5:14

11 Hindrances to Prayer

1. Unconfessed sin	Ps. 66:18
2. Insincerity	Matt. 6:5
3. Carnal motives	James 4:3
4. Unbelief	James 1:5-6
5. Satanic activity	Dan. 10:10-13
6. Domestic problems	1 Pet. 3:7
7. Pride	Luke 18:10-14
8. Robbing God	Mal. 3:8-10
9. Refusing to submit to biblical teaching	Prov. 1:24-28; 28:9; Zech. 7:11-14
10. Refusing to forgive or to be forgiven	Matt. 5:23-24; 6:12, 14
11. Refusing to help the needy	Prov. 21:3; 1 John 3:16-17

8 Things to Pray For

1. Ourselves	Gen. 24:12; Matt. 14:30; Luke 23:42
2. One another	James 5:16; Rom. 1:9
3. Pastors	Eph. 6:19-20; Col. 4:3
4. Sick believers	James 5:14-15
5. Rulers	1 Tim. 2:1-3
6. Our enemies	Matt. 5:44; Acts 7:59, 60

7. Israel   Ps. 122:6; Isa. 62:6-7

8. All men   1 Tim. 2:1

PRECIOUS METALS

1. Gold
   a. The tabernacle and temple vessels were made of gold.   Exod. 25; 1 Kings 6
   b. Part of the statue in Nebuchadnezzar's dream was gold.   Dan. 2:32
   c. Nebuchadnezzar made an entire statue of gold.   Dan. 3:1
   d. Aaron made for Israel a gold calf idol.   Exod. 32
   e. The Philistines made some gold mice.   1 Sam. 6:4
   f. Jeroboam made two gold calves.   2 Kings 10:29
   g. The wise men presented the infant Jesus with gold.   Matt. 2:11
   h. The 24 elders will wear crowns of gold.   Rev. 4:4
   i. The apparel of the ascended Christ was gold.   Dan. 10:4; Rev. 1:13; 14:14
   j. The streets of the New Jerusalem will be a transparent gold.   Rev. 21:18, 21
2. Silver
   a. Abraham purchased the cave of Machpelah for 400 pieces of silver.   Gen. 23:15
   b. Joseph was sold for 20 pieces of silver.   Gen. 37:28
   c. Moses made two silver trumpets.   Num. 10:2

d. Delilah betrayed Samson for 1,100 pieces of silver. — Judg. 16:5

e. David purchased a threshing floor for 50 shekels of silver. — 2 Sam. 24:24

f. Achan stole 200 shekels of silver. — Josh. 7:21

g. Haman offered King Ahasuerus 10,000 talents of silver to destroy the Jews. — Esther 3:9

h. Hosea bought his wife out of slavery for 15 pieces of silver. — Hos. 3:2

i. Part of the statue in Nebuchadnezzar's dream was silver. — Dan. 2:32

j. Jesus was sold out by Judas for 30 pieces of silver. — Matt. 26:15; 27:3-9

PRIESTS

Old Testament

1. Aaron, older brother of Moses and Israel's first high priest — Exod. 28; 39

2. Nadab and Abihu, wicked sons of Aaron who were slain by the Lord for offering strange fire — Lev. 10:1-2

3. Eleazar and Ithamar, godly sons of Aaron; Eleazar became Israel's second high priest — Lev. 10:6; Num. 20:26

4. Phinehas, son of Eleazar and Israel's third high priest — Num. 25:7

5. Eli, descendant of Ithamar who raised Samuel in the tabernacle — 1 Sam. 1–4

6. Hophni and Phinehas, godless sons of Eli who were slain by the Lord — 1 Sam. 2:12-36; 4:11

7. Ahimelech, head of a priestly compound at Nob, later killed by Saul for befriending David — 1 Sam. 21–22

8. Abiathar, one of Ahimelech's sons that escaped the bloodbath at Nob — 1 Sam. 22:20-23

9. Zadok, high priest in the days of David and Solomon — 2 Sam. 15; 1 Kings 1

10. Elishama and Jehoram, teaching priests in the days of Jehoshaphat — 2 Chron. 17:7-9

11. Amariah, high priest in the days of Jehoshaphat — 2 Chron. 19:11

12. Jahaziel, priest who assured Jehoshaphat he would be delivered from a terrible enemy threat — 2 Chron. 20:14-17

13. Jehoiada, high priest who saved young Joash from the purge of Queen Athaliah — 2 Kings 11–12

14. Amaziah, ungodly priest of Bethel who confronted the prophet Amos — Amos 7:10-11

15. Azariah, high priest who confronted King Uzziah when the ruler foolishly attempted to assume the work of a priest — 2 Chron. 26:16-20

16. Uriah, compromising priest who built a foreign altar for wicked King Ahaz — 2 Kings 16:10-16

17. Hilkiah, high priest who ministered in the days of King Josiah — 2 Kings 22–23

18. Pashur, false priest who persecuted the prophet Jeremiah — Jer. 20:1-6

19. Joshua, Judah's first high priest following the Babylonian captivity — Hag. 1:1; Zech. 3

20. Ezra, great scribe, teacher, and priest during the rebuilding of Jerusalem's walls — Ezra 7:11; Neh. 8

21. Eliashib, high priest during the days of Nehemiah — Neh. 3:1; 13:4-5

22. Shelemiah, priest who was in charge of the administration of storehouses in the time of Nehemiah — Neh. 13:13

New Testament

1. Zacharias, father of John the Baptist — Luke 1:5-23, 59-64
2. Annas, the wicked former high priest during the time of Jesus — John 18:13; Acts 4:6
3. Caiaphas, son-in-law of Annas and wicked high priest — Matt. 26:3; Luke 3:2; John 11:47-53; 18:13-14
4. Ananias, president of the Sanhedrin when Paul was brought before it — Acts 23:2; Acts 24:1
5. Sceva, false Jewish priest living in Ephesus who unsuccessfully attempted to mimic Paul's ministry — Acts 19:14

PRISONERS
See also Punishments

1. Joseph, beloved son of Jacob, imprisoned in Egypt — Gen. 39:20-23
2. A butler and baker, servants of Pharaoh, imprisoned in Egypt — Gen. 40:1-3
3. Simeon, brother of Joseph, held as a hostage for awhile in Egypt — Gen. 42:24
4. Samson, strong man bound in a prison in Gaza by the Philistines — Judg. 16:21
5. Micaiah, prophet imprisoned at Samaria by King Ahab — 1 Kings 22:27
6. Hoshea, last northern king of Israel, imprisoned in Assyria by King Shalmaneser — 2 Kings 17:4
7. Hanani, prophet imprisoned at Jerusalem by King Asa — 2 Chron. 16:7-10

8. Manasseh, cruel Judean king imprisoned temporarily by the king of Assyria   2 Chron. 33

9. Jehoahaz, king of Judah who was carried off to an Egyptian prison   2 Chron. 36:4

10. Jehoiachin, king of Judah imprisoned in Babylon by Evil-merodach   2 Kings 25:27

11. Jeremiah, prophet imprisoned in Jerusalem by Kings Jehoiakim and Zedekiah   Jer. 38

12. Zedekiah, last king of Judah, imprisoned in Babylon by Nebuchadnezzar   Jer. 39:7

13. Daniel, prophet imprisoned in a lions' den in Babylon   Dan. 6: 16-17

14. John the Baptist, imprisoned by Herod Antipas near the Dead Sea   Matt. 14:3-12

15. Barabbas, a robber and murderer released by Pilate in place of Jesus   Matt. 27:16-26

16. The apostles, placed in a Jerusalem prison for preaching Christ   Acts 4:3; 5:18

17. James, the brother of John, executed by Herod Agrippa I in a Jerusalem prison for preaching Christ   Acts 12:1-2

18. Peter, placed in a Jerusalem prison by Herod Agrippa I for preaching Christ   Acts 12:4

19. Paul and Silas, beaten and put in a Philippian prison by the magistrates for preaching Christ   Acts 16:23

20. Paul, temporarily imprisoned at Jerusalem by the Romans to protect him against the Jews   Acts 22:24

21. Paul, imprisoned at Caesarea by Roman governor Festus to appease the Jews   Acts 24:26-27

22. Paul, under house arrest for two years in Rome   Acts 28:30

PROMISES TO THE BELIEVER

1.	Abundant life	John 10:10
2.	A crown of life	Rev. 2:10
3.	A heavenly home	John 14:1-3
4.	A new name	Isa. 62:1-2
5.	Answers to prayer	1 John 5:14
6.	Assurance	2 Tim. 1:12
7.	Cleansing	John 15:3
8.	Clothing	Zech. 3:4
9.	Comfort	Isa. 51:3
10.	Companionship	John 15:15
11.	Deliverance	2 Tim. 4:18
12.	Divine sonship	1 John 3:1-2
13.	Everlasting life	John 3:16
14.	Fellowship of Jesus	Matt. 18:19
15.	Fruitfulness	John 15:4-5
16.	Gifts of the Spirit	1 Cor. 12
17.	Glory after death	Matt. 13:43
18.	God's protecting care	1 Pet. 5:6-7
19.	Growth	Eph. 4:11-15
20.	Guidance	Isa. 42:16
21.	Hope	Heb. 6:18-19
22.	Inheritance	1 Pet. 1:3-4
23.	Joy	Isa. 35:10
24.	Knowledge	Jer. 24:7
25.	Liberty	Rom. 8:2
26.	Peace	John 14:27
27.	Power for service	John 14:12
28.	Renewal	Titus 3:5
29.	Rest	Heb. 4:9, 11
30.	Restoration	Isa. 57:18; 1 John 1:9

31. Resurrection — Rom. 8:11
32. Rich rewards — Matt. 10:42
33. Spiritual fullness — John 6:35
34. Spiritual healing — Hos. 6:1
35. Spiritual light — John 12:46
36. Spiritual treasures — Matt. 6:19-20
37. Strength — Phil. 4:13
38. Temporal blessings — Matt. 6:25-33
39. Understanding — Ps. 119:104
40. Victory — 1 John 5:4
41. Wisdom — James 1:5

PROPHECIES
See also The Antichrist, Heaven, Hell, Jesus Christ, Judgments from God, The Tribulation

General Prophecies

1. The eating of the forbidden fruit to bring physical and spiritual death — Gen. 2:17
   Fulfillment: Gen. 3:7-8; 5:5

2. The Flood to occur in 120 years — Gen. 6:3
   Fulfillment: Gen. 7:10

3. The Flood never to be repeated — Gen. 9:15
   Fulfillment: testimony of history

4. Canaan to be a servant to his brothers — Gen. 9:25
   Fulfillment: Josh. 9:21-23, 27; Judg. 1:28

5. The people of Shem to be especially blessed by God — Gen. 9:26
   Fulfillment: John 4:22; Rom. 3:1-2; 9:4-5

6. The people of Japheth to share in Shem's blessing — Gen. 9:27

Fulfillment: Rom. 9:30; 11:11-12, 25

7. The firstborn of all unprotected homes in Egypt to die in one night — Exod. 12:12-13

Fulfillment: Exod. 12:29-30

8. The Red Sea to part — Exod. 14:13-18

Fulfillment: Exod. 14:26-31

9. The Jordan River to part — Josh. 3:13

Fulfillment: Josh. 3:14-17

10. Jericho to fall on the seventh day — Josh. 6:1-5

Fulfillment: Josh. 6:20

Prophecies Fulfilled by Jesus

1. That he would be born of a woman — Gen. 3:15; Gal. 4:4

2. That he would be from the line of Abraham — Gen. 12:3, 7; 17:7; Rom. 9:5; Gal. 3:16

3. That he would be from the tribe of Judah — Gen. 49:10; Heb. 7:14; Rev. 5:5

4. That he would be from the house of David — 2 Sam. 7:12-13; Luke 1:31-33; Rom. 1:3

5. That he would be born of a virgin — Isa. 7:14; Matt. 1:22-23

6. That he would be given the throne of David — 2 Sam. 7:11-12; Ps. 132:11; Isa. 9:6-7; 16:5; Jer. 23:5; Luke 1:31-32

7. That this throne would be an eternal throne — Dan. 2:44; 7:14, 27; Micah 4:7; Luke 1:33

8. That he would be called Emmanuel — Isa. 7:14; Matt. 1:23

9. That he would have a forerunner — Isa. 40:3-5; Mal. 3:1; Matt. 3:1-3; Luke 1:76-78; 3:3-6

10. That he would be born in Bethlehem — Micah 5:2; Matt. 2:5-6; Luke 2:4-6

11. That he would be worshiped by wise men and presented with gifts — Ps. 72:10; Isa. 60:3, 6, 9; Matt. 2:11

12. That he would be in Egypt for a season — Num. 24:8; Hos. 11:1; Matt. 2:15

13. That his birthplace would suffer a massacre of infants — Jer. 31:15; Matt. 2:17-18

14. That he would be called a Nazarene — Isa. 11:1; Matt. 2:23

15. That he would be zealous for the Father — Pss. 69:9; 119:139; John 6:37-40

16. That he would be filled with God's Spirit — Ps. 45:7; Isa. 11:2; 61:1-2; Luke 4:18-19

17. That he would heal many — Isa. 53:4; Matt. 8:16-17

18. That he would deal gently with the Gentiles — Isa. 9:1-2; 42:1-3; Matt. 4:13-16; 12:17-21

19. That he would speak in parables — Isa. 6:9-10; Matt. 13:10-15

20. That he would be rejected by his own — Ps. 69:8; Isa. 53:3; John 1:11; 7:5

21. That he would make a triumphal entry into Jerusalem — Zech. 9:9; Matt. 21:4-5

22. That he would be praised by little children — Ps. 8:2; Matt. 21:16

23. That he would be the rejected cornerstone — Ps. 118:22-23; Matt. 21:42

24. That his miracles would not be believed — Isa. 53:1; John 12:37-38

25. That his friend would betray him for 30 pieces of silver — Ps. 41:9; 55:12-14; Zech. 11:12-13; Matt. 26:14-16, 21-25

26. That he would be a man of sorrows — Isa. 53:3; Matt. 26:37-38

27. That he would be forsaken by his disciples — Zech. 13:7; Matt. 26:31, 56

28. That he would be scourged and spat upon — Isa. 50:6; Matt. 26:67; 27:26

29. That his price money would be used to buy a potter's field — Jer. 18:1-4; 19:1-4; Zech. 11:12-13; Matt. 27:9-10

30. That he would be crucified between two thieves — Isa. 53:12; Matt. 27:38; Mark 15:27-28; Luke 22:37

31. That he would be given vinegar to drink — Ps. 69:21; Matt. 27:34, 48; John 19:28-30

32. That he would suffer the piercing of his hands and feet — Ps. 22:16; Zech. 12:10; Mark 15:25; John 19:34, 37; 20:25-27

33. That his garments would be parted and gambled for — Ps. 22:18; Luke 23:34; John 19:23-24

34. That he would be surrounded and ridiculed by his enemies — Ps. 22:7-8; Matt. 27:39-44; Mark 15:29-32

35. That he would thirst — Ps. 22:15; John 19:28

36. That he would commend his spirit to the Father — Ps. 31:5; Luke 23:46

37. That his bones would not be broken — Exod. 12:46; Num. 9:12; Ps. 34:20; John 19:33-36

38. That he would be stared at in death — Zech. 12:10; Matt. 27:36; John 19:37

39. That he would be buried with the rich — Isa. 53:9; Matt. 27:57-60

40. That he would be raised from the dead — Ps. 16:10; Matt. 28:2-7

41. That he would ascend — Ps. 24:7-10; Mark 16:19; Luke 24:51

42. That he would then become a greater high priest than Aaron — Ps. 110:4; Heb. 5:4-6, 10; 7:11-28

43. That he would be seated at God's right hand	Ps. 110:1; Matt. 22:44; Heb. 10:12-13
44. That he would become a smiting scepter	Num. 24:17; Dan. 2:44-45; Rev. 19:15
45. That he would rule the heathen	Ps. 2:8; Rev. 2:27

Prophecies Made by Jesus

1. Concerning his ascension	John 1:50-51; 7:33-34; 8:14-15
2. Concerning being forsaken by his disciples	Matt. 26:31
3. Concerning his betrayal	Matt. 17:22; 26:21-25; Mark 14:18-21; Luke 9:44; 22:21-22; John 6:70-71; 13:18-33
4. Concerning the church	Matt. 16:18-19
5. Concerning his death	Matt. 26:2; John 3:14; 8:28; 10:17-18; 12:20-26, 32
6. Concerning his death and resurrection	John 2:19-22
7. Concerning the death of Peter	John 13:36
8. Concerning the destruction of Jerusalem	Luke 19:43-44; 23:28-31
9. Concerning the end times	Matt. 24:1-42; Luke 17:26-30; 23:28-31
10. Concerning the future resurrection	John 5:28-29
11. Concerning future rewards	Matt. 19:27-30; Mark 10:28-31; Luke 18:28-30
12. Concerning the Great White Throne judgment	Matt. 7:21-23; 12:41-42; Luke 11:31-32; 12:2-3
13. Concerning meeting his disciples in Galilee after his resurrection	Matt. 26:32; Mark 14:28; 16:7

14. Concerning Pentecost	John 7:37-39
15. Concerning Peter's first denial	Luke 22:34; John 13:38
16. Concerning Peter's second denial	Matt. 26:33-35; Mark 14:29-31
17. Concerning his resurrection	Matt. 12:28-40; 16:4, 21; 17:9, 23; 20:17-19; Mark 8:31; 9:9, 31; 10:32-34; Luke 9:22; 11:29-30; 18:31-34
18. Concerning his return	John 14:2-3
19. Concerning his second coming	Matt. 16:27; 25:29-31; 26:64; Mark 8:38; Luke 9:26; 22:69
20. Concerning the setting aside of Israel	Matt. 21:43-44
21. Concerning his sufferings	Matt. 17:12; Mark 9:12; Luke 17:25
22. Concerning his transfiguration	Matt. 16:28; Luke 9:27

Prophecies Concerning Births

1. Isaac's birth	Gen. 15:4; 17:19, 21; 18:10, 14
Fulfillment: Gen. 21:1-3	
2. Jacob and Esau's births	Gen. 25:19-23
Fulfillment: Gen. 25:24-26	
3. Samson's birth	Judg. 13:2-5
Fulfillment: Judg. 13:24	
4. Samuel's birth	1 Sam. 1:17-18
Fulfillment: 1 Sam. 1:20	
5. Birth of the Shunammite woman's son	2 Kings 4:16
Fulfillment: 2 Kings 4:17	
6. John the Baptist's birth	Luke 1:13-17
Fulfillment: Luke 1:57-64	
7. Jesus' birth	Luke 1:26-33
Fulfillment: Luke 2:4-7	

Prophecies Concerning Cities

1. Tyre
   a. The coastal city to be captured by Nebuchadnezzar — Ezek. 26:7
   b. The island city to later be scrapped and made flat, like the top of a rock — Ezek. 26:4, 14; 28:1-10
   c. Both cities to become a place for the spreading of nets — Ezek. 26:14
   d. Both to have their stones and timbers thrown into the sea — Zech. 9:3-4
   e. Neither to be rebuilt — Ezek. 26:14

2. Jericho
   a. To fall on the seventh day at the hands of Joshua — Josh. 6:1-5, 20
   b. The builder's youngest son (Segub) to die when the work was completed — 1 Kings 16:34

3. Nineveh
   a. The city to be totally destroyed — Nah. 1:3, 6
   b. This destruction to be effected (in part) by a mighty overflowing of the Tigris River — Nah. 1:8
   c. The attackers of the city to wear red — Nah. 2:3

4. Jerusalem
   a. To become God's chosen place — Deut. 12:5-6, 11; 26:2; Josh. 9:27; 10:1; 1 Kings 8:29; 11:36; 15:4; 2 Kings 21:4, 7; 2 Chron. 7:12; Ps. 78:68
   b. To be spared from invasion by Israel (ten northern tribes) and Syria — Isa. 7:1-7
   c. To be spared from invasion by the Assyrians — Isa. 37:33-35
   Fulfillment: Isa. 37:36-37

d. To be destroyed by the Babylonians — Isa. 3:8; Jer. 11:9; 26:18; Mic. 3:12

e. The temple of Solomon to suffer destruction — 1 Kings 9:7-9; Ps. 79:1; Jer. 7:11-14; 26:18; Ezek. 7:21-22; 24:21; Mic. 3:12

Fulfillment: Lam. 2:7; 2 Chron. 36:19

f. The temple vessels to be carried to Babylon and later returned to Jerusalem — Jer. 28:3

Fulfillment: 2 Kings 25:14-15; 2 Chron. 36:18; Ezra 1:7-11

g. To be rebuilt by the Jews after spending 70 years in Babylonian captivity — Isa. 44:28; Jer. 25:11-12; 29:10

Fulfillment: Ezra 1:1-4

h. To have its streets and walls rebuilt during a period of trouble — Dan. 9:25

Fulfillment: Ezra 4–5; Neh. 2:6

i. The walls to be rebuilt 483 years prior to the crucifixion of Jesus — Dan. 9:26

Fulfillment: testimony of history. From March 14, 445 B.C. [date of rebuilding of walls] until April 6 [crucifixion of Jesus] equals 483 years.

j. To be destroyed by the Romans — Luke 19:41-44

k. The temple of Herod also to be burned at this time — Matt. 24:1-2

Fulfillment: testimony of history. Accomplished by Titus in A.D. 70

l. To be trodden down by Gentiles until the Second Coming — Luke 21:24

Fulfillment: testimony of history

m. To be occupied by the Antichrist during the Tribulation — Zech. 12:2; 14:2

n. To become the worship center of the world during the Millennium — Isa. 2:2-3; Mic. 4:1

Prophecies Concerning Individuals
OLD TESTAMENT

1. Joshua and Caleb to enter Canaan after a period of 40 years — Num. 14:24, 30
Fulfillment: Josh. 3:7, 17; 14:6-12

2. Sisera to be defeated by a woman — Judg. 4:9
Fulfillment: Judg. 4:21

3. Hophni and Phinehas to die on the same day — 1 Sam. 2:34
Fulfillment: 1 Sam. 4:11

4. The priesthood to be removed from the line of Eli — 1 Sam. 2:27-36; 3:11-14
Fulfillment: 1 Kings 2:26-27

5. Saul to become Israel's first king and to save the country from the Philistines — 1 Sam. 9:15-16
Fulfillment: 1 Sam. 11, 14

6. Saul's kingdom not to continue — 1 Sam. 13:14; 15:28; 24:20
Fulfillment: 2 Sam. 3:1; 5:1-3

7. Saul to die in battle on a certain day — 1 Sam. 28:19
Fulfillment: 1 Sam. 31:1-6

8. Solomon to build the temple, not David — 1 Chron. 17:1-12
Fulfillment: 1 Kings 7:51

9. The sword not to depart from David's house because of sin — 2 Sam. 12:10-12
Fulfillment: 2 Sam. 13:28-29; 16:21-22

10. Jeroboam's dynasty to be destroyed 1 Kings 14:10-11
    Fulfillment: 1 Kings 15:27-28

11. Ahab to be victorious over the Syrians 1 Kings 20:28
    Fulfillment: 1 Kings 20:29-30

12. Ahab to die in battle for killing   1 Kings 21:19;
    Naboth   22:17
    Fulfillment: 1 Kings 22:37

13. The dogs would then lick his blood 1 Kings 21:19
    from his chariot
    Fulfillment: 1 Kings 22:38

14. Jezebel to be eaten by some wild dogs 1 Kings 21:23;
                    2 Kings 9:10
    Fulfillment: 2 Kings 9:35

15. Elisha to receive a double portion of 2 Kings 2:10
    Elijah's spirit
    Fulfillment: testimony of history. He
    performed twice the miracles of
    Elijah.

16. Naaman to recover from his leprosy 2 Kings 5:3, 8, 10
    Fulfillment: 2 Kings 5:14

17. The starving citizens of Samaria to 2 Kings 7:1
    enjoy an abundance of food in 24
    hours
    Fulfillment: 2 Kings 7:16-17

18. An arrogant aide of the king to see 2 Kings 7:2, 19
    this miracle, but not eat of the food
    Fulfillment: 2 Kings 7:17, 20

19. A Syrian king (Hazael) not to recover 2 Kings 8:10
    from his sickness
    Fulfillment: 2 Kings 8:15

20. Jehu to have four generations upon the 2 Kings 10:30
    throne of Israel
    Fulfillment: 2 Kings 15:12

21. Jehu's dynasty to then be destroyed Hos. 1:4
    Fulfillment: 2 Kings 15:8-12

22. Joash to defeat the Syrians on three occasions   2 Kings 13:18-19
    Fulfillment: 2 Kings 13:25

23. Jehoram to suffer with an intestinal disease because of his sin   2 Chron. 21:15
    Fulfillment: 2 Chron. 21:18-19

24. Amaziah to die for his idolatry   2 Chron. 25:16
    Fulfillment: 2 Chron. 25:20, 22, 27

25. Sennacherib not to invade Jerusalem   Isa. 37:33-35
    Fulfillment: Isa. 37:36-37

26. Sennacherib to fall by the sword in his own land   Isa. 37:7
    Fulfillment: Isa. 37:37-38

27. Hezekiah to be healed of a fatal disease   Isa. 38:5
    Fulfillment: Isa. 38:9

28. Jehoahaz to never return to Judah, but to die in his Egyptian captivity   Jer. 22:10-12
    Fulfillment: 2 Kings 23:33-34

29. Josiah to burn the decayed bones of Jeroboam's pagan priests upon the false altar Jeroboam had constructed   1 Kings 13:1-3
    Fulfillment: 2 Kings 23:4-6

30. Jehoiachin to be captured by Nebuchadnezzar   Jer. 22:25
    Fulfillment: 2 Kings 24:15

31. A false prophet named Hananiah to die within a year   Jer. 28:15-16
    Fulfillment: Jer. 28:17

32. Zedekiah to be captured by Nebuchadnezzar   Jer. 21:7
    Fulfillment: Jer. 52:8-9

33. Nebuchadnezzar to win over the Egyptians at Carchemish   Jer. 46
    Fulfillment: testimony of history

34. Nebuchadnezzar to invade Egypt	Jer. 43:9-13; 46:26; Ezek. 29:19-20

Fulfillment: testimony of history

35. Nebuchadnezzar to be reduced to an animal for his pride	Dan. 4:19-27

Fulfillment: Dan. 4:28-37

36. Belshazzar to have his kingdom removed from him	Dan. 5:5, 25-28

Fulfillment: Dan. 5:30

37. Cyrus to allow the Jews to go back and rebuild Jerusalem	Isa. 44:28

Fulfillment: Ezra 1:1-2

38. Alexander the Great to conquer Greece and establish a world empire	Dan. 2:32-39; 7:6; 8:5-8, 21; 11:3

Fulfillment: testimony of history

39. Alexander to defeat the Persians	Dan. 8:5-8

Fulfillment: testimony of history

40. Alexander to die suddenly and his kingdom to be divided into four parts	Dan. 8:8, 22; 11:4

Fulfillment: testimony of history

41. Antiochus Epiphanes to persecute the Jews and profane their temple	Dan. 8:11-25

Fulfillment: testimony of history

NEW TESTAMENT

1. Zacharias to be mute until the birth of his son	Luke 1:20

Fulfillment: Luke 1:57-64

2. John the Baptist to be Jesus' forerunner	Isa. 40:3-5; Mal. 3:1; Luke 1:76-77

Fulfillment: Matt. 3:1-11; Luke 3:2-6

3. Simeon to live until he had seen the Messiah	Luke 2:25-26

Fulfillment: Luke 2:28-32

4. Peter to deny Jesus   John 13:38
   Fulfillment: John 18:24-27
5. Peter to suffer martyrdom for Jesus   John 21:18-19;
                                           2 Pet. 1:12-14
   Fulfillment: testimony of history
6. Judas to give himself over to Satan   John 6:70
   Fulfillment: Luke 22:3; John 13:27
7. Judas to betray Jesus   John 6:71; 13:21
   Fulfillment: Matt. 26:47-50; Luke
   22:47-48; John 18:2-5
8. Paul
   a. To suffer much for Jesus   Acts 9:16
      Fulfillment: 2 Cor. 11:23-28; 12:7-
      10; Gal. 6:17; Phil. 1:29-30
   b. To be a minister to the Gentiles   Acts 9:15
      Fulfillment: Acts 13:46; 18:6;
      22:21; 26:17; 28:28; Rom. 11:13;
      Eph. 3:1; 1 Tim. 2:7; 2 Tim. 1:11
   c. To preach before kings   Acts 9:15
      Fulfillment: Acts 24–26
   d. To go to Rome   Acts 23:11
   Fulfillment: Acts 28:16

Prophecies Concerning Israel

1. The people of Shem to be especially   Gen. 9:26
   blessed of God
   Fulfillment: Matt. 1:1; John 4:22
2. A great nation to come from Abraham   Gen. 12:2
   Fulfillment: Num. 23:10
3. This nation to exist forever   Jer. 31:35-37
   Fulfillment: testimony of history

4. Israel's kings to come from the tribe of Judah   Gen. 49:10

Fulfillment: 1 Sam. 16:1-2; 1 Chron. 28:4; Luke 1:26-27

5. Canaan to be given to Israel forever   Gen. 13:15

Partial fulfillment: Josh. 21:43-45

Future fulfillment: Isa. 60:21; Ezek. 37:25

6. Israel to sojourn in another land (Egypt) for 400 years, there to serve and be afflicted   Gen. 15:13

Fulfillment: Exod. 12:40

7. This oppressive nation (Egypt) to be judged by God   Gen. 15:14

Fulfillment: Exod. 7:14–12:29

8. Israel to leave Egypt with great substance   Gen. 15:14

Fulfillment: Exod. 12:35-36

9. Israel to return to Canaan from Egypt in the fourth generation   Gen. 15:16

Fulfillment: Josh. 3:16-17

10. Israel to conquer Canaan gradually   Exod. 23:29-30

Fulfillment: Judg. 1:19-36

11. Those (over 20) who sinned at Kadesh-barnea would not see the Promised Land, but wander 40 years in the wilderness   Num. 14:32-34

Fulfillment: Num. 26:63-65

12. Israel to set a king over them   Deut. 17:14-20

Fulfillment: 1 Sam. 10:24

13. Israel to suffer a tragic civil war after the death of Solomon   1 Kings 11:11, 31

Fulfillment: 1 Kings 12:16-17, 19-20

14. The northern kingdom to be carried away into Assyrian captivity   1 Kings 14:15-16; Hos. 1:5; 10:1, 6

Fulfillment: 2 Kings 17:6-7, 22-23

15. This would happen 65 years after the Isaiah and Ahaz meeting

    Isa. 7:8

    Fulfillment: 2 Kings 17:24

16. The southern kingdom to be carried away into Babylonian captivity

    Jer. 13:19; 20:4-5; 21:10; Mic. 4:10

    Fulfillment: 2 Kings 24–25

17. The temple to be destroyed

    1 Kings 9:7; 2 Chron. 7:20-21; Jer. 7:14

    Fulfillment: 2 Kings 25:9

18. The length of the Babylonian captivity would be 70 years

    Jer. 25:11; 29:10

    Fulfillment: Dan. 9:2

19. Israel to then return to the land

    Jer. 29:10

    Fulfillment: Ezra 1

20. The temple vessels once carried into Babylon to be brought back to the land

    2 Kings 25:14-15; Jer. 28:3; Dan. 5:1-4

    Fulfillment: Ezra 1:7-11

21. Israel eventually to be scattered among the nations of the world

    Lev. 26:33; Deut. 4:27-28; 28:25-68; Hos. 9:17

22. Israel to "abide many days" without a king, an heir apparent, the Levitical offerings, the temple, or the Levitical priesthood

    Hos. 3:4

    Fulfillment: testimony of history

23. Israel also to be free from idolatry during this terrible time

    Hos. 3:4

    Fulfillment: testimony of history

24. Israel to become a byword among the nations

    Deut. 28:37

    Fulfillment: testimony of history

25. Israel to loan to many nations, but borrow from none

    Deut. 28:12

    Fulfillment: testimony of history

26. Israel to be hounded and persecuted   Deut. 28:65-67
    Fulfillment: testimony of history

27. Israel nevertheless to retain her identity   Lev. 26:44; Jer. 46:28
    Fulfillment: testimony of history

28. Israel to remain alone and aloof among the nations   Num. 23:9
    Fulfillment: testimony of history

29. Israel to reject her Messiah   Isa. 53:1-9
    Fulfillment: Luke 23:13-25

30. Israel to return to Palestine in the latter days prior to the Second Coming of Jesus   Deut. 30:3; Ezek. 36:24; 37:1-14
    Fulfillment: testimony of history since 1948

Prophecies Concerning Nations

1. Egypt
   a. To experience seven years of plenty and seven years of famine   Gen. 41:1-7, 17-24; 45:6, 11
      Fulfillment: Gen. 41:47-48, 53-57; 47:13, 20
   b. To host Israel for 400 years and afflict them   Gen. 15:13
      Fulfillment: Exod. 12:40; Acts 7:6
   c. To be judged for this by the ten plagues   Gen. 15:14; Exod. 3:20; 6:1; 7:5
      Fulfillment: Exod. 7:14; 12:29
   d. To pursue Israel but fail and perish   Exod. 14:3-4
      Fulfillment: Exod. 14:5-9, 23-28, 30-31
   e. To defeat Israel at Megiddo   Jer. 2:16-17, 19, 36-37
      Fulfillment: 2 Kings 23:29-35

    f. To stumble and fall before Babylon   Jer. 46:5-6, 10-12
       at Carchemish

       Fulfillment: testimony of history

    g. To be invaded by Nebuchadnezzar   Jer. 43:7-13;
                                                     46:13-26

       Fulfillment: testimony of history

    h. To decline from its exalted position   Ezek. 29:1-2, 15
        and become a base nation

       Fulfillment: testimony of history

    i. To suffer (perhaps to be double-   Dan. 11:40-43;
      crossed) at the hand of the   Joel 3:19
      Antichrist during the Tribulation

    j. To be restored and blessed by God   Isa. 19:21-25
      along with Assyria and Israel
      during the Millennium

2. Babylon

    a. To expand under Nebuchadnezzar   Hab. 1:5-10

       Fulfillment: testimony of history

    b. To defeat the Egyptians at   Jer. 46
       Carchemish

       Fulfillment: testimony of history

    c. To defeat the Assyrians   Nahum

       Fulfillment: testimony of history

    d. To be defeated by the Medes and   Isa. 13:17; Jer.
       Persians   51:11

       Fulfillment: Dan. 5

3. Three world powers to follow Babylon   Dan. 2, 7
   (Persia, Greece, Rome)

   Fulfillment: testimony of history

4. Persia

    a. To consist of an alliance between   Dan. 8:1-4, 20
      two peoples (the Medes and
      Persians)

       Fulfillment: testimony of history

  b. To defeat the Babylonians   Dan. 2:39; 7:5
    Fulfillment: Dan. 5
  c. To be defeated by the Greeks   Dan. 8:5-8, 21-22
    Fulfillment: testimony of history

5. Greece
  a. To be invaded by Persia   Dan. 11:2
    Fulfillment: testimony of history
  b. Alexander the Great to conquer   Dan. 2:32-39; 7:6;
    Greece and establish a world   8:5-8, 21; 11:3
    empire
    Fulfillment: testimony of history
  c. To defeat the Persians   Dan. 8:5-8
    Fulfillment: testimony of history
  d. To be divided into four parts after   Dan. 8:8, 22; 11:4
    Alexander's death
    Fulfillment: testimony of history

6. Rome
  a. To defeat the Greeks   Dan. 2:40; 7:7;
                11:18-19

    Fulfillment: testimony of history
  b. To destroy Jerusalem   Matt. 23:37-39
    Fulfillment: testimony of history
  c. To be revived during the   Dan. 2:41; 7:7-8;
    Tribulation   Rev. 13:1; 17:12
  d. To be destroyed by Jesus at the   Dan. 2:34-35, 44;
    Second Coming   7:9, 14, 27

7. Russia
  a. To invade Israel during the   Ezek. 28:8-11, 16
    Tribulation
  b. To be joined by various allies   Ezek. 38:4-7
  c. To come down for a "spoil"   Ezek. 38:12
  d. To suffer a disastrous defeat at the   Ezek. 39:2
    hand of God, losing some 83
    percent of its troops

End-Time Prophecies (A Basic Overview)

1. Prophecies concerning the Rapture — 1 Cor. 15:51-53; 1 Thess. 4:14-18; Heb. 9:24-28; Rev. 4:1

2. Prophecies concerning the judgment seat of Christ — Rom. 14:10; 1 Cor. 3:9-15; 2 Cor. 5:10

3. Prophecies concerning a seven-sealed book — Rev. 5–11

4. Prophecies concerning the marriage service of the Lamb — Matt. 22:2; 25:1; Luke 12:35-36; John 3:27-30; 2 Cor. 11:2; Eph. 5:22-32; Jude 24

5. Prophecies concerning the Second Coming — Zech. 14:4, 8; Matt. 24:29-30; 2 Thess. 1:7; Rev. 1:7; 11:15; 19:11-16

6. Prophecies concerning the binding of Satan — Rom. 16:20; Rev. 20:1-3

7. Prophecies concerning the resurrection of Old Testament and tribulational saints — Job 19:25-26; Ps. 49:15; Isa. 25:8; 26:19; Dan. 12:2; Hos. 13:14; John 5:28-29; Heb. 11:35; Rev. 20:4-5

8. Prophecies concerning the judgment of Israel — Matt. 25:1-30

9. Prophecies concerning the judgment of Gentiles — Matt. 25:31-46

10. Prophecies concerning the final revolt and defeat of Satan — Rev. 20:7-10

11. Prophecies concerning the judgment of fallen angels — Matt. 8:28-29; Mark 1:23, 24; 1 Cor. 6:3; 2 Pet. 2:4; Jude 6

12. Prophecies concerning the Great White Throne judgment — Ps. 9:17; Eccles. 12:14; Dan. 7:9-10; Matt. 12:36, 37; Heb. 9:27; Rev. 20:11-15

13. Prophecies concerning the destruction of this present earth and heaven — Matt. 24:35; Heb. 1:10-12; 2 Pet. 3:3-12

14. Prophecies concerning the creation of a new heaven and earth — Isa. 65:17; 66:22; 2 Pet. 3:13-14; Rev. 21:1

Prophecies Concerning the Last Days

1. Increase of wars and rumors of war — Joel 3:9-10; Matt. 24:6-7

2. Extreme materialism — 2 Tim. 3:1-2; Rev. 3:14-19

3. Lawlessness — Ps. 78:8; Prov. 30:11-14; 2 Tim. 3:2-3

4. Population explosion — Gen. 6:1

5. Increase in speed and knowledge — Dan. 12:4

6. Departure from the Christian faith — 2 Thess. 2:3; 1 Tim. 4:1, 3-4; 2 Tim. 3:5; 4:3-4; 2 Pet. 3:3-4

7. Intense demonic activity — Gen. 6:1-4; 1 Tim. 4:1-3

8. Unification of the world's religious, political, and economic systems — Rev. 13:4-8, 16-17; 17:1-18; 18:1-24

9. The absence of gifted leadership among the nations, thus making it easy for the Antichrist to take over

10. Universal drug usage (The word "sorceries" here can also refer to drugs.) — Rev. 9:21

11. Abnormal sexual activity — Rom. 1:17-32; 2 Pet. 2:10, 14; 3:3; Jude 18

12. Mass slaughter of innocents by unconcerned mothers (abortion) — Rom. 1:31; 2 Tim. 3:3

13. Widespread violence — Gen. 6:11, 13; Rev. 9:21

14. Rejection of God's Word	2 Tim. 4:3-4; 2 Pet. 3:3-4, 16
15. Rejection of God himself	Ps. 2:1-3
16. Blasphemy	2 Tim. 3:2; 2 Pet. 3:3; Jude 18
17. Self-seeking and pleasure-seeking	2 Tim. 3:2, 4
18. Men minus a conscience	1 Tim. 4:2
19. Religious hucksters	2 Pet. 2:3
20. Outright devil worshipers	Rev. 9:20; 13:11-14
21. Rise of false prophets and Antichrists	Matt. 24:5, 11; 2 Pet. 2:1-2
22. False claims of peace	1 Thess. 5:1-3
23. Rapid advances in technology	Gen. 4:22
24. Great political and religious upheavals in the Holy Land	Matt. 24:32-34

Prophecies Concerning the Nature of the Tribulation

1. Unbelievably bloody wars	Matt. 24:6-7; Rev. 6:2-4; 14:20
2. Drunkenness	Matt. 24:38; Luke 17:27
3. Illicit sex	Matt. 24:38; Luke 17:27; Rev. 9:21
4. Gross materialism	Luke 17:28; Rev. 18:12-14
5. Rise of false messiahs and prophets	Matt. 24:5, 11-24
6. Horrible persecution of believers	Matt. 24:10; Rev. 16:6; 17:6
7. Men to hide in the caves of the rocks in fear of God	Isa. 2:19-21; Rev. 6:15-17
8. The pangs and sorrows of death to seize men, similar to those of women in labor	Isa. 13:8; Jer. 30:6
9. Terrible worldwide famines	Rev. 6:5-6, 8
10. Humans to be slaughtered by predatory wild beasts	Rev. 6:8

11. Disastrous earthquakes	Rev. 6:12; 11:13; 16:18
12. Fearful heavenly signs and disturbances	Luke 21:25; Rev. 6:12-14; 8:12
13. Universal tidal waves and ocean disasters	Luke 21:25; Rev. 8:8-9; 16:3
14. The stars, moon, and sun to be darkened	Isa. 13:10; Joel 2:30-31; 3:15
15. The moon to be turned into blood	Joel 2:31; Rev. 6:12
16. The heavens to be rolled together like a scroll	Isa. 34:4; Joel 2:10; Rev. 6:14
17. Massive hailstones composed of fire and blood to fall upon the earth	Rev. 8:7; 16:21
18. Huge meteorites to fall upon the earth	Rev. 8:8-11
19. Stars of the heavens to fall upon the earth	Rev. 6:13
20. Both salt waters and fresh waters to become totally polluted	Rev. 8:8-11; 11:6; 16:3-4
21. Universal disaster of land ecology	Rev. 8:7
22. Events to steadily go from bad to worse	Amos 5:19
23. A time of thick darkness and utter depression	Joel 2:2
24. No period in history to even compare to it	Jer. 30:7; Dan. 12:1; Matt. 24:21-22
25. A time of famine of the very word of God itself	Amos 8:11-12
26. A time of absolutely no escape from God's fierce judgment	Amos 9:2-3
27. Worldwide drug usage	Rev. 9:21
28. Universal idolatry and devil worship	Rev. 9:20; 13:11-17
29. Murderous demonic invasions	Rev. 9:3-20
30. Subterranean eruptions	Rev. 9:1-2
31. Scorching solar heat	Rev. 16:8-9

32. Terrifying periods of total darkness	Rev. 16:10
33. Unchecked citywide fires	Rev. 18:8-9, 18
34. A plague of cancerous sores	Rev. 16:2
35. The total destruction of the earth's religious, political, and economic systems	Rev. 17–18
36. A universal dictatorial rule by the Antichrist	Rev. 13
37. An all-out, no-holds-barred attempt to destroy Israel	Rev. 12:1-17
38. Survivors of this period to be more rare than gold	Isa. 13:12
39. Men's blood to be poured out like dust and their flesh like dung	Zeph. 1:17
40. The slain to remain unburied and the mountains to be covered with their blood	Isa. 34:3; 66:24
41. The earth to be removed out of its orbit	Isa. 13:13
42. The earth to be turned upside down	Isa. 24:1, 19
43. The earth to reel to and fro like a drunkard	Isa. 24:20
44. The most frightful physical plague in all history	Zech. 14:12
45. A 200-mile river of human blood to flow	Rev. 14:20
46. Scavenger birds to eat the rotted flesh of entire armies of men	Matt. 24:28; Rev. 19:17-19

Prophecies Concerning the Events Occurring with the Tribulation

1. Formal organization of the harlot church	1 Tim. 4:1-3; 2 Tim. 3:1-5; Rev. 17
2. Appearance of the Antichrist and his false prophet	Rev. 13
3. Revival of the Roman Empire	Dan. 2:41; 7:7; Rev. 13:1; 17:12

4. The Antichrist's seven-year covenant with Israel — Isa. 28:18; Dan. 9:27

5. Pouring out of the first six seals — Matt. 24:4-8; Rev. 6:1-17

6. Mass return of the Jews to Palestine — Isa. 43:5-6; Ezek. 34:11-13; 36:24; 37:1-14

7. Conversion and call of the 144,000 — Matt. 24:14; Rev. 7:1-4

8. Abomination of desolation — Dan. 9:27; 12:11; Matt. 24:15; 2 Thess. 2:4; Rev. 11:2

9. Ministry of the two witnesses — Rev. 11:3-13

10. The Gog and Magog invasion of Palestine — Ezek. 38–39

11. The martyrdom of the two witnesses — Rev. 11:7

12. The martyrdom of the 144,000 — Rev. 14:1-5

13. The casting out of Satan from heaven — Rev. 12:3-15

14. The destruction of the false church — Rev. 17:16

15. The full manifestation of the Antichrist — Rev. 13:16-18

16. The worldwide persecution of Israel — Dan. 12:1; Zech. 11:16; Matt. 24:21; Rev. 12:13

17. The pouring out of the last seal judgment — Rev. 8–9; 11:15-19

18. The messages of three special angels — Rev. 14:6-12

19. The pouring out of the seven vials of judgment — Rev. 16

20. The sudden destruction of economic and political Babylon — Rev. 18

21. The battle of Armageddon — Ps. 2:1-5, 9; Isa. 34:1-6; 63:3-4, 6; Joel 3:2, 9-16; Zech. 12:2; 14:2-3, 12; Rev. 14:14-20; 16:16; 19:11-21

Millennial Prophecies

1. The temple to be rebuilt	Isa. 2:2; Ezek. 40-48; Joel 3:18; Hag. 2:7-9; Zech. 6:12-13
2. Israel to be regathered	Isa. 43:5-6; Jer. 24:6; 29:14; 31:8-10; Ezek. 11:17; 36:24-25, 28; Amos 9:14-15; Zech. 8:6-8; Matt. 24:31
3. Israel to recognize her Messiah	Isa. 8:17; 25:9; 26:8; Zech. 12:10-12; Rev. 1:7
4. Israel to be cleansed	Jer. 33:8; Zech. 13:1
5. Israel to be regenerated	Jer. 31:31-34; 32:39; Ezek. 11:19-20; 36:26
6. Israel to once again be related to God by marriage	Isa. 54:1-17; 62:2-5; Hos. 2:14-23
7. Israel to be exalted above the Gentiles	Isa. 14:1-2; 49:22-23; 60:14-17; 61:6-7
8. Israel to become God's witnesses	Isa. 44:8; 61:6; 66:21; Ezek. 3:17; Mic. 5:7; Zeph. 3:20; Zech. 8:3
9. Jesus to rule from Jerusalem with a rod of iron	Ps. 2:6-8, 11; Isa. 2:3; 11:4
10. David to aid in this rule as viceregent	Isa. 55:3-4; Jer. 30:9; Ezek. 34:23; 37:24; Hos. 3:5
11. All sickness to be removed	Isa. 33:24; Jer. 30:17; Ezek. 34:16
12. The original curse upon creation to be removed (see Gen. 3:17-19)	Isa. 11:6-9; 35:9; 65:25; Joel 3:18; Amos 9:13-15
13. The wolf, lamb, calf, and lion to lie down together in peace	Isa. 11:6-7; 65:25

14. A little child to safely play with once poisonous serpents and spiders — Isa. 11:8

15. Physical death to be swallowed up in victory — Isa. 25:8

16. All tears to be dried — Isa. 25:8; 30:19

17. The deaf to hear, the blind to see, and the lame to walk — Isa. 29:18; 35:5-6; 61:1-2; Jer. 31:8

18. Man's knowledge about God to be vastly increased — Isa. 41:19-20; 54:13; Hab. 2:14

19. No social, political or religious oppression — Isa. 14:3-6; 49:8-9; Zech. 9:11-12

20. Full ministry of the Holy Spirit — Isa. 32:15; 45:3; 59:21; Ezek. 36:27; 37:14; Joel 2:28-29

21. Jesus himself to be the Good, Great, and Chief Shepherd — Isa. 40:11; 49:10; 58:11; Ezek. 34:11-16

22. A time of universal singing — Isa. 35:6; 52:9; 54:1; 55:12; Jer. 33:11

23. A time of universal praying — Isa. 56:7; 65:24; Zech. 8:22

24. A unified language — Zeph. 3:9

25. The wilderness and deserts to bloom — Isa. 35:1-2

26. God's glory to be seen by all nations — Isa. 60:1-3; Ezek. 39:21; Mic. 4:1-5; Hab. 2:14

27. Longevity of man to be restored — Isa. 65:20

28. Universal peace — Isa. 2:4; 32:18

29. Universal holiness — Zech. 13:20-21

30. Solar and lunar light to increase — Isa. 4:5; 30:26; 60:19-20; Zech. 2:5

31. Palestine to become greatly enlarged and changed — Isa. 26:15; Obad. 17-21

32. A river to flow east-west from the Mount of Olives into both the Mediterranean and Dead Seas — Ezek. 47:8-9, 12; Joel 3:18; Zech. 14:4, 8, 10

33. Jerusalem to become known as Jehovah Isidkenu (the Lord our righteousness), and Jehovah Shammah (the Lord is there) — Jer. 33:16; Ezek. 48:35

34. Jerusalem to become the worship center of the world — Isa. 2:2-3; Mic. 4:1

35. Jerusalem's streets to be filled with happy boys and girls playing — Zech. 8:5

36. The city to occupy an elevated site — Zech. 14:10

37. The earthly city to be six miles in circumference — Ezek. 48:35

38. The heavenly, suspended city (New Jerusalem) to be 1,500 by 1,500 by 1,500 miles — Rev. 21:10, 16

PROPHETS AND PROPHETESSES

Old Testament

1. Enoch, who prophesied before the Flood on the theme of judgment — Jude 14-15

2. Noah, who predicted the destiny of his three sons' descendants — Gen. 9:24-27

3. Jacob, who predicted the future of his twelve sons' descendants — Gen. 48–49

4. An unnamed prophet, who explained to Israel the reason for their sufferings — Judg. 6:7-10

5. An unnamed prophet, who predicted the death of Hophni and Phinehas, Eli's two wicked sons — 1 Sam. 2:27-36

6. Gad, who predicted the nature of judgment that would fall upon David for the king's sin in numbering the people — 1 Sam. 22:5; 2 Sam. 24:11-19

7. Nathan, court prophet who took David to task for his sin of adultery and murder — 2 Sam. 7, 12; 1 Kings 1

8. Ahijah, who predicted that Jeroboam would rule over ten of the tribes after Israel's civil war — 1 Kings 11:29

9. An unnamed prophet, who predicted the name and reforms of King Josiah 315 years before he was even born — 1 Kings 13:1-24

10. Iddo, who prophesied against King Jeroboam — 2 Chron. 9:29

11. Shemiah, who warned King Rehoboam against a war with Jeroboam — 1 Kings 12:22

12. Oded I, who prophesied God's favor upon King Asa if he would honor and obey the word of the Lord — 2 Chron. 15:8

13. Azariah, who prophesied to King Asa as did his father Oded — 2 Chron. 15:1-2

14. Hanani, thrown in prison by Asa for rebuking the king's sin — 2 Chron. 16:7-10

15. Jehu, who rebuked King Baasha and King Jehoshaphat — 1 Kings 16:1-12; 2 Chron. 19:1-3

16. An unnamed prophet, who predicted God would deliver the Syrians into the hands of Ahab — 1 Kings 20:13-42

17. Micaiah, who predicted wicked king Ahab would not return alive from a battle — 1 Kings 22:8-28

18. Elijah, the great prophet who opposed Baal worship in the time of Ahab and Jezebel — 1 Kings 17— 2 Kings 2

19. Elisha, the successor to Elijah who performed many miracles and who predicted the healing of Naaman and the salvation of Samaria — 2 Kings 2–13

20. An unnamed prophet, who told King Amaziah he need not depend upon some northern hired troops to help him deport the Edomites — 2 Chron. 25:7-16

21. Zechariah, who ministered to King Uzziah — 2 Chron. 26:5

22. Uriah, who prophesied against the sins of Judah and was martyred by wicked King Jehoiakim — Jer. 26:20

23. Oded II, who prophesied in the days of King Ahaz — 2 Chron. 28:9-11

Note: This list includes only the non-writing prophets of the Old Testament.

New Testament

1. Zacharias, who predicted the ministry of his son John the Baptist — Luke 1:67-69

2. Simeon, who predicted the future ministry of Christ — Luke 2:25-35

3. John the Baptist, who predicted the ministry of Christ and final judgment — Matt. 11:9; Luke 1:57-80

4. Agabus, who predicted a famine and the imprisonment of Paul — Acts 11:28; 21:10

5. Judas and Silas, who exhorted believers in the days of the Jerusalem council — Acts 15:22

6. Two tribulational prophets, who will prophecy against the coming Antichrist — Rev. 11:3-12

Prophetesses

1. Miriam, Moses' older sister and Scripture's first recorded prophetess — Exod. 15:20

2. Deborah, who predicted the victory of Barak over the Canaanites — Judg. 4:4-9

3. Isaiah's wife, who bore Isaiah two sons whose names in themselves were prophetical of coming judgment — Isa. 8:3

4. Huldah, who predicted the prosperous reign of King Josiah — 2 Chron. 34:22-28

5. Anna, the 84-year-old widow who was present at the dedication of the infant Jesus in the temple — Luke 2:36-38

6. Philip's four daughters, who Paul met in Caesarea during his third missionary journey — Acts 21:8-9

False Prophets

1. Balaam, hired by the king of Moab to curse Israel — Num. 22–24

2. The old prophet from Bethel, whose lying words to another prophet cost the young man his life — 1 Kings 13:11-14

3. Zedekiah, who wrongly predicted victory for Ahab in his battle with the Syrians — 1 Kings 22:11-24

4. Hananiah, who attempted to refute Jeremiah's 70-year prophecy, saying the Babylonian captivity would last but 2 years — Jer. 28:1-17

5. Shemaiah, whose seed Jeremiah predicted would be wiped out — Jer. 29:24-32

6. Ahab, a lying prophet whose death Jeremiah predicted — Jer. 29:21

7. Zedekiah, whose death was also predicted by Jeremiah — Jer. 29:21

8. Noadiah, a false prophetess in the time of Nehemiah — Neh. 6:14

9. Elymas, a sorcerer who confronted Paul on Cyprus — Acts 13:6

10. Jezebel, a teacher of immorality in the church at Thyatira — Rev. 2:20

11. False prophet during the Tribulation, an aide to the Antichrist — Rev. 19:20

THE PSALMS IN SUBJECT CATEGORIES

1. Penitential psalms — 6, 32, 38, 51, 102, 130, 143

2. Imprecatory psalms (psalms that call down judgment upon God's enemies) — 35, 55, 58–59, 69, 83, 109, 137, 140

3. Degree or ascent psalms (psalms sung by the Jewish pilgrims as they ascended the temple mount) — 120–134

4. Hallelujah psalms (psalms sung during the Passover) — 113–118

5. Historical psalms — 78, 105–106

6. Acrostic psalms — 9–10, 25, 34, 38, 111–112, 119, 145

7. Messianic psalms (psalms that predicted the ministry of the Messiah) — 16, 22, 24, 31, 40–41, 55, 68–69, 72, 89, 109–110, 118, 129

8. "Omni" psalms (psalms describing the omniscience, omnipresence, and omnipotence of God) — 139, 147

9. Creation psalms — 8, 33

10. Psalm of the Exodus — 114

11. Ladder of faith psalm — 37

12. Psalms of Jerusalem — 44, 87, 122

13. Psalm of the Babylonian captivity — 137

14. Psalm of the release from the Babylonian captivity — 126

15. Psalm of the senior saint — 71

16. Family psalms — 127–128

17. The traveler's psalm — 121

18. House of God psalm — 84

19. Wealth of God psalm — 50

20. The word of God psalms — 19, 119

21. Providential care of God psalm — 104

22. The pursuit of God psalms — 27, 42, 63

23.	The mercy of God psalm	136
24.	The voice of God psalm	29
25.	The goodness of God psalm	107
26.	The manifestation of God psalm	18
27.	Psalms of the only true God	115, 135
28.	The evening psalm	4
29.	The morning psalm	5
30.	The security psalm	121
31.	Psalms of deliverance	31, 116
32.	The "If only" psalm	81
33.	The "How long" psalm	13
34.	Psalms of the wicked	10, 14, 58
35.	The folly of riches psalm	49
36.	The psalm of the question "Why"	73
37.	Psalm of deepest distress	88
38.	Psalm of the Good Shepherd	22
39.	Psalm of the Great Shepherd	23
40.	Psalm of the Chief Shepherd	24
41.	Psalms of supreme praise	100, 103
42.	Psalm of the godly man	1
43.	God the Father and God the Son psalm	2
44.	Psalm of death	90
45.	Psalm of life	91
46.	The unity psalm	133

PUNISHMENTS
See also Prisoners

1. Banishment	Ezra 7:26; Rev. 1:9
2. Beating	Deut. 25:1-3; 2 Cor. 11:24

3. Beheading	2 Kings 6:30-33; 2 Tim. 4:6
4. Burning	Lev. 20:14; Dan. 3:6
5. Confiscation	Ezra 7:26
6. Crucifixion	Matt. 27:31
7. Enforced labor	Judg. 16:21
8. Hanging	Gen. 40:22; Esther 7:10
9. Imprisonment	Gen. 39:20-23
10. Maiming	Deut. 25:11-22
11. Scourging	Matt. 27:26
12. Stoning	Lev. 24:14; 2 Chron. 24:21; Acts 7:59

RAISED FROM THE DEAD

1. Widow of Zarephath's son, raised by Elijah	1 Kings 17:22
2. Shunammite woman's son, raised by Elisha	2 Kings 4:34-35
3. Man raised when he came into contact with the bones of Elisha	2 Kings 13:20-21
4. Jairus's daughter, raised by Jesus	Luke 8:52-56
5. Widow of Nain's son, raised by Jesus	Luke 7:14-15
6. Lazarus of Bethany, brother of Mary and Martha, raised by Jesus	John 11
7. Dorcas, raised by Peter	Acts 9:40
8. Eutychus, raised by Paul	Acts 20:9-12

REVIVALS AND REFORMS

1. Under Jacob. On the return to Bethel, Jacob ordered his entire household to put away their false gods and to wash and change their garments. This they did as Jacob built an altar to the true God. The false gods were then buried under an oak in Shechem. — Gen. 35:1-4

2. Under Samuel. At the exhorting of Samuel the people put away their false gods and prepared their hearts to serve the only true God. — 1 Sam. 7:3-6

3. Under Moses. This occurred when complaining Israel saw the mighty hand of God in the parting of the Red Sea. On the safe (eastern) side of the sea, Moses led the people in a song of praise, while Miriam and the women furnished the special music. — Exod. 14:31–15:21

4. Under David
   a. When the Ark of the Covenant was brought into Jerusalem for the first time — 1 Chron. 15:25-28; 16:1-43; 29:10-25
   b. At the dedication of the materials to be used in building the future temple — 1 Chron. 29

5. Under Solomon. This occurred at the actual dedication of the temple. — 2 Chron. 7:1-3

6. Under Asa. He removed the Sodomites and all false idols out of the land. He even deposed his own grandmother because of her idolatry. — 1 Kings 15:11-15

7. Under Jehoshaphat. The king led a revival when he ordered the cleansing of the temple and the sanctification of the Levitical priests. — 2 Chron. 19

8. Under Elijah. This took place after the contest with the prophets of Baal on Mount Carmel.   1 Kings 18:21-40

9. Under Jehu. He exterminated all Baal worshipers and their temples.   2 Kings 10:15-28

10. Under Jehoiada. This godly high priest led the people in a covenant whereby they forsook their idols and worshiped God.   2 Kings 11:17-20

11. Under Hezekiah. Like Jehoshaphat, King Hezekiah experienced revival when he cleansed the temple of God.   2 Chron. 29–31

12. Under Manasseh. When wicked King Manasseh became converted, he led his people in a revival by ordering the destruction of all idols.   2 Chron. 33:11-20

13. Under Josiah. This revival began when the Book of the Law was accidentally discovered during a temple cleanup event. The public reading of God's Word had a profound effect upon both King Josiah and his people.   2 Kings 22–23

14. Under Ezra. Through Ezra's preaching on separation, the Jewish remnant ceased their ungodly marriage alliances with the heathen of the land.   Ezra 9–10

15. Under Nehemiah. After Nehemiah had rebuilt the walls around Jerusalem, Ezra stood by its gates and publicly read and taught from God's Word, causing a great revival.   Neh. 13

16. Under Jonah. The Ninevites, through Jonah's preaching, repented and stayed the destructive hand of God.   Jon. 3

17. Under Esther. This time of repentance and rejoicing followed the salvation of the Jews from the plot of wicked Haman.   Esther 9:17-22

18. Under John the Baptist. John preached the imminent appearance of Israel's Messiah, warning them to repent and submit to water baptism.   Luke 3:2-18

19. Under Jesus. The conversion of a sinful Samaritan woman instigated this revival in Samaria.   John 4:28-42

20. Under Philip. The strong preaching of Philip the evangelist concerning the kingdom of God produced a great revival in Samaria.   Acts 8:5-12

21. Under Peter
    a. At Pentecost, after his great sermon   Acts 2
    b. At Lydda, after he had healed Aeneas   Acts 9

22. Under Paul. One of the greatest revivals occurred in Ephesus during Paul's third missionary journey. This account should be carefully read.   Acts 19:11-20

RIVERS
See also Brooks

1. Pison, one of four rivers in the Garden of Eden   Gen. 2:11

2. Gihon, another river in Eden   Gen. 2:13

3. Hiddekel, a third river in Eden, also called Tigris   Gen. 2:14

4. Euphrates
    a. The fourth river in the Garden of Eden   Gen. 2:14
    b. Crossed by Jacob during his flight from Laban   Gen. 31:20-21

     c. Referred to by Joshua as the   Josh. 24:2-3
        dividing point in Abraham's life

     d. Constituted the northeast boundary   1 Kings 4:21
        of Solomon's empire

     e. Now a prison for four hellish angels   Rev. 9:13-15

     f. To be dried up during the   Rev. 16:12
        Tribulation

5. Nile

     a. Southern land boundary of the   Gen. 15:18
        Abrahamic covenant

     b. Seen by Pharaoh in his dream   Gen. 41:1-18

     c. Turned to blood by Moses   Exod. 7:17-25

6. Arnon, boundary river between Israel   Num. 21:13; Josh.
   and Moab   12:1; Judg. 11:22

7. Kanah, river that served as a   Josh. 16:8; 17:9
   boundary between the tribes of
   Ephraim and Manasseh

8. Kishon

     a. Located near the town of Megiddo   Judg. 5:21
        where Deborah and Barak defeated
        Sisera

     b. Near where Elijah defeated the   1 Kings 18:40
        priests of Baal

9. Ahava, river at which the returning   Ezra 8:21
   Babylonian Jews gathered before
   going back to Jerusalem

10. Chebar, where Ezekiel saw some of   Ezek. 1:1; 3:15,
    his visions   23; 10:15-22; 43:3

11. Abana and Pharpar, two of the   2 Kings 5:12
    Damascus rivers mentioned by
    Naaman

12. Jordan, the principal river in Palestine
    and most famous river in the Bible

     a. Parted by Joshua as Israel marched Josh. 3:13-17
        into the Promised Land

     b. Parted by Elijah for himself and   2 Kings 2:7-8
        Elisha

    c. Parted by Elisha to test the power   2 Kings 2:13-14
       of God

    d. The river where Naaman washed   2 Kings 5:10-14
       his leprosy away

    e. The place where John baptized   Matt. 3:13-17
       Jesus

13. Millennial river   Ezek. 47:1-12;
                              Zech. 14:8

14. Eternal river   Rev. 22:1-2

ROADS AND HIGHWAYS

1. The highway leading through Edom.   Num. 20:19
   This was blocked by the Edomites,
   thus forcing the weary Israelites to go
   around another way.

2. The highway from Bethel to Shechem.   Judg. 21:19
   The continuation of the tribe of
   Benjamin was settled through a
   celebration which took place
   alongside this road.

3. The highway from Ekron (a city in   1 Sam. 6:12
   Philistia) to the Israelite city of Beth-
   shemesh. Two cows carrying the Ark
   of the Covenant in a cart made their
   way along this road.

4. The Jerusalem to Jericho road. This   Luke 10:30
   road played an important part in
   Jesus' parable of the Good Samaritan.

5. The Bethphage to Jerusalem road.   Matt. 21:1-9
   Here Jesus mounted the foal of an ass
   and rode into Jerusalem on Palm
   Sunday.

6. The Jerusalem to Emmaus road.   Luke 24:13
   Christ appeared to two of his disciples
   on the first Easter Sunday.

7. The Jerusalem to Antioch road. Paul   Acts 9:3
   met Christ on this road.

8. The millennial highway. This will   Isa. 19:23; 35:8
   stretch from Egypt to Assyria, and
   will be used by many nations coming
   to worship in Jerusalem.

ROCKS AND STONES

1. The rock struck by Moses at   Exod. 17:1-6
   Rephidim, at which time he obeyed
   God

2. The rock struck by Moses in the   Num. 20:1-1?
   desert of Zin, at which time he
   disobeyed God

3. The two stones on which God had   Exod. 24:12
   written the Ten Commandments

4. The stone Jacob used as a pillow,   Gen. 28:11-2&
   which he anointed after his vision

5. The stone Jacob moved from the well   Gen. 29:10
   at Haran

6. The stone used as a pillar memorial   Gen. 31:45
   between Jacob and Laban

7. The stone Jacob anointed with oil   Gen. 35:14
   upon his return to Bethel

8. The 12 memorial stones taken from   Josh. 4:5
   the River Jordan

9. The great stone used by Joshua as a   Josh. 24:26
   memorial reminder to Israel

10. The stone used by the citizens of Beth-shemesh in sacrificing to celebrate the return of the Ark of God — 1 Sam. 6:14

11. The stone named Ebenezer by Samuel — 1 Sam. 7:12

12. The five smooth stones picked by David before he met Goliath — 1 Sam. 17:40

13. The stones thrown at David by Shimei — 2 Sam. 16:13

14. The huge 15-foot-high stones in the foundation of the temple — 1 Kings 7:10

15. The 12 stones used by Elijah in building an altar on Mount Carmel — 1 Kings 18:31

16. The stones used in the slaying of Zechariah, Israel's fearless high priest — 2 Chron. 24:21

17. The stones used in an attempt to kill Jesus — John 8:59; 10:31

18. The stone which sealed the tomb of Jesus — Matt. 27:60

19. The stones used to slay Stephen — Acts 7:59

SALVATION
See also The Christian Life

4 Facts about God's Salvation

1. Salvation is always by innocent blood. — Heb. 9:22

2. Salvation is always through a person. — Jon. 2:9; Acts 4:12; 1 Thess. 5:9; Heb. 5:9

3. Salvation is always by grace. — Eph. 2:8-9; Titus 2:11

4. Salvation is always through faith. — Rom. 5:1; Heb. 11:6

6 Reasons Why People Are Lost and in Need of Salvation

1. They are lost because of their rejection of biblical revelation.

   Acts 14:17; Ps. 19:1; Rom. 1:19-20

2. They are lost because of disobeying their own conscience.

   Rom. 2:14-16

3. They are lost because of their relationship to the world.

   Eph. 2:2; James 4:4; 1 John 2:15-17; 5:19

4. They are lost because of their relationship to Satan.

   John 8:42-44; 12:31; 2 Cor. 4:4; Col. 1:13; 1 John 3:10; 5:19

5. They are lost because of their relationship to sin.

   Gen. 2:17; Job 14:4; Jer. 17:19; Rom. 5:12; 7:14; Eph. 4:18

6. They are lost because of their relationship to God.

   Eph. 2:12; 1 John 5:12; Jude 1:19

17 Key Words in the Vocabulary of Salvation

1. Repentance—turning from sin

   Matt. 9:13; Acts 17:30; 26:20

2. Faith—turning to the Savior

   Acts 20:21; Eph. 2:8-9; Heb. 11:6

3. Substitution—Christ dying on the cross in our stead

   1 Pet. 3:18; John 10:11

4. Reconciliation—bringing together through a third party two opposing parties

   2 Cor. 5:18-20

5. Propitiation—Christ satisfying the holiness of God on the cross

   Rom. 3:25; Eph. 2:13; Col. 1:20; 1 John 2:2; 4:10

6. Remission—putting away or carrying away our sins—also synonymous with forgiveness

   Lev. 16:21-22; Heb. 9:26; 13:12-13; Rom. 3:25; Eph. 4:32; Col. 2:13

7. Regeneration—receiving a new nature through the second birth

   John 1:12-13; 3:3; 1 John 5:1

8. Redemption—obtaining by paying a ransom price

Luke 1:68; Gal 3:13; Heb. 9:12

9. Imputation—God adding the righteousness of Christ to the believing sinner

Isa. 53:5, 11; Rom. 4:3-8; Phil. 3:7-8

10. Adoption—wherein the believing sinner enjoys all the privileges and responsibilities of adult sonhood

Gal. 4:4-5; Rom. 8:15-23; Eph. 1:5

11. Supplication (prayer)—communicating with God

Luke 18:13; Acts 2:21; Rom. 10:13; Jude 20

12. Justification—God declaring a repentant sinner righteous

Rom. 5:1; 8:33

13. Sanctification—God setting us apart for growth and service

John 17:17; Eph. 5:26; 1 Thess. 4:3-4; 5:23

14. Glorification—the ultimate, eternal, and absolute physical, mental, and spiritual perfection of all believers

Rom. 8:18, 23, 30; 5:2; 1 Cor. 15:43; Col. 3:4; 1 Pet. 5:1

15. Election—being chosen by God

Eph. 1:4; 2 Thess. 2:13; 1 Pet. 2:9

16. Foreknowledge—that attribute of God which provided him in advance with all the facts concerning the elect

Acts 15:18; Rom. 8:29; 1 Pet. 1:2

17. Predestination—God's eternal plan whereby all believing sinners are conformed to the image of Christ

Rom. 8:29-30; Eph. 1:9-12

SATAN AND FALLEN ANGELS
See also Demon Possessions, Hell

16 Facts about Satan

1. He was named Lucifer before his fall.   Isa. 14:12

2. He was in Eden.   Ezek. 28:13

3. He was the anointed cherub of God.   Ezek. 28:14

4. He was adorned with precious stones.   Ezek. 28:13

5. He possessed great musical ability.   Ezek. 28:13

6. He was the perfection of wisdom and beauty.   Ezek. 28:12

7. He fell through pride.   Ezek. 28:17

8. He attempted to steal God's throne.   Isa. 14:13

9. He wanted to be like God.   Isa. 14:14

10. He possesses intelligence.   2 Cor. 2:11; 11:3

11. He possesses memory.   Matt. 4:6

12. He possesses a will.   2 Tim. 2:26

13. He possesses desire.   Luke 22:31

14. He possesses pride.   1 Tim. 3:6

15. He possesses wrath.   Rev. 12:12

16. He possesses great organizational ability.   1 Tim. 4:1; Rev. 2:9, 24

22 Names for Satan

1. Satan (adversary), his most common name, used some 52 times.

2. The devil (slanderer), used 35 times.

3. The prince of the power of the air   Eph. 2:2

4. The god of this age   2 Cor. 4:4

5. The king of death   Heb. 2:14

6. The prince of this world   John 12:31

7. The ruler of darkness   Eph. 6:12

8. Leviathan (one who dwells in the sea of humanity)   Isa. 27:1

9. Lucifer (light-bearer, shining one)   Isa. 14:12

10. The dragon   Rev. 12:7

11. The deceiver   Rev. 20:10

12. Apollyon (destroyer)   Rev. 9:11

13. Beelzebub (prince of demons)   Matt. 12:24

14. Belial (vileness, ruthlessness)   2 Cor. 6:15

15. The wicked one   Matt. 13:38

16. The tempter	1 Thess. 3:5
17. The accuser of the brethren	Rev. 12:10
18. An angel of light	2 Cor. 11:14-15
19. A liar	John 8:44; Gen. 3:4-5
20. A murderer	John 8:44
21. The enemy	Matt. 13:39
22. A roaring lion	1 Pet. 5:8

27 Activities of Satan

1. He has a false trinity.	Rev. 13:2; 16:13
2. He has his synagogues.	Rev. 2:9
3. He has his doctrines.	1 Tim. 4:1
4. He has his mysteries.	Rev. 2:24; 2 Thess. 2:7
5. He has his throne.	Rev. 2:13; 13:2
6. He has his kingdom.	Luke 4:6
7. He has his worshipers.	Rev. 13:4
8. He has his angels.	Rev. 12:7
9. He has his ministers.	2 Cor. 11:15
10. He has his miracles.	2 Thess 2:9; Matt. 7:21-23
11. He has his sacrifices.	1 Cor. 10:20
12. He has his fellowship.	1 Cor. 10:20
13. He has his armies.	Isa. 24:21; Rev. 14:14-17; 16:16
14. He sows tares among God's wheat.	Matt. 13:24-30, 36-43
15. He instigates false doctrine.	1 Tim. 4:1-3
16. He perverts the Word of God.	Gen. 3:1-4
17. He hinders the works of God's servants.	1 Thess. 2:18
18. He resists the prayers of God's servants.	Dan. 10:12-13
19. He blinds men to the truth.	2 Cor. 4:4

20. He steals the Word of God from human hearts.

Matt. 13:19

21. He accuses Christians before God.

Job 1:7-12; 2:3-6; Zech. 3:1-4; Rev. 12:10

22. He lays snares for men.

2 Tim. 2:26; 1 Tim. 3:7

23. He tempts.

Matt. 4:1; Eph. 6:11

24. He afflicts.

Job 2:7; Luke 13:16; 2 Cor. 12:7; Acts 10:38

25. He deceives.

Rev. 12:9; 20:8, 10

26. He undermines the sanctity of the home.

1 Cor. 7:3-5

27. He prompts both saints and sinners to transgress against the holiness of God.

1 Chron. 21:1; Matt. 16:22-23; John 13:2; Acts 5:3

20 Facts about Fallen Angels

1. Fallen angels have names.

Luke 8:30; Rev. 9:11

2. They speak.

Luke 4:34, 41; 8:28; Matt. 8:29; Mark 5:12; Acts 19:15; Mark 3:11

3. They know who Jesus is.

Luke 4:34

4. They know of future damnation.

Matt. 8:29

5. They know the saved from the unsaved.

Rev. 9:4

6. They are able to formulate a Satan-centered systematic theology.

1 Tim. 4:1

7. They possess great strength.

Exod. 8:7; 7:11-12; Dan. 10:13; Mark 5:2-4; 9:17-26; Acts 19:16; 2 Cor. 10:4-5; Rev. 9:15-19

8. They experience fear.

Luke 8:28; James 2:19

9. They display disdain.   Acts 16:15

10. There are unchained angels, having a certain amount of freedom at the present time.   Ps. 78:49; Eph. 6:12; Rev. 12:7-9

11. There are chained angels, having no freedom at the present time.   2 Pet. 2:4

12. There are evil angels who rule over the nations of this world.   Dan. 10:13

13. A wicked angel named Legion headed up a large group of fallen spirits that had possessed the maniac of Gadara.   Mark 5:9

14. The bottomless pit is under the control of an angel called Abaddon (in the Hebrew) and Apollyon (in the Greek).   Rev. 9:11

15. Four military angels will lead a hellish army 200 million strong during the latter part of the Tribulation.   Rev. 9:16

16. These four angels are now bound in the Euphrates River.   Rev. 9:14

17. Some angels are in a place called Tartarus.   2 Pet. 2:4; Jude 6

18. Three angels organize those events which lead to the battle of Armageddon.   Rev. 16:13-14

19. Evil angels will be judged by Christ and his Church.   1 Cor. 6:3

20. They will eventually be cast into the lake of fire forever.   Matt. 25:41; 2 Pet. 2:4; Jude 6

14 Activities of Fallen Angels

1. They oppose God's purpose.   Eph. 6:12

2. They execute Satan's program.   1 Tim. 4:1; Rev. 9; 16:12-14

3. They disseminate false doctrine.   2 Thess. 2:2; 1 Tim. 4:1

4. Some cause insanity.   Matt. 8:28; 17:15, 18; Mark 5:15; Luke 8:27-29

5. Some cause muteness of speech.   Matt. 9:33

6. Some cause disease.   Matt 10:1; **Mark**
1:23-26; 3:11;
Luke 4:36; Acts
5:16; 8:7; Rev.
16:13

7. Some cause deafness.   Mark 9:25

8. Some cause epilepsy.   Matt. 17:15-18

9. Some cause blindness.   Matt. 12:22

10. Some cause suicidal mania.   Mark 9:22

11. Some cause personal injuries.   Mark 9:18

12. Some cause physical defects.   Luke 13:11

13. They will inflict grievous torture upon   Rev. 9:3-4
unsaved mankind during the great
Tribulation.

14. Saul, Israel's first king, was often   1 Sam. 16:14;
troubled by an evil spirit.   18:10; 19:9

5 Examples of How God Uses Fallen Angels for His Glory

1. A demon was used to punish wicked   Judg. 9:23
King Abimelech.

2. A demon was used to prepare for the   1 Kings 22:19-23
execution of King Ahab in battle.

3. A demon brought out the true nature   1 Sam. 16:14
of unsaved King Saul.

4. Demons were used to punish   Ps. 78:49
rebellious Israel during the time of
wandering.

5. Demons will be used to bring ungodly   Rev. 16:13-16
nations to Armageddon for
slaughtering at the end of the
Tribulation.

SCIENTIFIC ACCURACIES IN THE BIBLE

1. The spherical shape of the earth — Isa. 40:22
2. The fact that the earth is suspended — Job 26:7
3. The fact that the stars are innumerable — Gen. 15:5
4. The existence of mountains and canyons in the sea — 2 Sam. 22:16
5. The existence of springs and fountains in the sea — Gen. 7:11; 8:2; Prov. 8:28
6. The existence of "watery paths" (ocean currents) in the sea — Ps. 8:8
7. The hydrologic cycle — Job 26:8; 36:27-28; 37:16; 38:25-27; Ps. 135:7; Eccles. 1:6-7
8. The fact that all living things are reproduced after their own kind — Gen. 1:21; 6:19
9. The nature of health and sanitation concerning sickness, community health, and circumcision — Gen. 17:9-14; Lev. 12–14
10. The facts concerning the human bloodstream — Lev. 17:11
11. The second law of thermodynamics concerning energy deterioration — Ps. 102:26; Rom. 8:18-23; Heb. 1:10-12

SEAS

1. The Mediterranean Sea, also called the Great Sea — Josh. 1:4; Acts 10:6; 27:40
2. The Dead Sea, also called the Salt Sea — Josh. 18:19
3. The Red Sea — Exod. 14:21
4. The Sea of Galilee — Matt. 4:18

SERMONS

1. Aaron's sermon to the Hebrew elders in Egypt	Exod. 4:29-31
2. Moses' sermon to the Hebrew elders at Sinai	Exod. 19:7-8
3. Moses' sermons to all Israel in the Moab desert	Deut. 1, 4–5, 26–27, 30
4. Joshua's sermon to all Israel	Josh. 23–24
5. Samuel's sermon to Israel at Ramah	1 Sam. 8:10-18
6. Samuel's sermon to Israel at Gilgal	1 Sam. 12:1-25
7. David's sermon to Israel in Zion	1 Chron. 29:1-5, 10-20
8. Solomon's sermon to Israel at the temple dedication	1 Kings 8:12-21, 54-61
9. Elijah's sermon to the Israel tribes on Mount Carmel	1 Kings 18:21
10. Josiah's sermon to Judah	2 Kings 23:2; 2 Chron. 35:3-6
11. Hezekiah's sermon to Judah's leaders	2 Chron. 29:3-11
12. Jonah's sermon to Nineveh	Jon. 3:4
13. John the Baptist's sermon to Israel near the Jordan River	Matt. 3:1-3, 7-12; Luke 3:4-18; John 1:15-34; 3:27-36
14. Jesus' Sermon on the Mount	Matt. 5–7
15. Jesus' sermon by the seaside	Matt. 13
16. Jesus' sermon on the Mount of Olives	Matt. 24–25
17. Peter's sermon to the Jews at Pentecost	Acts 2:14-40
18. Peter's sermon to the Jews at the Beautiful Gate	Acts 3:12-26
19. Peter's sermon to the Sanhedrin	Acts 4:5-12
20. Stephen's sermon to the Jewish leaders at Jerusalem	Acts 7:1-53
21. Peter's sermon to Cornelius at Caesarea	Acts 10:34-43

22. Paul's sermon to the assembled synagogue at Antioch in Pisidia — Acts 13:16-41

23. Peter's sermon to the Jerusalem council — Acts 15:7-11

24. James's sermon to the Jerusalem council — Acts 15:13-21

25. Paul's sermon to philosophers in Athens — Acts 17:22-31

26. Paul's sermon to Ephesian elders in Miletus — Acts 20:18-35

27. Paul's sermon to a Jerusalem mob — Acts 22:1-21

28. Paul's sermon to Felix and his court at Caesarea — Acts 24:10-25

29. Paul's sermon to Agrippa and his court at Caesarea — Acts 26:2-29

30. Paul's sermon to terrified shipmates on the high seas — Acts 27:21-26

31. Paul's sermon to curious Jews in Rome — Acts 28:17-20, 25-28

SEXUALLY IMPURE

1. The men of Sodom, who wanted to have intercourse with Lot's visitors — Gen. 19:5

2. Lot's two daughters, who got their father drunk and had sex with him — Gen. 19:30-38

3. Shechem the Hivite, who raped Jacob's daughter Dinah — Gen. 34:1-2

4. Reuben, who slept with one of his father Jacob's concubines — Gen. 35:22

5. Onan, who spilled his seed upon the ground rather than father a child by the wife of his dead brother — Gen. 38:9

6. Tamar, guilty of enticing her father-in-law Judah to have sex with her   Gen. 38:14-18

7. Zimri, who flouted the law of God by taking a Midianite woman as his harlot companion   Num. 25:6-14

8. Samson, who visited a harlot in Gaza   Judg. 16:1

9. Hophni and Phinehas, the priest Eli's sons who had sex right in the area of the tabernacle   1 Sam. 2:22

10. David, who committed adultery with Bathsheba   2 Sam. 11

11. Amnon, who raped his half sister Tamar   2 Sam. 13:14

12. Absalom, who had public sex with his father David's concubines   2 Sam. 16:22

13. Gomer, a harlot prior to marrying Hosea and an adulteress after the wedding   Hos. 1–2

14. The Samaritan woman, married five times and living out of wedlock at the time she met Jesus   John 4

15. The adulterous woman whose shameful past was forgiven by Christ   John 8:1-11

16. The woman who washed Jesus' feet. She repented of her immoral past in the home of a Pharisee and was forgiven by Christ.   Luke 7:36-39

17. A Corinthian church member who was committing fornication with either his mother or stepmother   1 Cor. 5:1

18. Jezebel II, the false prophetess who was encouraging sexual impurity in the church at Thyatira   Rev. 2:20

THE SHEKINAH GLORY CLOUD OF GOD

1. Led Israel across the wilderness — Exod. 13:21-22; Num. 9:17-22

2. Protected Israel at the Red Sea — Exod. 14:19-20, 24

3. Appeared when Israel murmured in the Zin wilderness — Exod. 16:10

4. Appeared when God spoke to Moses on Mount Sinai — Exod. 19:9, 16; 24:15-16, 18; 34:5

5. Filled the tabernacle during Moses' dedication — Exod. 40:34-38

6. Stood above the mercy seat in the Holy of Holies — Lev. 16:2

7. Appeared when God appointed the 70 — Num. 11:25

8. Appeared when Miriam spoke against Moses' wife — Num. 12:5

9. Appeared as Moses pleaded for Israel — Num. 14:14

10. Appeared during Korah's rebellion — Num. 16:42

11. Filled the temple during Solomon's dedication — 1 Kings. 8:10-11; 2 Chron. 5:13, 14

12. Was seen by Ezekiel — Ezek. 1:28; 8:11; 10:3-4

13. Appeared to the shepherds at Christ's birth — Luke 2:8-9

14. Was present at Christ's baptism — Matt. 3:16

15. Was present at Christ's transfiguration — Matt. 17:5

16. Was present at Christ's death — Matt. 27:45

17. Was present at Christ's ascension — Acts 1:9

18. Will appear at the Rapture — 1 Thess. 4:17

19. Will appear during the Tribulation at the funeral of God's two witnesses — Rev. 11:12

20. Will appear during the Second Coming — Dan. 7:13-14; Matt. 24:30; Rev. 1:7; 14:14

SHEPHERDS

1. Abel, who offered God a lamb from his flock — Gen. 4:2

2. Abraham, who owned many sheep and oxen — Gen. 12:16

3. Lot, who foolishly chose the plains near Sodom to graze his sheep — Gen. 13:5

4. Isaac, who, like his father, had many sheep and oxen — Gen. 26:14

5. Jacob, who shepherded both his own flocks and those belonging to his father-in-law, Laban — Gen. 30:32-25

6. Laban, who was the brother of Rebekah and father-in-law of Jacob — Gen. 31:19

7. Joseph, who cared for his father Jacob's sheep — Gen. 37:2

8. Judah, the fourth son of Jacob — Gen. 38:12

9. Reuel, also called Jethro, the father-in-law of Moses — Exod. 2:16

10. Moses, who was caring for sheep when God spoke to him from the burning bush — Exod. 3:1

11. David, the shepherd boy who cared for his father's sheep in Bethlehem and later wrote the Shepherd's Psalm, 23 — 1 Sam. 16:11

12. Nabal, a surly and stupid shepherd who insulted David — 1 Sam. 25:2

13. Amos, a shepherd when called by God to become a prophet — Amos 7:15

SIGNS
See also Memorials

1. The rainbow, a sign that the world would never again be destroyed by water — Gen. 9:13-17

2. The ten plagues in Egypt, signs of the power of God — Exod. 10:2

3. Unleavened bread, a sign of the deliverance from Egypt — Exod. 13:7-9

4. The Sabbath, a sign of completion and rest — Exod. 31:13

5. Twelve stones, signs of the parting of the Jordan — Josh. 4:6

6. A fleece, a sign of answered prayer and God's approval — Judg. 6:17

7. Two censers, signs of invoked punishment at the unlawful offering of incense — Num. 16:36-40

8. A "slow" sundial, a sign of Hezekiah's recovery — 2 Kings 20:8-11

9. The Virgin Birth, a sign of the Incarnation — Isa. 7:14

10. A torn altar, a sign of the destruction of a false religion — 1 Kings 13:5

11. A fire, a sign of the impending Babylonian invasion — Jer. 6:1

12. The prophet Jonah, a sign of the Resurrection of Christ — Matt. 16:4

13. Swaddling clothes, a sign of the birth of Christ — Luke 2:12

14. Tongues, a sign of God's power to unbelievers — 1 Cor. 14:22

SIN

Various Sins

1. Disobedience	Gen. 3:6
2. Drunkenness	Gen. 9:21
3. Self-worship	Gen. 11:1-9
4. Sodomy	Gen. 19; Rom. 1:24-32
5. Incest	Gen. 19:33-38
6. Lying	Gen. 26:7-8
7. Deceit	Gen. 27:11-15
8. Hatred	Gen. 27:41
9. Plotting murder	Gen. 37:18-22
10. Idolatry	Exod. 32
11. Murmuring	Num. 14:29
12. Breaking the Sabbath	Num. 15:32-36
13. Rebellion	Num. 16
14. Covetousness	Josh. 7
15. Compromise	Judg. 2:1-3
16. Intruding into the priests' office	1 Sam. 2:17
17. Taking bribes	1 Sam. 8:3
18. Pride	1 Sam. 14:12-14
19. Eating blood	1 Sam. 14:33
20. Jealousy	1 Sam. 18:8-12
21. Practicing witchcraft	1 Sam. 28:7-18
22. Despising a husband	2 Sam. 6:16-23
23. Adultery	2 Sam. 11:4, 27
24. Rape	2 Sam. 13:14
25. Causing division among God's people	2 Sam. 15:4
26. Mockery	2 Kings 2:23-24
27. Offering human sacrifices	2 Kings 17:17
28. Despising God's Word	2 Chron. 36:16
29. Scattering the sheep	Jer. 23:1

30. Self-will	Ezek. 28:17
31. Prayerlessness	Hos. 7:7
32. Attributing to Satan the work of the Holy Spirit	Matt. 12:24-32
33. Teaching false doctrine	Matt. 16:6
34. Lack of mercy	Matt. 18:23-35
35. Hypocrisy	Matt. 23
36. Denying Christ	Matt. 26:69-75
37. Polluting the house of God	John 2:14-16
38. Crucifying Christ	Acts 2:23
39. Being stiffnecked	Acts 7:51
40. Blasphemy	Acts 12:20-23
41. Unthankfulness	Rom. 1:21
42. Boasting	Rom. 1:30
43. Disobeying parents	Rom. 1:30
44. Lacking natural affection	Rom. 1:31
45. Living in the flesh	Gal. 3:3

7 Consequences of Sin

1. It brought immediate judgment upon Satan.	Rev. 12:7
2. It will someday doom Satan forever in hell.	Matt. 25:41; Rev. 20:10
3. It brought physical death upon man.	Gen. 5:5; Ps. 90:10
4. It brought spiritual death upon man.	Matt. 7:23; 25:41; Rev. 2:11; 20:6, 14; 21:8
5. It brought disorder and pain to nature.	Gen. 3:18; Rom. 8:19-22
6. It served as an object lesson for the angels.	1 Cor. 4:9; 1 Tim. 5:21; Gal. 3:19; 1 Pet. 1:12; Heb. 1:14
7. It caused God to end his rest after creation and begin his work of redemption.	John 5:17; 9:4; Phil. 1:6; Gen. 2:1-2

7 Losses When a Christian Sins

1.	The loss of light	1 John 1:6
2.	The loss of joy	Ps. 51:12; John 15:11; Gal. 5:22; 1 John 1:4
3.	The loss of righteousness	1 John 3:4-10
4.	The loss of love	1 John 2:5, 15-17; 4:12
5.	The loss of fellowship	1 John 1:3, 6-7
6.	The loss of confidence	1 John 3:19-22
7.	The possible loss of health and even physical life	1 Cor. 11:30

SORCERERS

1.	Jannes and Jambres, the Egyptian court sorcerers at the time of Moses	Exod. 7:11; 2 Tim. 3:8
2.	The witch of Endor, who called up Samuel for King Saul in his hour of desperation	1 Sam. 28
3.	Simon, the Samaritan sorcerer who attempted to buy the power of the Holy Spirit from Peter and John	Acts 8:9-24
4.	Bar-Jesus, or Elymas, sorcerer who withstood Paul on Cyprus	Acts 13:6-11
5.	The Philippian soothsaying girl, led to Christ by Paul	Acts 16:16-18
6.	Sceva, probably a self-styled "priest" who, with his seven sons, tried to practice magic using Jesus' name	Acts 19:13-16

SPEARS AND SWORDS
See also Weapons

1. The sword of the cherubim — Gen. 3:24
2. The swords used by Simeon and Levi on the Hivites — Gen. 34:25-26
3. The sword held by an angel against Balaam — Num. 22:23
4. The sword of the captain of the Lord's host — Josh. 5:13
5. Joshua's victorious sword against Ai — Josh. 8:18
6. The huge spear used by Goliath — 1 Sam. 17:7
7. The spears Saul used in attempting to kill David — 1 Sam. 18:11; 19:9
8. The spear Saul used in attempting to kill Jonathan — 1 Sam. 20:33
9. The spear David took from Saul while he slept — 1 Sam. 26:12
10. The one Saul fell upon to kill himself — 1 Sam. 31:4
11. The sword used to kill wicked Queen Athaliah — 2 Kings 11:20
12. The sword Peter used to cut off the ear of the servant of the high priest — Matt. 26:51
13. The spear used to pierce the side of Christ — John 19:34
14. The sword used by Herod to kill the apostle James — Acts 12:1-2
15. The sword almost used by the Philippian jailor to kill himself — Acts 16:27
16. The sword carried by the rider on the red horse — Rev. 6:4
17. The sword carried by the returning Christ — Rev. 19:15

STAFFS, STICKS, AND RODS

1. The rods Jacob used in an attempt to control the breeding of animals — Gen. 30:37

2. The staff Jacob carried over Jordan — Gen. 32:10

3. The staff Jacob used upon his deathbed — Heb. 11:21

4. The staff Judah unknowingly gave to his daughter-in-law — Gen. 38:18

5. The staff of Moses that turned into a serpent — Exod. 4:2

6. Aaron's rod, use to swallow up the rods-turned-snakes of the magicians in Egypt — Exod. 7:12

7. The staff of Moses used to bring down the ten plagues upon Egypt — Exod. 7:19

8. The staff of Moses used in parting the Red Sea — Exod. 14:16

9. The staff of Moses, held while he prayed for Israel — Exod. 17:9

10. The staff of Moses, with which he struck a rock — Exod. 17:6-7; Num. 20:8-11

11. Aaron's rod, use to demonstrate God's blessings upon him as the rod blossomed — Num. 17:8

12. The staff used by Balaam to beat his donkey — Num. 22:27

13. The staff used by the 12 spies to carry fruit found in the Promised Land — Num. 13:23

14. The staff used by an angel to consume Gideon's offering — Judg. 6:21

15. The rod used by Jonathan to secure honey from a hive — 1 Sam. 14:27

16. The stick used by Elisha which caused an axe head to float — 2 Kings 6:6

17. The rod and staff of the Good Shepherd — Ps. 23:4

18. The two sticks used by Ezekiel to predict the eventual union and millennial blessings of Israel's 12 tribes — Ezek. 37:16-28

19. The staff Zechariah broke to predict coming judgment upon Gentile nations — Zech. 11:10

20. The rod given John by an angel to measure the tribulational temple — Rev. 11:1

21. The rod Christ will use to rule all nations in the Millennium — Rev. 2:27; 12:5; 19:15

SUFFERING

25 Reasons Why Christians Suffer

1. To produce the fruit of patience — Rom. 5:3; James 1:3-4; Heb. 10:36

2. To produce the fruit of joy — Ps. 30:5; 126:5-6

3. To produce the fruit of maturity — Eccles. 7:3; 1 Pet. 5:10

4. To produce the fruit of righteousness — Heb. 12:11

5. To silence the devil — Job 1:9, 10, 20-22

6. To teach us — Ps. 119:67, 71

7. To purify our lives — Job 23:10; Ps. 66:10-12; Isa. 1:25; 48:10; Prov. 17:3; 1 Pet. 1:7

8. To make us like Christ — Heb. 12:9, 10; 1 Pet. 4:12-13; Phil. 3:10; 2 Cor. 4:7-10

9. To glorify God — Ps. 50:15; John 9:1-3; 11:1-4; 21:18-19; Phil. 1:19-20

10. To prevent us from sinning	2 Cor. 12:7, 9-10
11. To make us confess when we do sin	Judg. 10:6-7, 15-16; Ps. 32:3-5; Hos. 5:15; 6:1; 2 Chron. 15:3-4
12. To chasten us for our sin	1 Pet. 4:17
13. To prove our sonship	Heb. 12:5-6
14. To reveal ourselves to ourselves	Job 42:6; Luke 15:18
15. To help our prayer life	Isa. 26:16
16. To become an example to others	2 Cor. 6:4-5; 1 Thess. 1:6-7
17. To qualify us as counselors	Rom. 12:15; Gal. 6:2; 2 Cor. 1:3-5
18. To further the gospel witness	Acts 8:1-5; 16:25-34; Phil. 1:12-13; 2 Tim. 4:6-8, 16-17
19. To make us more than conquerors	2 Cor. 2:14; Rom. 8:35, 37
20. To give us insight into God's nature	Job 42:5; Rom. 8:14-15, 18
21. To drive us closer to God	1 Pet. 4:14; 2 Cor. 12:10
22. To prepare us for a greater ministry	1 Kings 17–18; John 12:24
23. To provide for us a reward	Matt. 5:10-12; 19:27-29; Rom. 8:16-17; 2 Cor. 4:17
24. To prepare us for the kingdom	2 Thess. 1:5; 2 Tim. 2:12
25. To show God's sovereignty	Rom. 8:28; 1 Cor. 10:13; Ps. 66:10-12; Gen. 45:5-8; 50:20

13 Proper Reactions to Suffering

1. Expect suffering.	John 15:19-20; 16:2, 20, 33; Heb. 12:9-10; 2 Tim. 3:12

2. Commit your soul to God at the very beginning of your suffering.

Ps. 3:5-6; 37:3; 31:5; Dan. 3:14-18; Heb. 6:17-20; 1 Pet. 4:19

3. Don't try to understand all the reasons for your suffering.

Rom. 8:28

4. Realize others suffer.

1 Cor. 10:13; 1 Pet. 5:8-9

5. Pray while in your suffering.

Ps. 50:15; Job 42:10; James 5:13; Mark 9:20-24

6. Don't despise your suffering.

Heb. 12:5

7. Don't faint because you're suffering.

Prov. 24:10; Heb. 12:5

8. Patiently endure your suffering in a steadfast way.

Rom. 12:12; 2 Tim. 2:3; James 5:10; 1 Pet. 2:20

9. Thank God for your sufferings.

Ps. 42:5; 1 Thess. 5:18

10. Rejoice because of your sufferings.

Acts 5:40-41; 16:25; Phil. 4:4; James 1:2; 5:11

11. Don't become a self-made martyr because of your sufferings.

Heb. 12:12-13

12. Don't suffer needlessly.

1 Pet. 2:20; 3:17; 4:15-17

13. Weigh your current suffering against the coming glory.

John 16:20-21; Rom. 8:18

5 Sources of Suffering

1. Suffering may be caused by satanic activity.

Job 1–2; Luke 13:15-16; Acts 10:38

2. Suffering may be caused by ungodly men.

2 Tim. 4:14

3. Suffering may be caused by this world's system.

2 Pet. 2:8

4. Suffering may be caused by the believer's own fallen nature.

Rom. 7:14-23

5. Suffering may be caused by carnal Christians.

Phil 1:15-16; 2 Tim. 4:10

SUICIDES

1. Abimelech, the son of Gideon, who had his armor-bearer kill him after being injured by a woman

Judg. 9:54

2. Samson, the strong man who destroyed a building, thus killing himself and a multitude of Philistines

Judg. 16:26-30

3. Saul, who killed himself after losing a battle to the Philistines

1 Sam. 31:4

4. Saul's servant, who killed himself as his master had done

1 Sam. 31:5

5. Ahithophel, who hanged himself after his advice was rejected by Absalom

2 Sam. 17:23

6. Zimri, who set the palace on fire with himself inside rather than being taken prisoner

1 Kings 16:18

7. Judas Iscariot, who hanged himself after betraying Jesus

Matt. 27:5

SUPERNATURAL CONCEPTIONS

1. Isaac, born to Abraham and Sarah, who were physically too old to conceive

Gen. 21:1-3

2. Son of the Shunammite woman, born to a barren mother, a friend of Elisha

2 Kings 4:14-17

3. John the Baptist, born to Zacharias and Elisabeth, who were physically too old to conceive — Luke 1:36-37

4. Jesus, conceived by the Holy Spirit and born of the Virgin Mary — Luke 1:35; 2:7

SYMBOLS AND EMBLEMS
See also Parables, Types, Foreshadows

Symbols of Christ

1. Alpha and Omega	Rev. 1:11
2. An anchor	Heb. 6:19
3. Bread, manna	John 6:31-35
4. An eagle	Exod. 19:4; Rev. 4:7
5. The firstfruits of a crop	1 Cor. 15:20
6. A hen	Matt. 23:37
7. A lamb	John 1:29; Rev. 5:6
8. Light	John 1:9
9. A lily	Song of Sol. 2:1
10. A lion	Ezek. 1:10; Rev. 4:7; 5:5
11. An ox or calf	Ezek. 1:10; Rev. 4:7
12. A rock	Matt. 16:18; 1 Pet. 2:8
13. A root	Isa. 11:1; Rev. 5:5; 22:16
14. A rose	Song of Sol. 2:1
15. A serpent	John 3:14
16. A star	Rev. 22:16
17. A living stone	1 Pet. 2:4

18. A cornerstone	1 Pet. 2:6
19. A precious stone	1 Pet. 2:7
20. A stumbling stone	Rom. 9:33; 1 Pet. 2:8
21. A rejected stone	Matt. 21:42; Acts 4:11
22. A crushing stone	Dan. 2:34
23. The sun	Rev. 22:5
24. A temple	John 2:19
25. A vine	John 15:1
26. A worm	Ps. 22:6

Symbols of the Church and Believers

1. An athlete	1 Cor. 9:24-27; 2 Tim. 2:5; Heb. 12:1
2. A body	1 Cor. 12:27; Eph. 3:6; 4:4; Col. 1:18
3. Branches	John 15:1
4. A bride	2 Cor. 11:2; Rev. 21:2
5. A building	1 Cor. 3:9
6. Candlesticks, lampstands	Rev. 1:20
7. A family	Eph. 3:15
8. A farmer	2 Tim. 2:6
9. Lights	Matt. 5:14; John 12:36; Eph. 5:8; Phil. 2:15; 1 Thess. 5:5
10. Pearls	Matt. 13:45-46
11. Priests	1 Pet. 2:9; Rev. 1:6; 5:10; 20:6
*12. Salt	Matt. 5:13
13. Sheep, lambs	Luke 10:3; John 10:11; 21:15-17
14. Soldiers	2 Tim. 2:3
15. Stewards	1 Cor. 4:2; 1 Pet. 4:10

16. Stones	Eph. 2:19-22; 1 Pet. 2:5
17. A temple	2 Cor. 6:16; 2 Pet. 2:5
18. A vessel	2 Cor. 4:7; 2 Tim. 2:21
19. Wheat	Matt. 13:29-30
20. A wife	Rev. 21:9

Symbols of Israel

1. A linen girdle	Jer. 13:10
2. A marred clay vessel	Jer. 18:4
3. Two baskets of figs	Jer. 24:1
4. Three bunches of hair	Ezek. 5:1-2
5. Dross in a furnace	Ezek. 22:18
6. A valley of dry bones	Ezek. 37:1-2
7. Two sticks	Ezek. 37:16-17
8. A barren fig tree	Matt. 21:19; Luke 13:6
9. An empty vine	Hos. 10:1
10. An unturned, half-baked cake	Hos. 7:8
11. A backslidden heifer	Hos. 10:11
12. A silly dove	Hos. 7:11
13. A wild ass	Hos. 8:9
14. Dust	Gen. 13:16
15. Sand	Gen. 22:17
16. Sheep	Ps. 100:3
17. Stars	Gen. 22:17; Dan. 12:3
18. Three servants	Matt. 25:14-15
19. Ten servants	Luke 19:12-13
20. Ten virgins	Matt. 25:1
21. A harlot wife	Hos. 4:15
22. Three wedding guests	Luke 14:16-24
23. A hidden treasure	Matt. 13:44

24. A persecuted woman — Rev. 12:13
25. Precious jewels — Mal. 3:17
26. Trees of righteousness — Isa. 61:3

Symbols of Satan

1. A dragon — Rev. 12:3, 7
2. A serpent — Rev. 20:2
3. A roaring lion — 1 Pet. 5:8
4. A sower of weeds — Matt. 13:39
5. An angel of light — 2 Cor. 11:14
6. A prince — John 12:31

Symbols of Apostates

1. Waterless clouds — Jude 12
2. Fruitless trees — Jude 12
3. Raging, wild waves — Isa. 57:20; Jude 13
4. Wandering stars — Jude 13
5. Dogs — 2 Pet. 2:22
6. Hogs — 2 Pet. 2:22
7. Brute beasts — Jude 10
8. Goats — Matt. 25:33
9. Tares — Matt. 13:30

Symbols of the Bible

1. A mirror — James 1:23-25
2. A seed — Matt. 13:18-23; James 1:18; 1 Pet. 1:23
3. Water — Eph. 5:25-27
4. A lamp — Ps. 119:105; Prov. 6:23; 2 Pet. 1:19
5. A sword — Heb. 4:12; Eph. 6:17
6. Gold — Pss. 19:10; 119:127
7. Silver — Ps. 12:6

8. Milk	1 Pet. 2:2
9. Meat	Heb. 5:12-14
10. Bread	John 6:51
11. Honey	Ps. 19:10
12. A hammer	Jer. 23:29
13. A fire	Jer. 20:9; Luke 24:32

Symbols of the Holy Spirit

1. A dove	John 1:32
2. Water	Isa. 44:3; John 7:37-39
3. Oil	Luke 4:18; Acts 10:38; Heb. 1:9; 1 John 2:27
4. A seal	2 Cor. 1:22; Eph. 1:13; 4:30
5. Wind	John 3:8; Acts 2:1-2
6. Fire	Acts 2:3
7. A guarantee	2 Cor. 1:22; 5:5; Eph. 1:14

Symbols of the Kingdom of Heaven

1. A field	Matt. 13:3-30
2. A tree	Matt. 13:31-32
3. The sea	Matt. 13:47-48
4. The marriage feast	Matt. 22:2

Symbols of Coming Judgment

1. A sickle	Rev. 14:14
2. A dragnet	Matt. 13:47
3. A wine press	Isa. 63:3
4. A falling stone	Dan. 2:34
5. Four horses	Rev. 6:2-8
6. A white throne	Rev. 20:11

Symbols of Wickedness and Uncleanness

1.	Leaven	Matt. 16:6
2.	Leprosy	Lev. 13:44
3.	An ephah	Zech. 5:6

Symbols of the Antichrist

1.	A little horn	Dan. 7:8
2.	A seven-headed, ten-horned beast from the sea	Rev. 13:1

Symbols of Sorrow

1.	Ashes	Esther 4:1; Job 2:8; Dan. 9:3; Jon. 3:6
2.	Sackcloth	Esther 4:1; Jon. 3:6
3.	Torn clothing	1 Sam. 4:12; 2 Sam. 13:31; Ezra 9:3; Job 1:20; 2:12; Matt. 26:65

Symbols of the Death and Resurrection of Christ

1.	The great fish	Jon. 1–2
2.	Baptism	Rom. 6:2-10

Symbol of Rewards

1.	Crowns	Rev. 4:4
2.	A white stone	Rev. 2:17
3.	Hidden manna	Rev. 2:17
4.	A morning star	Rev. 2:28
5.	White raiment	Rev. 3:18; 19:8

TEACHERS

1. Moses wrote and taught Scripture's first five books. — Deut. 4:5

2. Samuel taught during the early days of the kingdom. — 1 Sam. 12:23

3. David wrote and taught the Psalms. — Prov. 4:4

4. Solomon wrote and taught the Proverbs. — 1 Kings 4:32

5. Men of Jehoshaphat's reign taught the law of God throughout Judah. — 2 Chron. 17:7-9

6. Josiah taught the law of Moses. — 2 Chron. 34:30

7. Ezra taught the law of God. — Ezra 7:10

8. Men of Ezra's time taught the law of God. — Neh. 8:1-8

9. Jesus taught the Old Testament and its fulfillment in him. — Matt. 4:23; Luke 24:27

10. Barnabas, Simeon, Lucius, and Manaen taught in the church at Antioch. — Acts 13:1

11. Paul taught the word of God. — Acts 18:11; 20:20

12. Apollos taught the message of John the Baptist and, later, of Christ. — Acts 18:25, 28

13. Aquila and Priscilla taught Apollos. — Acts 18:26

14. Timothy taught church doctrine. — Titus 2:1

15. Author of the Epistle to the Hebrews taught the Old Testament's fulfillment in Christ. — Heb. 5:11-14

TEAMS

1. Moses and Aaron, two brothers, one (Moses) the great lawgiver and the other (Aaron) Israel's first high priest — Exod. 7:1

2. Caleb and Joshua, the two spies who gave the only positive report after searching out the land of Kadesh-barnea — Num. 14:6-9

3. Zerubbabel and Joshua, Judah's first political and religious leaders who headed up the return from Persia to Jerusalem — Hag. 1:1

4. Ezra and Nehemiah, the two men who headed up the project to rebuild the walls of Jerusalem — Neh. 8:9

5. Peter and John, the two key apostles in the early Jerusalem church — Acts 3:1

6. Paul and Barnabas, the team that carried out the world's first missionary journey — Acts 13:2

7. Paul and Silas, the team that carried out the second missionary journey — Acts 15:40

8. Barnabas and Mark, the uncle and nephew team that conducted a successful missionary trip on Cyprus — Acts 15:39

TEMPLES

1. The temple (tabernacle) of Moses — Exod. 40
2. The temple of Solomon — 1 Kings 6

3. The temple of Zerubbabel   Ezra 3

4. The temple of Herod   John 2:20

5. The temple of Christ's body   John 2:21

6. The temple of the believer's body   1 Cor. 6:19;
                                             2 Cor. 6:16

7. The temple of collective believers   Eph. 2:20-22;
                                             1 Pet. 2:5

8. The tribulational temple   Matt. 24:15; Rev.
                                             11:1

9. The millennial temple   Ezek. 40; Acts
                                             15:16

10. The heavenly temple   Rev. 11:19; 14:15;
                                            15:5-6, 8; 16:1, 17

TRAITORS
See also Plots, Troublemakers

1. Delilah, the Philistine woman who   Judg. 16
   betrayed Samson

2. Ahithophel, David's advisor who   2 Sam. 15:12
   sided with Absalom during the
   rebellion

3. Ziba, the servant of Mephibosheth   2 Sam. 16:3
   who attempted to betray his master to
   David

4. Judas Iscariot, the apostle who   Matt. 26:47; Mark
   betrayed Christ for 30 pieces of silver   14:43-44; Luke
                                             22:47-48; John
                                             12:4

TREES
See also Plants

1. Acacia	Exod. 25:5, 10; 26:26
2. Algum	2 Chron. 2:8
3. Almond	Num. 17:8
4. Almug	1 Kings 10:11-12
5. Apple	Prov. 25:11; Song of Sol. 2:3, 5; 7:8; Joel 1:12
6. Box	Isa. 41:19; 60:13
7. Bramble	Judg. 9:14-15
8. Cassia	Exod. 30:24
9. Cedar	1 Kings 6:15
10. Chestnut, plane	Gen. 30:37; Ezek. 31:8
11. Cinnamon	Exod. 30:23; Prov. 7:17; Rev. 18:13
12. Cypress	1 Kings 6:15-35; Isa. 55:13; 60:13
13. Fig	Judg. 9:10-11; Isa. 38:21; Matt. 21:19
14. Fir, pine	1 Kings 5:10; Isa. 37:24
15. Frankincense	Matt. 2:11
16. Mulberry	2 Sam. 5:23-24
17. Myrtle	Isa. 41:19; 55:13
18. Oak	Gen. 35:4; Ezek. 27:6; Zech. 11:2
19. Olive	Gen. 8:11; Deut. 24:20; Ps. 52:8; Isa. 17:6; 24:13; Hos. 14:6
20. Palm	Num. 33:9; 2 Chron. 28:15; John 12:13; Rev. 7:9

21. Pistachio	Gen. 43:11
22. Poplar	Gen. 30:37; Hos. 4:13
23. Sycamine (mulberry)	Luke 17:6
24. Sycamore	Amos 7:14; Luke 19:4
25. Tamarisk	Gen. 21:33; 1 Sam. 22:6; 31:13
26. Terebinth (oak)	2 Sam. 18:9-10
27. Thyine (citron)	Rev. 18:12
28. Willow	Ps. 137:1-5; Isa. 44:4

THE TRIBULATION
See also The Antichrist, Prophecies

---

12 Names for the Coming World Calamity

1. The Day of the Lord	Isa. 2:12; 13:6, 9; Ezek. 13:5; 30:3; Joel 1:15; 2:1, 11, 31; 3:14; Amos 5:18, 20; Obad. 15; Zeph. 1:7, 14; Zech. 14:1; Mal. 4:5; Acts 2:20; 1 Thess. 5:2; 2 Thess. 2:2; 2 Pet. 3:10
2. The indignation	Isa. 26:20; 34:2
3. The day of God's vengeance	Isa. 34:8; 63:1-6
4. The time of Jacob's trouble	Jer. 30:7
5. The overspreading of abominations	Dan. 9:27
6. The time of trouble such as never was	Dan. 12:1
7. The seventieth week	Dan. 9:24-27
8. The time of the end	Dan. 12:9

9. The great day of his wrath	Rev. 6:17
10. The hour of his judgment	Rev. 14:7
11. The end of this world	Matt. 13:40, 49
12. The great Tribulation	Matt. 24:21

7 Reasons for the Great Tribulation

1. To harvest the crop that has been sown throughout the ages by God, Satan, and mankind	Matt. 13
2. To prove the falseness of the devil's claim	Isa. 14:12-15
3. To prepare a great martyred multitude for heaven	Rev. 7:9, 14
4. To prepare a great living multitude for the Millennium	Matt. 25:32-34
5. To punish the Gentiles	Rom. 1:18; 2 Thess. 2:11-12; Rev. 19:15
6. To purge Israel	Ezek. 20:23, 38; Zech. 13:8-9; Mal. 3:3
7. To prepare the earth itself for the Millennium	Rev. 16:20

25 Individuals and Groups Appearing in the Great Tribulation

1. God	Rev. 7:9-17; 11:17; 17:3
2. The devil	Rev. 12:12
3. Two special witnesses	Rev. 11:3
4. The Antichrist	2 Thess. 2:3-4, 9
5. The false prophet	Rev. 13:11
6. 144,000 Israelite preachers	Rev. 7:4
7. An army of locusts like demons from the bottomless pit	Rev. 9:2-3
8. An army of horse and rider demons from the Euphrates River	Rev. 9:14-16

9. Three evil spirits	Rev. 16:13-14
10. A cruel, power-mad ruler from the north	Ezek. 38:1-3
11. An angel with the seal of the living God	Rev. 7:2
12. Seven angels with seven trumpets	Rev. 8–9, 11
13. An angel with a golden censer	Rev. 8:3
14. An angel with a little book and a measuring reed	Rev. 10:1-2; 11:1
15. An angel with the everlasting gospel	Rev. 14:6
16. An angel with a harvest sickle	Rev. 14:14-19
17. Seven angels with seven vials of wrath	Rev. 16
18. An angel with a message of doom	Rev. 18:1, 21
19. An angel with a strange invitation	Rev. 19:17
20. An angel with a key and a great chain	Rev. 20:1
21. A persecuted woman (Israel)	Rev. 12:1-2
22. A vile and bloody harlot (the false church)	Rev. 17:3-5
23. An arrogant queen (the world's political and economic systems)	Rev. 18:2, 7
24. A pure, chaste bride (the true Church)	Rev. 19:7-8
25. A mighty warrior from heaven	Rev. 19:11, 16

TROUBLEMAKERS
See also Plots, Traitors

1. Korah, rebel who instigated a revolt against Moses	Num. 16
2. Balaam, the false prophet who attempted to curse Israel and later succeeded in causing immorality in their camp	Num. 22–24

3. Achan, whose disobedience and greed caused Israel to lose a battle — Josh. 7:1

4. Absalom, who led a rebellion against his father, David — 2 Sam. 13–18

5. Ziba, a servant of Mephibosheth who attempted to stir up trouble between his master and David — 2 Sam. 16:3

6. Sheba, a Benjaminite who led a rebellion against David — 2 Sam. 16:3

7. Hadad, an Edomite who made trouble for King Solomon — 1 Kings 11:14

8. Bishlam and Rehum, who wrote letters to the Persian king slandering the Jews who had returned to build their temple — Ezra 4:7-9

9. Geshem and Tobiah, who opposed Nehemiah's project in rebuilding the walls of Jerusalem — Neh. 2:19

10. Sanballat, a Horonite who opposed Nehemiah — Neh. 2:19

11. Demetrius, a silversmith and worshiper of Artemis, who made trouble for Paul in Ephesus — Acts 19:24

12. Diotrephes, a godless and arrogant troublemaker in the early church — 3 John 9

TRUMPETS

1. Moses' two silver trumpets — Num. 10:2
2. Joshua's seven rams' trumpets — Josh. 6:4
3. Ehud's trumpet — Judg. 3:12-30
4. Gideon's 300 trumpets — Judg. 7
5. David's trumpet — 2 Sam. 6:15

6. Zadok's trumpet	1 Kings 1:39
7. Solomon's trumpets	2 Chron. 5:13
8. Ezra's trumpets	Ezra 3:10
9. The trumpet of the Rapture of the Church	1 Cor. 15:52; 1 Thess. 4:16
10. The seven judgment trumpets	Rev. 8:2
11. The regathering of Israel trumpet	Matt. 24:31

TYPES, FORESHADOWS
See also Symbols and Emblems

A type is an event, person, or thing in the Old Testament that foreshadows something in the New Testament.

Types of Christ
INDIVIDUALS

1. Adam: his headship over a new creation	Gen. 1:28; Rom. 5:17-19; 1 Cor. 15:22, 45, 47; Heb. 2:7-9
2. Noah: his saving life	Gen. 6:13-14, 17-18; 1 Pet. 3:18-22
3. Abraham: his fatherhood	Gen. 22:7-8; Matt. 26:36, 42-43
4. Melchizedek: his priestly ministry	Gen. 14:18-20; Ps. 110:4; Heb. 5-8
5. Isaac: his death	Gen. 22:2, 8, 10; Matt. 26:36, 42-43
6. Joseph: most perfect type of Christ in the Old Testament	
a. Hated without a cause	Gen. 37:4, 8; John 15:25
b. Ridiculed	Gen. 37:19; Luke 22:63
c. Plotted against	Gen. 37:20; John 11:53

d. Stripped of his robe

Gen. 37:23; John 19:23-24

e. Sold for silver

Gen. 37:28; Matt. 26:14-16

f. Lied about

Gen. 39:14; Matt. 26:61

g. Placed in captivity with two guilty men

Gen. 40:1-3; Luke 23:32-33

h. Unrecognized by his own

Gen. 42:8; John 1:11

7. Moses: his prophetical ministry

Deut. 18:15-18; Heb. 3:5-6

8. Joshua: his victorious life

Josh. 1:3, 5-6, 8-9; John 10:17-18; 19:30

9. David: his kingly ministry

2 Sam. 7:1-17; Mark 11:10; Rev. 5:5; 22:16

10. Solomon: his wisdom

1 Kings 3:11-13; Luke 4:22; John 7:46

11. Elijah: his forerunner

Isa. 40:3-4; Matt. 17:11-12

12. Elisha: his miracles

2 Kings 2:9; John 3:2

13. Jonah: his resurrection

Jon. 1:17; Matt. 12:40; 16:4; Luke 11:29

14. Jeremiah: his sorrows

Jer. 3:20; 5:1-5; 8:20-22; 9:1; 10:19; 11:19

15. Daniel: his acceptance by the Father

Dan. 9:23; 10:11, 19; Matt. 3:17; 17:5

16. Ezekiel: his parables

Ezek. 17:2; 20:49; Matt. 13:3

17. Ezra: his zeal for the scriptures

Neh. 8; Matt. 21:42; 22:29; Mark 12:10, 24; Luke 4:21; 24:27; John 10:35

18. Nehemiah: his zeal for the Holy City — Neh. 1–2; Matt. 23:37-39; Luke 19:41

ANIMALS

1. Lamb — Exod. 29:38; John 1:29

2. Dove — Lev. 5:11; Luke 2:24

3. Eagle — Exod. 19:4; Matt. 23:37

4. Lion — Hos. 11:10; Rev. 5:5

5. Sheep — Lev. 1:10; Isa. 53:7

6. Heifer — Gen. 15:9; Num. 19

7. Scapegoat — Lev. 16

8. Ram — Gen. 22:13

9. Pigeon — Gen. 15:9; Lev. 5:11

10. Ox — Num. 7:87

11. Bullock — Exod. 29:11

12. Serpent — Num. 21:8-9; John 3:14

EVENTS

1. The coats of skin for Adam and Eve — Gen. 3:21

2. The Passover — Exod. 12; 1 Cor. 5:7-8

3. The sacrifice on the Day of Atonement — Lev. 16

4. The giving of manna — Exod. 16:14-22; John 6

5. The ark and the Flood — Gen. 6–8; 1 Pet. 3:18-22

6. The striking of the rock — Exod. 17:5-7; 1 Cor. 10:4

7. The passage through the Red Sea — Exod. 14; 1 Cor. 10:1-2

8. The branch cast into the waters at Marah — Exod. 15:23-26

FEASTS

1. Passover, which points to Calvary — Lev. 23:4-8; 1 Cor. 5:7

2. The Feast of Firstfruits, which points to the Resurrection — Lev. 23:9-14; 1 Cor. 15:23

3. Pentecost, which points to the coming of the Holy Spirit — Lev. 23:15-22; Acts 2:1-4

4. The Feast of Trumpets, which points to the Rapture and Second Coming — Lev. 23:23-25; 1 Thess. 4:13-18

5. The Day of Atonement, which points to the Tribulation — Lev. 23:26-32; Rev. 6–19

6. The Feast of Tabernacles, which points to the Millennium — Lev. 23:33-44; Rev. 20:1-6

THE OFFERINGS

1. The burnt offering, which points to Christ's willingly offering himself — Lev. 1

2. The meal offering, which points to his purity and sinlessness — Lev. 2

3. The peace offering, which points to his accomplishments on the cross — Lev. 3

4. The sin offering, which points to his dealing with sin's guilt — Lev. 4

5. The trespass offering, which points to his dealing with sin's injury — Lev. 5

Types of the Antichrist

1. Cain, murderer of the righteous son — Gen. 4:5-14; 1 John 3:12

2. Nimrod, builder of Babylon and the Tower of Babel — Gen. 10–11; Rev. 17–18

3. Pharaoh, oppressor of God's people — Exod. 1:8-22; Rev. 12

4. Korah, the rebel — Num. 16:1-3; Rev. 13:6

5. Balaam, who attempted to curse Israel — Num. 23–24; Dan. 7:25

6. Saul, who intruded into the office of the priesthood — 1 Sam. 13:9-13; Matt. 24:15; Rev. 13:15-18

7. Goliath, the proud and boastful one — 1 Sam. 17; Dan. 11:36

8. Absalom, who attempted to steal the throne of David — 2 Sam. 15:1-6; 2 Thess. 2:3-4, 9

9. Jeroboam, creator of a false religion — 1 Kings 12:25-31; Rev. 13:15

10. Sennacherib, who tried to destroy Jerusalem — 2 Kings 18:17; Zech. 14:2

11. Nebuchadnezzar, maker of a golden statue — Dan. 3:1-7; Rev. 13:15

12. Haman, who tried to exterminate the Jews — Esther 3; Rev. 12:13-17

13. Antiochus Epiphanes, defiler of the temple — Dan. 11:21-35; Matt. 24:15

Types of the Church

1. Eve, Adam's wife — Gen. 2:23-25; 3:20

2. Rebekah, Isaac's wife — Gen. 24

3. Ruth, Boaz's wife — Ruth 4

Types of Israel
CONCERNING HER IMMORALITY

1. Gomer, the wife of Hosea — Book of Hosea

2. Jezreel, Lo-ruhamah, and Lo-ammi, children of Hosea — Book of Hosea

CONCERNING HER IMMORTALITY

1. Jonah in the fish — Jon. 2

2. The three Hebrew men in the fiery furnace — Dan. 3

3. Daniel in the lions' den — Dan. 6

4. The infant Moses in the water — Exod. 14

5. Esther in Persia — Esther 3–7

Types of the Father

1.	Abraham	Gen. 22
2.	Jacob	Gen. 37:3
3.	David	2 Sam. 9
4.	Hosea	Hos. 1–3

Types of False Religion

1.	Adam's fig leaves	Gen. 3:7
2.	Cain's ground offering	Gen. 4:3
3.	Nimrod's tower	Gen. 11:1-9
4.	Aaron's golden calf	Exod. 32
5.	Jezebel's teachings	1 Kings 18:19; 2 Kings 9:22; Rev. 2:20
6.	Nebuchadnezzar's statue	Dan. 3

Types of the Rapture

1.	Noah, a type of Israel which will endure through the Tribulation	Gen. 6–8; Matt. 24:3; Rev. 12
2.	Lot, a type of the Church which will escape from the Tribulation	Gen. 19:22; 1 Thess. 1:10; 5:9

Types of the Tribulation

1.	The Flood, foreshadowing the scope of the Tribulation	Gen. 6–8; 2 Pet. 3:1-9
2.	The destruction of Sodom, foreshadowing the nature of it	Gen. 19; 2 Pet. 3:10-13
3.	The ten plagues upon Egypt, foreshadowing the intensity of it	Exod. 7–12; Rev. 6–19

Types of the Millennium

1.	The Sabbath	Exod. 20:8-11; Lev. 23:3
2.	The jubilee year	Lev. 25:10-12
3.	The tabernacle	Exod. 25:8; 29:42-46; 40:34
4.	The Feast of Tabernacles	Lev. 23:34-42

5. The Promised Land — Deut. 6:3; Heb. 4:8-10

6. The reign of Solomon
   a. The vastness of his kingdom — 1 Kings 4:21
   b. The security of it — 1 Kings 4:25
   c. His great wisdom — 1 Kings 4:29, 34
   d. His great fame — 1 Kings 10:7
   e. His great riches — 1 Kings 10:27

Old Testament Individuals Who Foreshadow New Testament Individuals

1. Elijah, foreshadowing John the Baptist — 1 Kings 17:1; 18:21; Matt. 17:10-13; Mark 6:14-20

2. Abel, foreshadowing Stephen — Gen. 4:8; Acts 7:57-58

3. Joshua and Zerubbabel, foreshadowing the two witnesses in the Tribulation — Zech. 4; Rev. 11

VESSELS, PITCHERS, AND WATER POTS

1. The vessel carried by Hagar — Gen. 21:14
2. The pitcher Rebekah filled for Abraham's servant — Gen. 24:16
3. The vessels in the tabernacle — Exod. 40:9; Heb. 9:21
4. The old vessels carried by the Gibeonites — Josh. 9:13
5. The vessel of milk given Sisera by Jael — Judg. 4:19
6. The 300 pitchers used by Gideon to defeat the Midianites — Judg. 7:16

7. The vessel of wine used in the dedication of Samuel — 1 Sam. 1:24

8. The vessel of oil used in anointing Saul — 1 Sam. 10:1

9. The vessel of wine David carried to his brothers doing battle with the Philistines — 1 Sam. 16:20

10. Two vessels of wine sent to David by Abigail — 1 Sam. 25:18

11. The vessel belonging to the widow of Zarephath — 1 Kings 17:12-16

12. The borrowed vessels of a widow in which God supernaturally created oil — 2 Kings 4:3-7

13. The vessels in the temple
    a. Description — 2 Chron. 4:19
    b. Taken by Nebuchadnezzar — Dan. 1:2; 2 Chron. 36:7
    c. Desecrated by Belshazzar — Dan. 5:2-3
    d. Returned by Zerubbabel — Ezra 1:7-11

14. The vessel made as Jeremiah watched — Jer. 18:4-5

15. The vessel that Jeremiah broke — Jer. 19:10

16. The vessel Ezekiel used — Ezek. 4:9

17. The waterpots filled with water that Jesus changed to wine at a wedding in Cana — John 2:6

18. The waterpot carried by a Samaritan woman who met Jesus by a well — John 4:28

19. The waterpot carried by a young man whom Jesus told Peter and John to follow — Mark 14:13

20. The vessels carried by the ten virgins — Matt. 25:4

21. The vessel that Peter saw in a vision — Acts 10:11

22. Symbolic vessels
    a. Earthen vessels—the bodies of believers — 2 Cor. 4:7
    b. Weaker vessel—the believer's wife — 1 Pet. 3:7

    c. Vessels of honor—the saved   Rom. 9:21-23;
                                                  2 Tim. 2:20-21

    d. Vessels of dishonor—the unsaved   Rom. 9:21-22;
                                                  2 Tim. 2:20

VINEYARDS

1. The vineyard planted by Noah   Gen. 9:20
2. The vineyard of Naboth   1 Kings 21:1
3. The vineyard of Timnah where   Judg. 14:5
   Samson killed a lion
4. The vineyards of Shiloh, where the   Judg. 21:20
   remaining 400 Benjaminite soldiers
   found wives
5. Parabolic vineyards   Isa. 5:1-7; Matt.
                                        20:1-16; 21:28-41;
                                        Luke 13:6-9

VOWS

1. Of Jacob at Bethel   Gen. 28:20
2. Of the Nazarite   Num. 6:2, 21
3. Of Jephthah concerning the offering   Judg. 11:30
   of a sacrifice
4. Of Hannah concerning a yet unborn   1 Sam. 1:11
   child
5. Of Absalom, used to deceive David   2 Sam. 15:7
6. Of Jezebel to kill Elijah   1 Kings 19:1-2
7. Of Jonah inside the fish   Jon. 2:9
8. Of Paul   Acts 18:18

9. Of four men and Paul   Acts 21:23-26
10. Of certain Jews to kill Paul   Acts 23:12

WALLS

1. The wall where the angel of the Lord trapped Balaam — Num. 22:24

2. The walls of Jericho that fell — Josh. 6:20; Heb. 11:30

3. The wall in Saul's palace where an attempt was made to kill David — 1 Sam. 19:10

4. The wall of Beth-shan where the Philistines fastened the body of Saul — 1 Sam. 31:10

5. The walls of Rabbah where Uriah was killed by an enemy arrow — 2 Sam. 11:24

6. The wall of Abel, over which the head of Sheba was thrown — 2 Sam. 20:21-22

7. The walls of Jerusalem
   a. Built by Solomon — 1 Kings 9:15
   b. Destroyed by Nebuchadnezzar — 2 Kings 25:10
   c. Rebuilt by Nehemiah — Neh. 2:17; 6:15

8. A wall in Moab where the Moabite king sacrificed his own son — 2 Kings 3:27

9. A wall in Samaria where an Israelite king heard a horrible story about cannibalism — 2 Kings 6:26

10. The wall in Damascus over which Paul escaped from a plot on his life — Acts 9:25; 2 Cor. 11:33

11. The wall in the millennial temple — Ezek. 42:20

12. The wall surrounding the New Jerusalem — Rev. 21:14-19

WARS AND BATTLES
See also Military Men

1. Abraham's war against a Mesopotamian king to rescue his nephew Lot — Gen. 14:1-16

2. Wars of Israel en route to Canaan
   a. Victory over the Amalekites — Exod. 17:8-16
   b. Defeat by the Amalekites — Num. 14:39-45
   c. Victory over the southern Canaanites — Num. 21:1-4
   d. Victory over the Amorites — Num. 21:21-31
   e. Victory over the king of Bashan — Num. 21:33-35
   f. Victory over the Midianites — Num. 31:6-12

3. Wars of Israel in conquering Palestine
   a. Victory over Jericho — Josh. 6:1-27
   b. Defeat by Ai — Josh. 7:1-5
   c. Victory over Ai — Josh. 8:1-29
   d. Victory over the king of Jerusalem and his four allies — Josh. 10:8-26
   e. Victory over Libnah — Josh. 10:29-30
   f. Victory over Lachish — Josh. 10:31-32
   g. Victory over Gezer — Josh. 10:33
   h. Victory over Eglon — Josh. 10:34-35
   i. Victory over Hebron — Josh. 10:36-37
   j. Victory over Debir — Josh. 10:38-39
   k. Victory over Jabin, king of Hazor, and his allies — Josh. 11:1-15

4. Wars during the period of the judges
   a. Othniel's defeat of the Mesopotamians — Judg. 3:10
   b. Ehud's defeat of the Moabites — Judg. 3:26-29
   c. Shamgar's defeat of the Philistines — Judg. 3:31
   d. Deborah and Barak's defeat of the northern Canaanites — Judg. 4:1-16

e.	Gideon's defeat of the Midianites	Judg. 7:9-25
f.	Abimelech's defeat by the citizens of Shechem	Judg. 9:43-57
g.	Jephthah's defeat of the Ammonites	Judg. 11:32-33
h.	Jephthah's defeat of the tribe of Ephraim	Judg. 12:1-6
i.	Samson's victory over the Philistines	Judg. 15:9-15
j.	The tribe of Dan's defeat of the city of Laish	Judg. 18:27-29
k.	Eleven tribes' defeat of Benjamin	Judg. 20:18-48
l.	Israel's defeat by the Philistines	1 Sam. 4:1-22
m.	Israel's defeat of the Philistines	1 Sam. 5:7-14

5. Wars during the United Kingdom period

a.	Saul's defeat of the Ammonites	1 Sam. 11:1-11
b.	Jonathan's defeat of the Philistines	1 Sam. 13:5; 14:31
c.	Saul's defeat of the Amalekites	1 Sam. 15:7-9
d.	David's defeat of the Philistine Goliath	1 Sam. 17
e.	David's defeat of the Philistines	1 Sam. 18:27
f.	David's defeat of the Amalekites	1 Sam. 27:8; 30:1-20
g.	Saul's defeat by the Philistines	1 Sam. 31
h.	The house of David's defeat of the house of Saul	2 Sam. 3:1
i.	David's defeat of the Jebusites	2 Sam. 5:6-9
j.	David's defeat of the Philistines	2 Sam. 5:17-20
k.	David's defeat of Moab	2 Sam. 8:2
l.	David's defeat of Zobah	2 Sam. 8:3-4
m.	David's defeat of Syria	2 Sam. 8:5-6
n.	David's defeat of Ammon-Rabbah	2 Sam. 11:1; 12:26-31
o.	David's defeat of Absalom's followers	2 Sam. 18:1-8

p. David's defeat of Sheba		2 Sam. 20:1-2, 14-22
q. David's defeat of the Philistines		2 Sam. 21:15-22

6. Wars during the Divided Kingdom period

   a. The civil wars between Israel's tribes

(1)	The original revolt	1 Kings 12:1-21
(2)	Fighting between Rehoboam (Judah) and Jeroboam (Israel)	1 Kings 15:6
(3)	Fighting between Asa (Judah) and Baasha (Israel)	1 Kings 15:16
(4)	Fighting between Amaziah (Judah) and Jehoash (Israel)	2 Kings 14:8-14
(5)	Fighting between Ahaz (Judah) and Pekah (Israel)	2 Kings 16:5; Isaiah 7:1-14

   b. Wars allowed by God to punish Judah's unfaithful rulers

(1)	Egypt against Jerusalem in Rehoboam's reign	1 Kings 14:25-28
(2)	The Philistines against Joram	2 Chron. 21:16-17
(3)	The Syrians against Joash	2 Chron. 24:23-24
(4)	Edom against Ahaz	2 Chron. 27:16-19
(5)	Assyria against Manasseh	2 Chron. 33:11

c. Amaziah's defeat of Edom		2 Chron. 25:5-13
d. Uzziah's defeat of the Philistines		2 Chron. 26:6-7
e. Ahab's war with Syria		1 Kings 20:13-30; 22:29-38
f. Jehoshaphat and Jehoram's defeat of Moab		2 Kings 3:16-27
g. Jehoram's defeat of Syria		2 Kings 6:8-23
h. Four lepers' defeat of the Syrian army		2 Kings 6:24-25; 7:3-11
i. The war between Edom and Judah		2 Kings 8:20-22
j. The allied war of Ahaziah (Judah) and Joram (Israel) against Syria		2 Kings 8:28-29

k. Syria's war against Israel's eastern two-and-a-half tribes — 2 Kings 10:32-33

l. Assyria's war against Israel — 2 Kings 15:29; 17:5-6

m. Assyria's war against Damascus — 2 Kings 16:7-9

n. Babylon's war against Assyria — Nah. 2–3

o. Asa's war against Ethiopia — 2 Chron. 14:6-15

p. Jehoshaphat's war against the Ammonites and Moabites — 2 Chron. 20:1-30

q. Josiah's defeat by the Egyptians — 2 Kings 23:29-30

r. Babylon's war against Judah — 2 Kings 25:1-3

7. Wars during the Babylonian captivity period

   a. The battle of Carchemish, between Egypt and victorious Babylon — Jer. 46:1-8

   b. The battle between the victorious Medo-Persians and Babylon — Dan. 5

8. War of the Persian Jews against their enemies — Esther 9

9. Wars between Satan and God

   a. The historical fall of Satan — Isa. 14:12-15; Ezek. 28:11-19

   b. The future casting of Satan out of heaven — Rev. 12:7-12

   c. The final revolt of Satan — Rev. 20:7-10

10. Wars during the Tribulation

   a. Gog's invasion of Palestine — Ezek. 38–39

   b. The battle of Armageddon — Rev. 14:14-20; 16:16; 19:11-21

WEAPONS
See also Spears and Swords

1. Battering ram	Ezek. 4:2; 21:22; 26:9
2. Battle ax, mace	Ps. 2:9; 35:3; Prov. 25:18; Ezek. 26:9
3. Bow and arrow	Gen. 27:3; 2 Sam. 22:35
4. Breastplate, coat of mail	1 Sam. 17:5, 38; Isa. 59:17; Eph. 6:14
5. Girdle, belt	2 Sam. 20:8
6. Greaves, leg protection	1 Sam. 17:6
7. Helmet	1 Sam. 17:5; Isa. 59:17; Eph. 6:17
8. Rock-throwing engine	2 Chron. 26:14-15
9. Shield	1 Sam. 17:7, 41; Eph. 6:16
10. Sling	1 Sam. 17:4
11. Spear, lance, javelin, dart	Josh. 8:18; Judg. 5:8; 1 Sam. 18:11
12. Sword	Gen. 27:40; Eph. 6:17

WEEPING AND MOURNING
See also Burials and Funerals

1. Hagar wept for Ishmael in the desert.	Gen. 21:16
2. Abraham wept at the funeral of Sarah.	Gen. 23:2
3. Esau wept upon hearing of Jacob's treachery.	Gen. 27:34; Heb. 12:17
4. Jacob wept for joy upon finding Rachel.	Gen. 29:11

5. Esau and Jacob both wept at their reunion. — Gen. 33:4

6. Jacob wept over the apparent death of Joseph. — Gen. 37:35

7. Joseph wept at the reunion of his brothers. — Gen. 45:14

8. Joseph wept at the funeral of his father Jacob. — Gen. 50:1

9. Israel wept for freedom in Egypt. — Exod. 2:23; 3:7

10. The Egyptians wept over the death of their firstborn. — Exod. 12:30

11. Israel wept because of their sins. — Num. 11:4, 10; 14:1; Judg. 2:4; 3:9, 15; 4:3; 6:6-7; 10:10

12. Moses wept over Miriam's sin. — Num. 12:13

13. Israel wept at the funeral of Aaron. — Num. 20:29

14. Israel wept at the death of Moses. — Deut. 34:8

15. Joshua wept over the defeat of Israel. — Josh. 7:6-9

16. Sisera's mother wept at his death. — Judg. 5:28

17. Samson's wife wept to secure a favor. — Judg. 14:16

18. Naomi wept as she left Moab. — Ruth 1:9

19. Hannah wept over her barrenness. — 1 Sam. 1:10

20. Samuel wept over fickle Israel. — 1 Sam. 7:9

21. Israel wept over the threatened city of Jabesh-Gilead. — 1 Sam. 11:4

22. Samuel wept over the failure of Saul. — 1 Sam. 15:35

23. David and Jonathan wept over Saul. — 1 Sam. 20:41

24. Saul wept over his own stupidity. — 1 Sam. 24:16

25. Israel wept at the death of Samuel. — 1 Sam. 25:1

26. David wept at the destruction of Ziklag. — 1 Sam. 30:4

27. David wept at the death of Saul and Jonathan. — 2 Sam. 1:17

28. David wept at the murder of Abner. — 2 Sam. 3:32

29. David wept over his great sin. — Ps. 32:4; 51:17

30. David wept at the death of his infant child. — 2 Sam. 12:15-23

31. Tamar wept upon being raped by Amnon. — 2 Sam. 13:19

32. David wept at the murder of Amnon. — 2 Sam. 15:23

33. David wept at the death of Absalom. — 2 Sam. 18:33

34. Israel wept at the death of Jeroboam's son. — 1 Kings 14:18

35. Elisha wept over the future cruelty of King Hazael. — 2 Kings 8:11-12

36. Joash wept at the death of Elisha. — 2 Kings 13:14

37. Hezekiah wept at the announcement of his impending death. — 2 Kings 20:2-3

38. Hezekiah and Isaiah wept over the threat to Jerusalem. — 2 Chron. 32:20

39. The Jewish captives wept en route to Babylon. — Ps. 137:1

40. Jeremiah wept over the sins of Jerusalem. — Jer. 9:1

41. Some old Jews wept at the dedication of Zerubbabel's temple. — Ezra 3:12-13; Hag. 2:3-9

42. Daniel wept over Israel's sin. — Dan. 10:2

43. Ezra wept over Jerusalem's sin. — Ezra 10:1

44. Nehemiah wept over Jerusalem's broken walls. — Neh. 1:4

45. Mordecai wept over the wicked plot of Haman. — Esther 4:1

46. Esther wept as she pleaded for her people. — Esther 8:3

47. Job wept for his sons. — Job 1:18-22

48. Job's friends wept for him. — Job 2:12

49. Some Bethlehem parents wept for their children. — Matt. 2:18

50. Mary and Joseph wept over the missing Jesus. — Luke 2:48

51. A maniac in Gadara wept at the sight of Jesus. — Mark 5:7

52. A Canaanite mother wept over her child. — Matt. 15:22

53. Jairus's household wept over his little girl. — Mark 5:39

54. A father wept over his demoniac son. — Mark 9:24

55. A widow wept over her dead son. — Luke 7:13

56. An immoral woman wept over her sin. — Luke 7:38

57. A rich man wept in hell. — Luke 16:24

58. Mary and Martha wept over Lazarus. — John 11:33

59. Jesus wept over Lazarus. — John 11:35

60. Jesus wept over Jerusalem. — Luke 19:41

61. Some Jerusalem women wept for Jesus. — Luke 23:28

62. Jesus wept in the Garden of Gethsemane. — Mark 14:32-42; Heb. 5:7

63. Mary Magdalene wept over Jesus. — John 20:11

64. The disciples wept over the departure and death of Christ. — John 16:6; Mark 16:10

65. Peter wept over his sin. — Matt. 26:75

66. Dorcas's friends wept at her funeral. — Acts 9:39

67. Paul wept over the Ephesian church. — Acts 20:36-37

68. Paul wept over the Corinthian church. — 2 Cor. 2:4

69. Paul wept over Israel. — Rom. 9:2

70. The Ephesian elders wept over Paul. — Acts 20:37

71. The Christians at Caesarea wept over Paul. — Acts 21:13

72. Timothy wept over his ministry. — 2 Tim. 1:4

73. John wept over a seven-sealed book. — Rev. 5:5

74. The faithful martyrs wept during the Tribulation. — Rev. 7:17

75. Israel will weep at the Second Coming of Christ. — Zech. 12:10-12

76. The nations will weep at the Second Coming of Christ.   Matt. 24:30

77. The world's merchants will weep over fallen Babylon.   Rev. 18:18

WELLS

1. The well in the Kadesh wilderness, where God spoke to Hagar   Gen. 16:14

2. The well in the Paran wilderness, where he met her the second time   Gen. 2:19

3. The well in Beersheba, where Abraham made a covenant with Abimelech Gen. 21:30

4. The well in the city of Nahor, where Abraham's servant discovered Rebekah   Gen. 24:11-20

5. The wells in the Valley of Gerar, as dug by Isaac   Gen. 26:18

6. The well in Haran, where Jacob met Rachel   Gen. 29:1-12

7. The well in Midian, where Moses met Zipporah   Exod. 2:15-21

8. The well in the wilderness, dug by the Israelites   Num. 21:16-18

9. The well in the village of Bahurim, where two of David's spies hid from Absalom   2 Sam. 17:18-19

10. The well in Ramah, where Saul sought after David   1 Sam. 19:18-24

11. The well in Sirah, where Joab met Abner   2 Sam. 3:26

12. The well in Bethlehem, where David longed to drink   2 Sam. 23:15

13. The well in Elim, where Israel drank from 12 wells en route to Mount Sinai — Exod. 15:27

14. The well in Samaria, where Jesus met the Samaritan woman — John 4:6

WICKED MEN IN THE OLD TESTAMENT

1. Cain, murderer of his righteous brother Abel — Gen. 4:8

2. Bera, king of the perverted city of Sodom — Gen. 14:2, 21

3. Esau, materialistic and fornicating son of Isaac and brother of Jacob — Gen. 27:41; Heb. 12:16

4. Pharaoh Thutmose I, Egyptian king who enslaved Israel — Exod. 1:8

5. Pharaoh Thutmose III, Egyptian king who attempted to kill Moses — Exod. 2:15

6. Amenhotep II, Egyptian king during the ten plagues — Exod. 5–14

7. Korah, Israelite who organized a revolt against Moses — Num. 16:1

8. Abimelech, bloody son of Gideon who murdered 70 of his brothers in an attempt to become king — Judg. 9:1-6

9. Nahash, cruel Ammonite king who threatened to destroy the right eye of all Israelites living in Jabesh-gilead — 1 Sam. 11:2

10. Saul, Israel's first king, who attempted to kill David and ordered the slaughter of 85 godly priests at Nob — 1 Sam. 13:13-14

11. Doeg, Edomite soldier who carried out Saul's bloody order to slay 85 priests at Nob — 1 Sam. 22:18

12. Absalom, David's favorite son who led a revolt against his own father — 2 Sam. 15–18

13. Shimei, descendant of Saul who cursed David during the revolt led by Absalom — 2 Sam. 16:5-8

14. Joab, David's army commander who killed Abner, Absalom, and others in cold blood — 1 Kings 2:5

15. Rehoboam, Solomon's son whose insensitivity triggered the Israelite civil war — 1 Kings 12:8-11

16. Jeroboam, first king of northern Israel, who led the ten tribes astray by constructing idols — 1 Kings 12:20, 25-33

17. Ahab, weak and greedy husband of Jezebel who allowed Naboth to be murdered to possess his vineyard — 1 Kings 16:33; 20:15-16

18. Menahem, Israel's brutal ruler who ripped open the wombs of pregnant women belonging to his enemies — 2 Kings 15:14-22

19. Ahaz, king of Judah who sacrificed his own children to idols — 2 Chron. 28:1-4

20. Manasseh, Israel's most wicked king, later repentant in captivity — 2 Chron. 33:1-9

21. Pashhur, ungodly priest who persecuted the prophet Jeremiah — Jer. 20:1-6

22. Jehoiakim, king of Judah who burned the scroll written by Jeremiah — Jer. 36

23. Sennacherib, vicious Assyrian king who surrounded Jerusalem only to have his troops destroyed by the death angel — 2 Kings 19:16-37

24. Belshazzar, arrogant Babylonian king who ridiculed God and was condemned by God through the handwriting on the wall — Dan. 5

25. Haman, Persian prime minister who attempted to carry out history's first holocaust during the time of Esther — Esther 3

26. Sanballat, Nehemiah's enemy who did everything possible to prevent the walls of Jerusalem from being rebuilt — Neh. 4:1-3, 7-8

WICKED MEN IN THE NEW TESTAMENT

1. Herod the Great, wicked Edomite ruler who attempted to kill the infant Jesus — Matt. 2:1-18

2. Herod Antipas, Herod the Great's youngest son who killed John the Baptist — Matt. 14:1-11

3. Annas, Jewish ex-high priest who plotted the crucifixion of Jesus — John 18:13-24; Acts 4:6

4. Caiaphas, high priest and son-in-law of Annas who aided in the plot to condemn Jesus — John 18:24; Acts 4:6

5. Barabbas, murderer and robber whom Pilate released instead of Jesus — Mark 15:7; John 18:40

6. Pilate, Roman governor who officially allowed the crucifixion of Jesus — John 19:1-6

7. Judas Iscariot, disciple who betrayed Christ — John 6:70-71; 12:6

8. Simon the sorcerer, greedy citizen of Samaria who attempted to buy the power of the Holy Spirit — Acts 8:9, 18-19

9. Herod Agrippa I, grandson of Herod the Great who killed James the apostle — Acts 12

10. Bar-Jesus (Elymas), false prophet on Cyprus who attempted to prevent the governor from accepting Christ — Acts 13:6

11. Alexander, a coppersmith who caused Paul much harm — 2 Tim. 4:14

12. Diotrephes, an unsaved troublemaker in the early church denounced by John the apostle — 3 John 9-10

WICKED WOMEN IN THE OLD AND NEW TESTAMENTS

1. Lot's wife, destroyed by God as she looked back toward Sodom — Gen. 19:26

2. Potiphar's wife, who falsely accused Joseph of rape when he refused her sexual advances — Gen. 37:7-20

3. Delilah, Philistine woman who betrayed Samson into the hands of his enemies — Judg. 16:4-20

4. Witch of Endor, medium who brought up Samuel's spirit from the dead — 1 Samuel 28

5. Maachah, idol-worshiping mother of King Asa — 1 Kings 15:13

6. Jezebel, wicked and bloody Baal-worshiping wife of Ahab — 1 Kings 16:31; 21:25

7. Athaliah, cruel daughter of Ahab and Jezebel who instituted a blood purge to obtain the throne of Judah — 2 Chron. 22:10

8. Gomer, sexually impure wife of Hosea the prophet — Hos. 1–2

9. Zeresh, heartless wife of Haman in the Book of Esther — Esther 5:14

10. Herodias, cruel queen who demanded   Matt. 14:1-11
    and received the head of John the
    Baptist out of revenge

11. Mary Magdalene, woman out of   Mark 16:9; Luke
    whom Jesus cast seven demons   8:2

12. Jezebel, false prophetess in the church Rev. 2:20-21
    at Thyatira who encouraged its
    members to commit fornication

WIDOWS

1. Tamar, whose first two husbands, Er   Gen. 38:6-7
   and Onan, were slain by God

2. Naomi, whose husband, Elimelech,   Ruth 1:3, 5
   died in Moab

3. Orpah, widow of Chilion and   Ruth 1:3, 5
   daughter-in-law of Naomi

4. Ruth, widow of Mahlon and devoted   Ruth 1:3, 5
   daughter-in-law of Naomi

5. Phinehas's wife, daughter-in-law of   1 Sam. 4:19
   Eli and mother of Ichabod

6. Abigail, whose foolish husband,   1 Sam. 25:37-39
   Nabal, was slain by God

7. Bathsheba, wife of Uriah, who was   2 Sam. 11:26
   ordered killed in battle by David

8. Hiram's mother, whose son helped   1 Kings 7:13-14
   Solomon in the building of the first
   temple

9. Zeruah, mother of Jeroboam, first   1 Kings 11:26
   king of Israel's ten tribes

10. Jezebel, whose husband, Ahab, was   1 Kings 16:31;
    killed in battle   22:40

11. The widow of Zarephath, whose son   1 Kings 17:9
    was raised from the dead by Elijah

12. A wife of one of the prophets, for whom Elisha worked a miracle to help her out of terrible debt — 2 Kings 4:1

13. Poor widow in the temple, pointed out by Jesus as an example of faithful giving — Mark 12:42

14. Anna, the 84-year-old prophetess who was present at Christ's dedication — Luke 2:36-37

15. The widow of Nain, whose son was raised from the dead by Jesus — Luke 7:12-15

16. Sapphira, slain by God for lying to the Holy Spirit, just as her husband, Ananias, had been slain earlier — Acts 5:5-10

WINDOWS

1. The window in the ark — Gen. 8:6

2. The window through which Abimelech saw Isaac and Rebekah — Gen. 26:8

3. The window of Rahab the harlot — Josh. 2:15, 18, 21

4. The window of Michal in Gibeah, from which David escaped the wrath of Saul — 1 Sam. 19:12

5. The window of Michal in Jerusalem through which she viewed a celebration led by her husband David and later criticized him for it — 2 Sam. 6:16

6. The window in Jezreel from which Jezebel was thrown to her death — 2 Kings 9:30, 32

7. Solomon's window, where he viewed a young man enticed by a harlot — Prov. 7:6

8. Elisha's window, where he ordered a king to shoot an arrow — 2 Kings 13:17

9. The eastern window of Daniel's
upstairs room that opened toward
Jerusalem, in front of which he prayed
three times a day — Dan. 6:10

10. The window in Troas through which
Eutychus fell to his death during
Paul's long message — Acts 20:9

11. The window (opening) in the wall of
Damascus through which Paul
escaped the plot of some Jews — 2 Cor. 11:33

12. Symbolic windows:
  a. The flood windows of heaven — Gen. 7:11; 8:2
  b. The blessing windows of heaven — Mal. 3:10

WINDSTORMS

1. During Noah's flood — Gen. 8:1
2. During the locust plague in Egypt — Exod. 10:13, 19
3. During the Red Sea crossing — Exod. 14:21
4. During the quail plague in the
wilderness — Num. 11:31
5. After the Mt. Carmel contest — 1 Kings 18:45
6. During God's meeting with Elijah on
Mt. Horeb — 1 Kings 19:11
7. During the translation of Elijah — 2 Kings 2:11
8. During Daniel's vision of the four
beasts — Dan. 7:2
9. During Jonah's sea trip — Jon. 1:4
10. During Jonah's visit to Nineveh — Jon. 4:8
11. As God talked with Job — Job 38:1
12. As the disciples crossed the Sea of
Galilee from west to east — Matt. 8:26

13. As the disciples crossed the Sea of   Matt. 14:24
    Galilee from east to west
14. During Pentecost   Acts 2:2
15. During Paul's trip to Rome   Acts 27:14-15

WORSHIPING GOD
See also The Christian Life, The Church's Tasks, Commands
to Believers

---

1. Through reading God's Word   Col. 4:16; 1 Thess.
   5:27; 1 Tim. 4:13;
   Rev. 1:3

2. Through studying God's Word   Acts 6:2; 2 Tim.
   2:15; 3:15

3. Through teaching God's Word   Acts 2:42; 6:7;
   12:24; 18:28;
   19:20; 1 Tim. 4:6;
   2 Tim. 1:13; 2:2

4. Through preaching God's Word   2 Tim. 4:2

5. Through the keeping of the ordinances   1 Cor. 11:2

6. Through the singing of psalms,   Eph. 5:19; Col.
   hymns, and spiritual songs   3:16; James 5:13

7. Through the lifting up of prayers,   Acts 2:42, 46; 3:1;
   intercessions, supplications, and   4:31; Eph. 6:18;
   thanksgiving   Phil. 4:6; Col. 4:2;
   1 Thess. 5:17;
   1 Tim. 2:1-2, 8

8. Through the receiving of his Son   John 1:11-12

9. Through the sacrifice of our bodies   Rom. 12:1

10. Through the sacrifice of our praise   Heb. 13:15

11. Through the sacrifice of our good   Heb. 13:16
    works

12. Through the sacrifice of our substance   Phil. 4:18